HENRI DE LUBAC

THE MOTHERHOOD
OF THE CHURCH

HENRI DE LUBAC

THE MOTHERHOOD
OF THE CHURCH

followed by

PARTICULAR CHURCHES
IN THE UNIVERSAL CHURCH

and an interview conducted by
Gwendoline Jarczyk

translated by
Sr. Sergia Englund, O.C.D.

IGNATIUS PRESS   SAN FRANCISCO

Title of the French original:
*Les églises particulières dans l'Église universelle,
suivi de La maternité de l'église, et d'une
interview recueillie par G. Jarczyk*
©1971 Aubier Montaigne, Paris

CONTENTS

APPENDIX

THE PRIESTHOOD

INTRODUCTION

On February 11, 1913, Pastor Jules-Émile Roberty wrote to Charles Péguy, who, in a moment of distress, had confided to him the difficulties of his position in the Church: "The Gospel existed before the Church. It is about the only thing of which we can be certain in this world."[1]

In one sense, the pastor was right. It is obvious that the Church would not exist if Jesus had not first come and preached the Gospel. This is consequently true of the Gospel itself. But if it is a question of the Gospel for us, it is no less obvious that the relation between the two is reversed. The books which make the Gospel of Jesus known to us—these little pieces of "minor literature", so simple and so profound, of a unique singularity, in which the minute examinations of the sharpest critics like the motionless gaze of the most contemplative souls never cease to make discoveries —have been prepared, formed, edited and circu-

[1] Letter published in *Évangile et liberté* (July 2, 1969), 5.

lated within the Church; they have been preserved and canonized within the Church. They cannot be separated from the tradition of the Church. Today, just as from the very beginning, it is still through the Church that the Gospel is transmitted to us. Thus, if one thing is certain in this world, it is that, for us, the Church precedes the Gospel.

The Church appears first to us in everything. The disciples of Christ were called Christians very early, and, indeed, a better name could not be found. Yet would we say that they were adherents of Christianity? But "Christianity" is a neutral, abstract word; without further specification, it could signify only a body of doctrine or a way of life or a set of personal opinions. In reality, what characterized these first disciples of Christ was their having gathered together into a new and original society that was as concrete as it was mysterious: they were united with the Church of Christ.

There has never been Christianity without the Church. *"Unus christianus, nullus christianus"*, Saint Cyprian will later say; and later still, Karl Barth: one does not become Christian "in a vacuum".[2] Christianity spread from Jerusalem by

[2] *Dogmatique*, vol. 4, t. 2, fasc. 3; *Labor et fides* (Geneva, 1971), 2. Likewise, the Orthodox theologian Georges Florovsky, *Le Corps du Christ vivant* (Delachaux and Niestlé,

the creation of churches which proceeded "fully equipped from the mother churches"; its expansion was "a multiplication of churches and like a proliferation of cells"[3] which were always linked to one another. Subsequent history is as expressive as the beginning. In spite of the strong individualistic tendencies known to us, Protestant communities were formed automatically, so to speak, without interval, at the very time when those whom we call their founders broke away from the ancient body they judged to be decrepit. We can cite that as an exemplary case in point. And "Christians without a Church"[4] have never been able to live and survive except as parasites, on the fringe of the Church but in her shadow, or, to be more exact, by intercepting—for whatever uncertain length of time—one or another of her rays of light.

This practical necessity of the Church—of a Church—for the faithful, moreover, has not es-

---

1948), 15: "Christian existence presupposes and implies an incorporation." Cf. Yves-Noël Lelouvier, *Perspectives russes sur l'Église* (Centurion, 1968), 69–72.

[3] Pierre Batiffol, *Cathedra Petri* (Cerf, 1939), 4.

[4] This is the improper title (for it is concerned at length with, among others, Saint John of the Cross, Bérulle, Surin, Angelus Silesius) of a work by Leszek Kolakowski, trans. from the Polish by Anna Posner: *Chrétiens sans Église, la conscience religieuse et le lien confessionnel au XVIIe siècle* (Gallimard, 1969).

caped the attention of many who do not share our faith. André Suarès, who was also one of Péguy's friends, wrote in 1916, borrowing not his thought but his vocabulary: "The passage from pure religion to the Church represents the very fall from the mystical to the political. Now it happens that without Church, religion does not endure: it dies along with the God who founded it and its first believers, who cannot live without her. It is through the Church that religion endures. Thus the Church is the politics of religion." "But", Suarès added, "should it endure? That is the question."[5]

A wholly pragmatic concept, expressed many times this last century and still popularized rather often today. It was Renan's concept. We read in his *Marc Aurèle*: "The episcopacy established order over freedom. . . . The work of Jesus was not born viable; it was chaos. . . . Unrestrained prophecy, charisms, glossolalia, personal inspiration, that was more than enough to reduce everything to the proportions of an ephemeral sect. . . . With freedom there must be law. . . . Inspiration passes from the individual to the community. The Church has become all in Christianity."[6] This

[5] Introduction to the *Oeuvres complètes* of Charles Péguy, vol. 4 (NRF, 1916).

[6] *Marc Aurèle et la fin du monde antique*, 3d ed. (Calmann-

was again the almost identical concept of Rudolf Sohm, for whom the enthusiastic faith of the first Christian generations knew only "the power of love and of the Spirit"; it was the concept again of, among others, Auguste Sabatier, who saw the "drama" of the Church's history in the substitution of the word of the bishop for the Word of God, of the sacrament for repentance, of discipline for fraternal love, of obedience for inspiration; in the victory of the religion of authority over the religion of the Spirit, who had to "go back underground" to live on more or less secretly "in the secret life of humble and pious souls and in the speculative work of a few elite minds."[7] Monsignor Pierre Batiffol rightly said of this anarchic view of Christian origins: "What a fable!"[8] Alfred Loisy wanted to correct it. He insisted on the fact that Jesus' entourage consti-

---

Lévy, 1882), 407–8. Renan also wrote in a subsequent edition of his *Vie de Jésus* that Jesus "with rare sure-sightedness, lay the foundations of a Church destined to endure". But there would be no end to pointing out his fluctuations. Some of them are noted in J. Lagrange, *La vie de Jésus d'après Renan* (Gabalda, 1923).

[7] *Les religions d'autorité et la religion de l'esprit* (1904), 483–84.

[8] *L'Église naissante et le catholicisme*, 3d ed. (Gabalda, 1909), 156. A fundamental work which has just been republished by Cerf with a preface by Cardinal Jean Daniélou (1971). The

tuted a "society of men", an embryo of the future "kingdom", at the same time as he tried to justify more positively the existence of the Church, which had become necessary as a result of the delay of the awaited parousia and which was, moreover, as conformable to human nature as it was indispensable to the propagation of the Gospel.[9] Nevertheless, on both sides—and this is the only point on which our comparison rests— the Church, extrinsic to Jesus' message, was a secondary phenomenon, even if considered essential.

Now we think, on the contrary, that the Gospel of Christ "does not aim only at a new relation of individuals as such with the Father, outside of any social and institutional framework, but indeed at a 'new covenant' whose consequence is the new people of God", a people who will be characterized by its status as the "Body of Christ".[10] This new people will be very different from the old,

---

"fable" of which Batiffol was speaking appears in more than one new edition today and continues to sustain dreams.

[9] *L'Évangile et l'Église* (Picard, 1902), etc.

[10] Jorge Medina Estevez, *"Annexe sur le caractère spécifique de l'Église"*, in: *Le ministère sacerdotal* (Cerf, 1971), 108. Cf. Annie Jaubert, *La notion d'alliance dans le judaïsme aux abords de l'ère chrétienne* (Seuil, 1963), conclusion.

this new covenant will be a radical transformation of the old—but the very transformation presupposes a rootedness and continuity. The earliest Christianity was not a simple spiritual movement nor a pure brotherhood, not a school of wisdom nor a "gnosis", not a "popular philosophy", a learned society, a group of illuminati, a simple cultural association, nor, as Renan said, "a religion made for the interior consolation of a small number of elect."[11] It was, in all reality, a Church. Or rather, it was, in its singularity, *the Church*.

A number of scholars and critics have attributed their own mentality to Jesus and his disciples. They have not sufficiently taken into account the structure of Jewish society and the categories of Jewish thought within which the Christian revolution took place, even if it did explode them. They have not sufficiently understood that if Jesus considered himself the Messiah of Israel, he "could not but envisage the formation of a community."[12] Today we also have the benefit of a whole series of valuable analogies drawn from the Jewish community milieu of the same period, thanks

[11] *Marc Aurèle*, 626.

[12] Oscar Cullmann, *Saint Pierre, disciple, apôtre, martyr* (Neuchâtel, 1952), 171. Cf. Pierre Benoit, *Exégèse et théologie*, 2 (Cerf, 1965), 296.

particularly to the Qumran discoveries.[13] And as far back as we can go, the Church in her essential structure is "already there". Whatever the relative obscurity in which the history of the first Christian generation will always remain submerged for us,[14] we are called to this conclusion by a certain number of facts and accurate texts, which are corroborated, moreover, by what we see subsequently, as soon as the light becomes a little more abundant.

From the day of Pentecost—the exact date or precise form of the event which bears this name, or even of the series of events which this name summarizes, are of little importance—it is at the

[13] J. Schmitt, *"L'organisation de l'Église primitive et Qumrân"*, in: *Recherches bibliques*, 4 (DDB, 1959), 217–31; *"Sacerdoce judaïque et hiérarchie ecclésiale"*, in: *Revue des sciences religieuses*, 29 (1955), 250–61. J. Coppens, *"L'Église nouvelle alliance de Dieu avec son peuple"*, in: *Recherches bibliques*, 7 (1965), 13–22.

[14] Christians then had other things to do besides composing memoirs or chronicles for the benefit and according to the norms of twentieth-century scholars. Some excessively critical ones today misuse the argument *a silentio*, seeming to imply "that the New Testament offers a description of the early Church which is sufficient in itself and which does not, in any way imaginable, have to be completed or, indeed, enlightened by any tradition whatsoever": Report of the subcommittee (of the International Theological Commission) on the recognition of ministries (1971), 7.

call of Peter and his companions, "invested with power from above",[15] that the first nucleus of faithful assembled. They entered, we maintain, a Church which was calling them together; they did not create her by their arrival. The Church is not a result; at least she is not a mere result, the simple fruit of a confluence. She has not been formed by individuals who, having believed in Jesus Christ each on his own part and each in his own way, decided to join together in order to organize their belief and their life in common. The Church, composed of men, was not made by the hands of men. She is not an organization. She is a living organism, what Saint Irenaeus called "the ancient organism of the Church".[16] "The source of her life and of her unity does not arise from the desire to live in common on the part of the individuals she gathers together; it is she who communicates it to them."[17]

Those who look in the Church for a founding

[15] Lk 24:49. Acts 1:8: "You will receive power, that of the Holy Spirit who will descend upon you; you will then be my witnesses."

[16] *Adversus Haereses*, l. 4, c. 33, n. 8: τὸ ἀρχαῖον τῆς ἐκκλησίας σύστημα (A. Rousseau, SC, 102:819).

[17] Yves de Montcheuil, S.J., commenting on Moehler in Pierre Chaillet, *L'Église est une, hommage à Moehler* (Bloud and Gay, 1939), 237.

charter analogous to what might be the legal document announcing the creation of a new state or
the protocol establishing a commercial firm or
a professional association, will obviously not find
it. Even if the facts were better known, they
would not show it. All the analogies drawn from
our human societies would be misleading. We
must not speak so much of a foundation of the
Church, in the artificial sense this word suggests,
as of her *birth*. She is seen rising in broad day-
light with the first preaching of the Twelve—
and through that she is directly connected to the
preaching of Jesus himself. For if there is a well-
certified fact, in spite of the arguments which have
sought to weaken it, it is the selection Jesus made
of these twelve men in the course of his earthly
life.[18] Just as Yahweh had chosen Moses and
Aaron to guide his people,[19] and just as he then
had set the tribe of Levi apart, he separated them

[18] Cf. Augustin George, *"Des Douze aux Apôtres et à leurs
successeurs"*, in: *Le ministère sacerdotal*, papers, Faculty of Theology of Lyons (1970), 23–53. This term "the Twelve", used
frequently in the Gospels (eight times in Matthew, eleven in
Mark, seven in Luke, four in John) and which appears a single
time in Paul, in the passage where he hands over "what he has
received" (1 Cor 15:1–5), will disappear very quickly. It
belongs "to the most ancient fabric of our Gospels". See
below, 242–43.

[19] Cf. 1 Sam 12:6.

from the other disciples "in order that they might be with him",[20] to prepare them to become his messengers, his witnesses and his fellow workers. The fact that the traitor Judas was designated as one of them is sufficient indication of the existence of their very distinct group before the Passion. For Jesus, the ages were fulfilled; what the prophets and kings of the Old Covenant had so longed to see and hear could even now be seen and heard; in him "the power of the sovereign God vehemently found its way; he communicated it to the little group which he had chosen and formed".[21] Now these men are conscious of the mission that rests with them and which rests with them jointly; and thus we see them concerned very soon, after Judas' defection, with completing their number,[22] in view of the universal work of gathering which they have to accomplish. They have a presentiment of this work without yet being able to imagine the conditions of it clearly or to measure

[20] Mk 3:13–14.

[21] Mk 1:14–15. Lk 10:24. Mt 11:12, etc. Heinz Schürmann, *"Le groupe des disciples de Jésus"*, in: *Christus*, 50 (1966), 192–93. Paul will be united with them: Gal 1:17. 1 Cor 11 and 15. Acts 9:17–18. Cf. Lucien Cerfaux, *La théologie de l'Église suivant saint Paul* (Cerf, 1965), 355–60.

[22] Acts 1:15–26. This number, an obvious allusion to the twelve tribes and a sign of universality, prefigures the total gathering of the eschatological people (George).

its scope or to foresee where it will lead them. They must be the "unifying center" of the new Israel[23] born of the New Covenant, the pillar of the new messianic community, the foundation of the new Jerusalem. They are not going to communicate the secret of some intimate experience to a few privileged individuals; from the first day, they are going to speak, through the mouth of Peter, "to the whole house of Israel".[24] There could no more have been Christianity without the Church than there could have been a Jewish religion without the chosen people. "The possibility of non-ecclesial Christianity, existing outside of worship rendered in common within the Church, could only have aroused supreme astonishment and total incomprehension in the New Testament community."[25] For all the New Testament writers, "to be Christian and to be a member of the one Church is one and the same thing."[26]

[23] The expression of Heinrich Schlier, *"L'unité de l'Église d'après le Nouveau Testament"*, in: *Essais sur le Nouveau Testament*, trans. A. Liefooghe (Cerf, 1968), 23. See below, 242–44. They are already the "germ" of this new Israel: cf. Yves Congar, *Ministères et communion ecclésiale* (Cerf, 1971), 18–19.

[24] Acts 2:36.

[25] Barth, *Dogmatique*, loc. cit., 31.

[26] Schlier, *Essais*, 218.

The preaching of the Twelve, however, was not the creative force. The Church that already lived in them after having been prepared by their formation in the company of their Master was conceived, so to speak, in the institution of the Eucharist,[27] was born from the side of Christ on Calvary[28] and arose with him from the tomb. Without the death and Resurrection of Jesus, their word would lack not only efficacy but an object. But in proclaiming the death and Resurrection of Jesus, they are not only giving witness to the facts that place the seal on the Good News, they are communicating a Life. The idea of a foundation still appears absolutely insufficient here in that it

[27] Lk 22:20. 1 Cor 11:25: "This cup is the New Covenant in my blood." Cf. J. Coppens, *"L'Eucharistie fondement de l'Église"*, in: *Recherches bibliques*, 7 (1965), 125–58. Jean-Jacques von Allmen, *Essai sur le repas du Seigneur* (Neuchâtel, 1966), 12: "Reduced to the essential, it is possible to say that it is in instituting the Last Supper that Jesus instituted the Church." Joseph Ratzinger, *Le nouveau peuple de Dieu*, trans. R. Givord and H. Bourboulon (Aubier, 1971), 9: "Let us not forget that the first night of Easter was the precise moment of the birth of the people of Israel."

[28] *"Formata est ergo ei conjux de latere ejus"* (Saint Augustine). A frequent theme with the Fathers and taken up again by Vatican II, in the constitution *Sacrosanctum Concilium*, n. 5. Cf. Henri de Lubac, *Paradoxe et mystère de l'Église* (Aubier, 1967), 42–44.

implies, in the beginning, the intervention of a
founder who remains exterior to his work and
who will soon disappear. The Church has a vital
principle, a soul, and this soul is the Spirit of
Christ. Visible and invisible at one and the same
time, organized society and mystical participation,
institution and communion, unfolding in history
and already breathing within the Eternal, she is the
stem in the midst of our universe, as Péguy said,
or the axis, the axial current, as Teilhard liked to
say,[29] charged with channeling in order to liberate
our miserable and sublime humanity, not only
nor in the first place from its thousand historical bondages, but from its congenital bondage,
from the evil that leads it to death. Heiress of the
Twelve, proclaiming after them "the Word of
Life" who dwells in her and who will not abandon
her, even in ages when her members seem to be
scarcely alive, she carries the hope of the world.

In order to *understand his faith*, as far as this word
"understand" applies to a reality which his reason
neither embraces nor measures, the Christian thus
needs to understand his Church. That is neither an
adventitious nor a supererogatory task. He needs
to understand her essential structure, her inward

[29] Texts in Henri de Lubac, *Teilhard et notre temps* (Aubier,
1971), 99–104.

scope. The complete Christian mystery forms one body with that of the Church.[30]

It is often said, and the comment is accurate, that treatises on the Church are late in origin. Point out the earliest ones, trace their genealogy, and you see them end in those increasingly numerous and extensive studies which characterize our twentieth-century theology and find their consummation, as it were, in the Vatican II consitution *Lumen Gentium*. You can even wonder if there is not a plethora there, and perhaps sometimes a sign of collapse, as if theological thought, reflecting the spirit of the community from which it flowed, no longer dared to plunge into the mystery of God, or no longer had the strength to do so. But the comment would be justified only with respect to the studies that assume a positivist conception of the Church or that systematically confine themselves to her exterior aspects, without linking her structure to her underlying nature. Or else it might proceed from too unreal an idea of this mystery of God which is in fact the intimate homeland into which all men, whether they know it or not, dream of being admitted. In its reflection on divine things, the human mind, however pure

[30] Cf. Henri Bouillard, *Comprendre ce que l'on croit* (Aubier, 1971), particularly 139–42, *"L'Esprit dans l'Église"*.

the impulse that carries it there may be, is too
weak to withstand the light and soon falls back on
itself, and it is to be feared that its failure only
imprisons it more within its own darkness. But it
is a salutary obscurity, a shadow strewn with
signs, or, to speak the early language of the
Church, an "economy", a "dispensation", which,
by making known to us what God is for us in the
work of our salvation, reveals to us in that way,
"in the opacity of signs and shadows", what it is
possible for us to glimpse of God himself.[31] Now
this work of salvation, completely contained within our Catholic creed, is not merely made known
to us by the Church; it is effected within the
Church; it is the Church herself in the depth of her
life—and it is in this way that we have access,
within the mystery of the Church, to the mystery
of God.[32]

That is what the Church Fathers understood so
profoundly, what they felt so intensely. If there is
no particular treatise on ecclesiology by them, it is
precisely because the Church is everywhere in
their thinking.[33] For them, she is the indispensable framework for all reflection just as for all

[31] See the admirable page by Saint Augustine, *De moribus
Ecclesiae catholicae*, l. 1, c. 7, n. 11 (PL, 32:1315).

[32] Cf. Henri de Lubac, *La foi chrétienne, essai sur la structure
du symbole des apôtres*, 2d ed. (Aubier, 1971).

[33] Melito of Sardis, however, did write a *Peri Ecclesias*

Christian life. Rather than being one particular article of their faith, rather than being a preliminary condition to the establishment of their relation to God or a society to which, because of its benefits, they are bound by a feeling of gratitude, she is in their eyes the reality at once historical and mystical that embodies everything, the universal place outside of which they would be in exile, lost. The more strictly they adhere to her and assert the demands of her discipline, dreading the sin of schism more than anything else, the more they exalt her fullness and her universal character. Athanasius, Moehler tells us, "depends on the Church like a tree depends on the earth into which it deeply extends its roots."[34] The same can be said of them all. Whatever the particular nature of their spirit or their action, whatever the aspects of doctrine that circumstances obliged them to probe or defend, they all have one common characteristic: they are men of the Church. The Fathers "had a clear *vision* of what the Church really was, even if this vision was never reduced to a *concept* or to a definition".[35]

---

which is lost today.

[34] *Athanase le Grand*; cited by P. Faynel, *L'Église*, 1 (Desclée, 1971), 124.

[35] Georges Florovsky, cited by Lelouvier, *Perspectives*, 52.

After a period in which the juridical mind predominated in the works and discussions concerning the Church and in which the spiritual life was often narrowed to an individualistic perspective unfavorable to authentic interiority, one might have thought that this spirit of the Fathers was about to rise again to experience a new springtime. At its dawning, the twentieth century was hailed from various quarters as destined to be the century of the Church. Protestant voices mixed with Catholic voices to proclaim it. Again, not long ago, at the suggestion of Cardinal Montini, who soon became Paul VI,[36] the Council convoked by John XXIII consecrated, as it were, the work accomplished during the preceding fifty years[37] by condensing the essence of its doctrinal teaching in its constitution *Lumen Gentium*. In this "fundamental text" (in which, as Jean-Jacques von Allmen, following Cardinal Garrone, tells

[36] It is known that toward the end of the first year of the Council, on December 5, 1962, Cardinal Montini, criticizing the excessive volume and scattered arrangement of the materials prepared, proposed to remove part of them and regroup the remaining subjects into a large schema on the Church of christological inspiration.

[37] See the well-documented work of Stanislas Jaki, O.S.B., *Les tendances nouvelles de l'ecclésiologie* (Rome: Herder, 1957).

us, Vatican II "has found its *raison d'être*"[38]), the first chapter sets forth precisely—just as the first schema *De Ecclesia* prepared for Vatican I had already proposed to do—"the mystery of the Church".[39]

A renewed youth, a stronger cohesiveness for a new start, a more lively and better-founded enthusiasm in the accomplishment of the great mission of unity received from Christ could be expected from it for the whole Catholic universe. The hope, it seemed, could be all the more firm because the Council set a "profound interior renewal"[40] as the fundamental condition for the spread of the Gospel, and because all its doctrinal work was accompanied by a program of reforms, the methodical accomplishment of which the Church authority immediately undertook by calling for the cooperation of all. Now everyone knows what has happened: the old seeds of dissolution gaining in virulence—a certain paraconciliar agitation foisting itself on public opinion as the only authentic interpreter of the Council's spirit—a resentment against the abuses of yesterday producing blindness to the benefits received from

[38] *"Remarques sur la constitution dogmatique Lumen Gentium"*, in: *Irenikon* (1966), 5.

[39] Henri Rondet, *Vatican I* (Lethielleux, 1962).

[40] *Ad Gentes*, n. 35.

the Church—the opening-up to the world to be evangelized turning into a mediocre and sometimes scandalous worldliness—numerous priests and religious losing the consciousness of their identity in losing that of their mission—the trust that the Council had placed in all the faithful in appealing to their initiative betrayed by influential groups—disdain of the tradition which the Council had exalted—the arrogance of theologians wishing to impose their own thinking on the Church, all the more tyranically as it is the more ill-considered and arbitrary—small pressure groups getting control of the information media and doing their best to intimidate the bishops—an insidious campaign against the papacy—under the pretext of a fight against that eccentricity which is dogmatism, a rejection of dogmatics, which is to say a rejection of the Christian faith in its original twofold character comprising an objective content received from authority—the worst neglect hiding behind the mask of flattering slogans—a full flowering of pseudo-prophetic pretensions—in the course of the century, a will toward destruction and a spirit of universal contestation against which even a more enlightened faith would have to be on guard —moral laxity presented as the adult man's irreversible progress which the Church must confirm —an intellectual and spiritual obscuration leading, on the one hand, to the unchecked reign of "human sciences" which could reasonably be only auxiliaries, and, on the other hand, to a politicization of the Gospel.

We are not painting the picture darker than it is. We do not fail to understand the reality of the problems which sometimes give rise to these excesses. Some would be inclined to reproach us, all the same, with a "negative attitude", a "distrust of the modern world", an excessive attachment to the past. They would regret that we do not seek to read "the signs of the times" better. We are fortunate if they do not take pity on our "anguish". Those are what have become the ritual formulas by which they draw a veil, as it were, in order to keep from seeing reality. There is no point in allowing ourselves to be intimidated by them. But we also know quite well that the Church, misunderstood in her history as well as in the great efforts undertaken to be everywhere more accessible and more evangelical, with flagrant insults heaped on the person of her chief shepherd, nonetheless pursues her course through the storm. In many regions, a Christianity that is more aware and more sober, because more tried, does not waste its heritage—in the coming hour, it will be able to breathe new vigor into us. The Spirit of God is always at work in the depths of many hearts, and he is preparing there new, unforseeable forces in silence. More than one sign of this is already discernable. Today as yesterday, in the most diverse situations, many faithful live the Gospel heroically. A whole generation of youth rediscovers the taste for the spiritual life. Here and there a work of profound doctrinal and spiritual investigation takes place, one which does not need to be supported by loud advertising in order to prepare syntheses of the future. We are confident that the fruits of the Council will ripen in their time. Now is the time for patience, that is, for hope, and hope does not deceive.

What storms the Church has already gone through! It was at the height of one of them that Saint Cyprian of Carthage wrote the following lines: "Evangelical vigor has not so subsided in the Church of God, the force of courage and of Christian faith has not so weakened, that there will not always be bishops to sustain the honor of God and of his priesthood. . . . It may be that there are betrayers within the Church who have undertaken to protest against the Church herself and, at the same time, to shake faith and truth. But with a great number, there remains a sincere and pure religion, a heart devoted to her Lord, a Christian faith which the infidelity of others has not caused to waver, but which, on the contrary, finds occasion in it to be strengthened, thinking of the words of the Apostle, 'And so! If some have not believed, has their lack of faith destroyed God's fidelity? Please God, no! God is truthful, and all mankind is false.' "[41]

Since the Catholic framework has been completely shaken, now is also the hour to become rooted in the essential. Whatever one might think of it, this is not a bad starting position for action and progress. Now a large number of the current negations, protests, or agitations, whatever the particular point at which they are aimed, apparently proceed from a loss of awareness among Catholics themselves of what constitutes the unique originality of their Church. From which arise—apart from the always limited problems of practical adaptation—all sorts of artificial problems, all sorts of false oppositions which, like so many uncriticized a prioris, encumber New Testament exegesis as well as doctrinal reflection or plans for reform—to say nothing of disputes of a pettier order. This is also the source, in more than one sincere search for renewal and progress, of diverse errors in orientation which lead to dead ends. This is why I hope that it will prove useful to seek to recall, on the subject of the Church, some

[41] *Epist.* 67, c. 8 (Hartel, 2:741 and 742).

of the essential truths which are historically and structurally at the foundation of the entire mystery of faith.

I am in complete agreement with all those who today issue an appeal for the social commitment of the Christian, for courageous combat for justice, for relentless work that demands the development of all people and of the whole human being. I understand no less than they that the best means of living the Christian tradition is not to turn always toward the past but to face the future in order to achieve there the work desired by God. They are right to think that the Spirit sent by Jesus does not cease to suggest new ways to his disciples in accord with new, or newly perceived, needs. But experience also shows that if the foundation should happen to be deficient, if faith grows tepid or disappears, if the fabric of the Church disintegrates, their most fervent appeals will remain useless, finding scarcely more of an echo than so many verbal demonstrations poured out by so many politicians, or that they would inevitably be perverted to encourage all kinds of miserable utopias. There is no fidelity to the Spirit without fidelity to the one who sent him. Now, the essential structures of the Church are not "ancient forms" which could be abandoned any more than the fundamental dogmas of our faith are out-of-date ideas in which a change of language would leave nothing subsisting. To the world of today just as to that of yesterday and to that of the first century, it is the same Christ who must be proclaimed, and it is the same Church who has the mission of proclaiming him. If, therefore, I seek to say plainly what a particular Church is, or what a bishop is, or the ministerial priesthood, or the papacy, without regularly making any definite allusion to the contemporary context of society, this is not at all to humor myself with abstract views nor to seek refuge in some other social context of the past by cultivating nostalgia for "a tranquil world in which the bishop tranquilly celebrates and preaches in his cathedral". It was not in a tranquil world that Faulhaber and von Gallen, under Nazi domination, preached yesterday in their cathedrals of Munich and Muenster; neither was it in a tranquil world that Ignatius of Antioch, in chains, dictated his letters to the churches or that Cyprian of Carthage addressed his to those who suffered persecution for Christ. Neither was tranquility always perfect when Augustine of Hippo preached in his cathedral, and his hard battle against the rival church of Donatus' party was always there to resume. As for the troubled era into which we have entered, it is perhaps one more invitation to the head of the Church to

celebrate and to preach, in his cathedral or elsewhere. The names of Ignatius, Cyprian, Augustine
would be references for us, still more so, those
of Peter, Paul and John, the first witnesses, the
founders, and I would not wish to advance anything that is not entirely conformed to their spirit
such as the tradition of the Church brings it to us.

Furthermore, it is far from my intention to treat
the subject in all its breadth. Neither am I unaware
that, even in limiting myself strictly to the internal
life of the Church, many other more immediately
relevant studies would be more appropriate, at
least for a time, to respond to the anxieties of
many. It would be wrong to disregard them,
and it would be fruitless to undertake them if
one were ever satisfied with classical solutions
when they often demand a genuinely innovative
effort. But when it is a matter of essential truths
—and sometimes of well-established historical
facts besides—one is never too classical: to affect
new views would then be an infidelity. If I were
told that priests of a certain age would rediscover
here "the main themes of the theology taught
them in the seminary", I would not take these
words as the gentle mockery they were intended
to be, but as the very expression of my desire:
in such a matter, the "main themes" of theology
have not moved aside to give place to any in-

vention whatever, and the younger priests have a right to receive in their turn the outline of these "main themes" which do not change. That can be affirmed without wishing in any way to canonize the manner in which I have endeavored to retrace them here nor, a fortiori, the more personal reflections which surround them on occasion. Without question, moreover, I do not believe that problems of structure are in themselves the most important. *I do not believe that structural reforms*, about which there has been much debate for some years, *are ever the main part of a program that must aim at the only true renewal, spiritual renewal*. I even fear that the present-day inflation of such projects and discussions furnishes an all-too-convenient alibi to avoid it. The conciliar formula *"Ecclesia semper purificanda"* seems to me as to others "much superior to the '*Ecclesia semper reformanda*' which is used so extensively nearly everywhere."[42] But *I do believe, on the other hand, that any disturbance, any change, or any relaxation of the essential structure of the Church would suffice to endanger all spiritual renewal.*

The two brief studies brought together here,

---

[42] Cf. von Allmen, *"Remarques"*, 40. It must be said, however, that we do not reject, for all that, the second formula.

due to two independent requests made of me,[43] approach the same fundamental problem from two points of view. They seek to throw a light on their subject only in terms of this problem. They tend towards the same end: to demonstrate that the mystery of faith, which is a mystery of life, is entrusted to "the living Church of God, pillar and support of the truth",[44] which is herself included within this mystery. Of the two intimately connected characteristics of this Church, institutional and mystical, hierarchical and communal, if the second is assuredly the principal in value, the more pleasant to contemplate and the one which alone will continue to exist, the first is its necessary condition. It is correct to say that it is the Spirit who is the "maker of the Koinônia"; but the Spirit, through the imposition of hands, gives the Church her pastors. It has been thus since the beginning, and it must be the same until the return

[43] A sketch of the first part was given at a conference in Venice, under the auspices of the Benedictines of San Giorgio Island and of the Cini Foundation; the second develops an article which appeared in the documents *Omnis Terra* of January 1971. At the request of several people, we have added as an appendix, despite its extemporaneous character and inevitable simplifications, an interview on the question of the priesthood given to *France catholique* and which appeared in its October 8, 1971, issue.

[44] 1 Tim 3:15.

of the Lord. Communion is the objective—an objective which, from the first instant, does not cease to be realized in the invisible; the institution is the means for it—a means which even now does not cease to ensure a visible communion. But their relations of reciprocal interiority could not be understood, nor, in consequence, could the nature and role of authority in the Church, just like the objectivity of dogma and the value of the sacrament, be recognized in their true sense if we did not believe, in giving our faith to Jesus, that the Christian life is a life received from above, a life to which we are begotten and in which we are nourished by a ministry coming from Jesus himself and which realizes historically a communion victorious over all history.

This life, said the old apostle John—and it is again to us that his word is addressed—"we proclaim to you so that you may enter into communion with us and so that our communion may be with the Father and with his Son, Jesus Christ, so that your joy may be perfect."[45]

[45] I Jn 1:2–5.

PART ONE

THE MOTHERHOOD
OF THE CHURCH

I

THE NEW TESTAMENT

When the Christian who knows what he is saying speaks of the Church as his mother, he is not giving way to some sentimental impulse; he is expressing a reality. "The motherhood of the Church", wrote Scheeben, "is not an empty title; it is not a weak analogy of natural motherhood. It does not signify only that the Church acts like a tender mother toward us. . . . This motherhood is as real as the presence of Christ is real in the Eucharist, or as real as the supernatural life that exists in the children of God." This is what I hope to show in the following account by studying the meaning of this expression in Christian tradition, and more particularly among the Fathers of the first centuries who made it one of their favorite themes. From this, I will then draw a few conclusions whose current relevance seems to command attention.

It could be said that the idea of the motherhood of the Church derives from the whole of New Testament teaching. I will only note here the few passages that introduce the expression itself.

Jesus' exclamation, reported by Saint Matthew, comes to mind: "Jerusalem, Jerusalem, you that kill the prophets and stone those who are sent to you, how often have I longed to gather your children, as a hen gathers her chicks under her wings!"[1] Here, still in the form of a simple comparison, is the idea of a double motherhood, of one motherhood which is going to take the place of another, of a double Jerusalem, as Saint Paul explains it in his Letter to the Galatians. Jesus compares himself to a mother, and the old Jerusalem, the mother-city of the Israelite people, is going to become, in the transformation effected by the passage from the Old Covenant to the New, "the Jerusalem above, our mother".[2] In other words, the Church will be the heir of the "Synagogue"—that *mater Synagoga* whose death Saint Thomas Aquinas evokes with a mixture of

[1] Mt 23:37.

[2] Gal 4:26. Cf. Tertullian, *Adversus Marcionem*, l. 5, c. 4 (Kroymann, CSEL, 47:581–82). Concerning this passage which gave rise to the Church, cf. Henri de Lubac, *Exégèse médiévale*, 1 (Aubier, 1959), particularly chap. 5, 305–63. Because of the serious misunderstandings on this subject

tenderness and ingenuousness when he says, with regard to the first Jewish converts to the new faith, who continued for some time to observe the Jewish rites, *"Hoc modo erat Mater Synagoga deducenda ad tumulum cum honore."*[3] Saint Augustine returns to the image of the mother hen in order to apply it to the Church, which has been charged by Jesus with continuing the maternal work of gathering together which he came to begin.[4]

The idea of spiritual motherhood holds an important place in Saint Paul's thought.

According to Paul, the Church, which is the Spouse of Christ, both virgin and fruitful at the same time, is the mother of all those who are born (reborn) in the Spirit and for whom she proclaims and maintains the pure and authentic doctrine of Christ.[5] Paul, in his role as apostle, compares

---

caused by an article appearing in *Esprit*, June 1971 (*"La rupture instauratrice"* by Michel de Certeau), I must declare that to read this chapter "in the perspective" recommended by this article is to go in direct opposition to the whole of my thought.

[3] "It is in this way that the mother Synagogue must be conducted with honor to her tomb" (*In 4 Sent.*, dist. 1, q. 2, art. 5, q. 4, solutio 3).

[4] *Contra Faustum*, l. 14, c. 9: *"sub alas Catholicae matris pullis fugientibus"* (PL, 42:299). *In Jo.* tract. 15, c. 4, n. 7 (PL, 35:1512–13).

[5] Eph 5. Gal 4. 2 Cor 11:2–4.

himself to a mother: is it not in fact through him that the Church brings forth her new Christians —coming from the Gentiles as from the Jews— who were converted by his appeal? "As a mother feeds and takes care of her children, such was our tenderness towards you", he writes to the first faithful of Thessalonica, "that we would have wished to hand over to you, along with the Gospel of God, our own life."[6] But he compares himself to a father as well, and does so in addressing the same Thessalonians and even in the same passage: "As you know, we have been for each one of you what a father is for his children, exhorting you, consoling you, entreating you to lead a life worthy of God, who is calling you to his kingdom and to his glory." And in fact, they receive the Apostle's preaching not "as a human message, but as the very Word of God, which it really is, the Word which is at work deep within those who believe."[7] Writing later to the Galatians, Paul returns to the image of motherhood: "My children, you for whom I continue to experience the pains of childbirth until Christ is formed in you!"[8] And in the First Letter to the Corinthians, it is again the image of paternity that prevails: "I am warn-

[6] 1 Th 2:7–8.
[7] 1 Th 2:10–13.
[8] Gal 4:19.

ing you as my beloved children; for, while you might have ten thousand teachers in Christ, you do not have more than one father, seeing that it was I who begot you in Christ Jesus through the Gospel."[9]

In this last text at the very least, there is clearly already much more than a mere image. It is a real paternity that Paul is attributing to himself.

Thus the Apostle is, on the one hand, one who, as a father or mother, tends to the education of his children. This is a long and exacting task, for Christ will not be formed in them, i.e., they will not attain the adult age of the Christian, in the course of one day; nor will it be in one day that they will become strong enough not to let themselves be led astray like children by every new doctrine in the air, or clearsighted enough not to let themselves be taken in by the deception and guile of men who wish to lead them into error.[10] But there is more. If the Apostle is an educator, it is because he is, first of all, truly a father: he has truly begotten sons "by the Gospel". He is fully aware of this. He knows that his relationship with

[9] 1 Cor 4:14–15. Citing this text in his *Journal* (July 1929), Paul Claudel noted by way of contrast, in considering the "teachers" or pedagogues: "The mind is easily reached, but the soul is not enriched", 1 (Gallimard, 1958), 869.

[10] Gal 4:19. Eph 4:14.

the Christians of Corinth and elsewhere is not simply that of master to disciple. His role among them is not restricted to that of philosopher or rabbi. He can say to them in complete truth: "I speak to you as to my children."[11] He has imparted a new life to these new Christians. He has made them pass into another sphere of existence: he has in actual fact begotten them in their Christian existence, that is, in their life in Christ. They have been regenerated, they are "reborn". From now on, they form a part of the new creation. In an incipient way, at least, they already constitute what he calls, in that eminently concrete language that corresponds to Christian reality, the "new man".[12]

That has been accomplished, he says, "by the Gospel". The Word of God is, in fact, in the fullest sense of the term, the "word of salvation". It not only announces salvation, it produces it in the one who receives it. It is not like human words, which, by the statement of a doctrine, can at the very most enlighten or dispose the intelligence to accept it by some external power of persuasion. It is alive and effective. "Word of life",[13] it penetrates to the innermost being. It converts and

---

[11] 2 Cor 6:13.

[12] Gal 6:15. 2 Cor 5:17, etc.

[13] Phil 2:16. Heb 4:12. Regarding the Word of God as understood by Vatican II according to Scripture and tradition:

renews. James and Peter express themselves in the same way as Paul. "God", says James, "wanted to make us his children by a word of truth so that we would be the first fruits of his creatures. . . . Receive this word into yourselves, therefore, as a seed that can produce the fruit of salvation in you."[14] And Peter: "Love one another with a pure heart. You were begotten anew (reborn) not from a corruptible seed but from an incorruptible one: the Word of the living and eternal God."[15]

These various texts echo numerous Old Testament passages that celebrate the fruitfulness of the divine Word, beginning with the work of the first creation.[16] These texts are themselves quoted and commented upon many times. In the fourth Gospel, faith, which receives the Word, is equally understood as rebirth, the passage from death to life.[17] And in the Second Letter of Saint John,

Henri de Lubac, commentary on the preamble and first chapter of the constitution *Dei Verbum*, in: *La Révélation divine* (*Unam Sanctam*, 70, 1968), 159–302. Cf. Heinrich Schlier, "*Traits fondamentaux d'une théologie néotestamentaire de la Parole de Dieu*", in: *Concilium*, 33:15–22.

[14] James 1:18, 21.

[15] 1 Pet 1:23–25.

[16] Thus Ps 33:9; 147:15, 18. Is 55:2, 10–11. Wis 9:1; 18:15. Cf. Pedro Gutierrez, *La paternité spirituelle selon saint Paul*, *Études bibliques* (Gabalda, 1968).

[17] Jn 3:5–8, etc. Cf. Donatien Mollat, "*La foi dans le quatrième évangile*", in: *Lumière et vie*, 22 (1955), 91–107.

moreover, we find the motherhood of the Church —of each particular church—evoked directly.[18] John, who is undoubtedly residing at Ephesus at the time, writes to the Christians of another city, which he does not identify, in order to place them on guard against seducers. "I, the Elder, to the chosen Lady and to her children, whom I love in truth. . . ." Thus begins the Letter. Who could this "chosen Lady" be if not the Church John is addressing? Clement of Alexandria and Tertullian, among others, have understood it in this way.[19] John continues: "I greatly rejoiced to meet some of your children who are living in the truth according to the commandment we have received from the Father." Then, at the very end, in the name of the community of Ephesus: "The children of your sister Chosen One send greetings to you."[20]

Such is the New Testament kernel of the patristic doctrine on the motherhood of the Church whose broad outline I must now retrace. As will be seen, the Fathers, in all their developments of this doctrine, do no more than bring out the inherent value of this "kernel". By making it bear fruit, they prove themselves faithful stewards.

[18] See below, part two, chap. 2.
[19] Clement, *Adumbratio* in 2 Jn 1 (PG, 9:737–38). Cf. below, chap. 5, 86.
[20] 2 Jn 1:4, 13.

II

PATRISTIC TESTIMONY

With the exception of the Apologists, who are addressing men outside of her, the Church is very frequently called "mother" in the writings of the early centuries. We will recall only a few examples of this.

In the Pastor of Hermas, the Church, personified, addresses the Christians of Rome in these terms:

> Listen to me, my children! It is I who have brought you up in all simplicity, innocence and holiness by the mercy of the Lord; it is I who have caused justice to fall on you drop by drop. . . . Listen to me, make peace among yourselves . . . so that, standing joyfully before the Father, I can render him a favorable account of you.[1]

We will see that in Gaul, Saint Irenaeus speaks in the same way. And likewise the Africans, too.

[1] *Pastor*, Vision 3, c. 17, 9 (R. Joly, SC 53 *bis*: 123–24).

Tertullian comforts the confessors of the faith who are in prison by assuring them that "the Mother Church" can from her maternal breasts provide enough to meet their spiritual needs.[2] For Saint Cyprian, "the Church is so obviously mother that this single word, *Mater*, suffices him to designate her without ambiguity."[3] He says, for example, that "it is impiety to abandon the Mother."[4] He multiplies these striking phrases:

> There is only one single Church, which, by her ever-increasing fertility, embraces an ever more plentiful multitude. . . . We are born from her womb, nourished by her milk, animated by her spirit.[5]
> The greater the number of virgins, the greater the joy of the mother in her glorious fertility.[6]

And again, in his letters:

> Let no one draw the Christians away from the Gospel of Christ! Let no one rob the Church of

[2] See below, chaps. 3 and 5. Cf. *De monogamia*, c. 7, n. 9 (CSEL, 4:58).

[3] Adrien Demoustier, "*L'ontologie de l'Église selon saint Cyprien*", in: *Recherches de science religieuse*, 52 (1964), 555.

[4] *Epist.* 44, c. 3 (Hartel, 2:598), etc.

[5] *De Ecclesiae catholicae unitate*, c. 5 (Hartel, 1:214).

[6] *De habitu virginum*, c. 3 (1:189). *Epist.* 46, c. 1 (2:604).

her sons!—Let them return to their mother, I mean to the Catholic Church![7]

In her love, this mother rejoices and suffers with her children; she welcomes them, gathers them. "She alone can give them true wealth."[8] And here is the celebrated phrase: "The Spouse of Christ brings forth sons spiritually for God. . . . He alone can have God as his Father who first has the Church as his mother!"[9]

Around the same time, in Palestine where he had been forced into exile, Origen expresses the same idea in the same terms: "He who leaves the Church", he says, "makes himself responsible for his own death. . . . He who does not have the Church for mother cannot have God for father."[10] Saint Augustine repeats it: "The Church is a

[7] *Epist.* 43, c. 5 (2:594). *Epist.* 47 (605). *De lapsis*, c. 2 (1:238).

[8] *Epist.* 10, 1; 16, 4; 41, 2; 59, 3; 73, 24 (2:490, 520, 588, 680, 797).

[9] *Epist.* 74, c. 7: "*Ut habere quis possit Deum Patrem, habeat antea ecclesiam matrem*" (2:804). Cf. Augustine addressing Faustus, who was claiming to hold sublime secrets and was rejecting the humility of faith: "*Audes insultare matronali verecundiae conjugis unici Filii Dei!*" *Contra Faustum*, l. 15, c. 6 (PL, 42:309).

[10] *In Leviticum*, hom. 11, c. 3 (Baehrens, 453–54). Cf. *In Matt.* 15:25: Priests and bishops are the spiritual fathers of Christians (GCS, 40:124).

mother for us. . . . It is from her that we were
born spiritually. . . . No one can find a paternal
welcome from God if he scorns his mother, the
Church."[11] In the sixth century, Saint Avitus of
Vienne exalts the unity of all the faithful in the
one same faith "under the sole God the Father and
the one mother Church."[12] I will return to some
of these phrases, which are particularly rich in
meaning. Let me note here that the motherhood of
the Church was also invoked in Africa in funeral
inscriptions. Thus on the tomb of a child in the
third century: "When you left this world, our
holy mother the Church took you into her arms
with love!" Saint Cyril of Jerusalem teaches cate-
chumens that the "Catholic Church is the proper
name of this holy mother of us all; spouse of
Our Lord Jesus Christ, . . . she bears the seal and
likeness of the Jerusalem above, which is free
and which is our mother. She began by being

---

[11] *Sermo*, May 94, c. 1: "*Manifestum esse non dubito . . .
ita nos ex Deo Patre et Matre Ecclesia spiritualiter nasci*"
(*Misc. Agost.*, 1:333); 92, c. 1: "*Neque poterit quispiam propitium
habere Deum Patrem, qui Ecclesiam, contempserit matrem*"
(ibid.). *In psalm.* 88, *Sermo* 2, c. 14 (PL, 37:1141). *Sermo* 359,
c. 6 (PL, 39:1595); etc.

[12] *Epist.* 1: ". . . *sub uno Deo Patre et una Ecclesia Matre*"
(PL, 59:200 A).

barren, but now she has numerous children."[13]
Optatus of Milevis gives multiple testimonies of
his affection towards her whom he names the
catholica mater. He knows that peace is attained
when, renouncing schism, one finally recognizes
this "catholic mother".[14] His expression will become quite popular; it is soon found again in
Augustine, then in Fulgentius, Caesarius of Arles
and still others.[15] It is especially common with
Augustine.[16] The great apostle of unity does not
cease to invite the Donatists to "come back to the
Mother Church, to the Catholic mother."[17]

Still more characteristic is the reference to the
Church in the official creed of the African Church.
This expression of faith is known to be very close
to the Roman creed. It does contain one word,

[13] *Catechesis XVIII*, c. 26 (PG, 32:1048 B).

[14] *De schismate Donatistarum* l. 7, c. 5: "*ab schismate recedentes,
agnita matre Catholica, secuti sunt pacem*" (CSEL, 26:178).

[15] Texts in Pierre Batiffol, *Le catholicisme de saint Augustin*,
5th ed. (Gabalda, 1929), 270–74.

[16] *Epist.* 58, 3; 185, 32 and 46 (PL, 33:226, 807, 913). *Sermo*
12, 5 (PL, 38:102–03). *Contra Gaud.* l. 1, 50 (PL, 43:737).
Contra duas epist. Pelag. l. 2, 5 (PL, 44:573). *Confessions*, l. 7,
n. 1: "*in fide spiritualis matris nostrae, catholicae tuae.*" *De moribus
Ecclesiae*, l. 1, c. 30, n. 62–63: "*Merito Ecclesia catholica mater
christianorum verissima . . .*" (PL, 32:1336), etc.

[17] *Contra Cresconium*, l. 4, c. 5, n. 6; c. 51, n. 61 (PL, 43:
550–51, 581).

however, that the Roman one does not; it explicitly affirms: *"Credo in . . . sanctam* matrem *Ecclesiam."*[18]

The motherhood of the Church is a frequent theme in the instructions for baptism. Thus in the sermons of Zeno of Verona: "Hurry to your mother. . . . Enter, be happy. You are soon going to be nursed, joyously, all together."[19] As for Zeno, so too for Saint Augustine the baptismal font is the *uterus* of the mother Church. He develops the image with a sustained realism.[20] The inscriptions in the baptisteries are expressed in the same way. One such inscription is that which Sixtus III had placed on the architrave of the Lateran baptistery between 432 and 440:

[18] Cf. Karl Delahaye, *Ecclesia Mater chez les Pères des trois premiers siècles*, trans. Vergriete and Bouis (Cerf, 1964), 98, 108.

[19] *Tract.* 32 and 33: *"Currite ad matrem. . . . Intrate felices, omnes simul subito futuri lactantes. . . . Fontanum semper virginis matris dulcem ad uterum convolate . . ."* (PL, 11, 478 A and 479 A). Other translated texts in *Le baptême d'après les Pères de l'Église*, coll. Ictys, 5 (1962), 75–79.

[20] *Sermo* 216, n. 7–8: *"Ecce uterus Matris Ecclesiae, ecce ut te pariat atque in lucem fidei producat, laborat in gemitu suo. . . . Illum Patrem, christiane, agnosce, qui . . . suscepit te ex utero matris tuae. . . . Pater Deus est, Mater Ecclesia"* (PL, 38:1080 and 1081). *Sermo* 56, c. 4, n. 5: *"tanquam utero Ecclesiae in fonte pariendi"* (379).

Gens sacranda polis hic semine nascitur almo,
  quam foecunditatis Spiritus edit aquis.
Virgineo foetu genitrix Ecclesia natos
  quos spirante Deo concipit, amne parit . . .
Fons hic est vitae, qui totum diluit orbem,
  sumens de Christi vulnere principium . . .
Nulla renascentum est distantia, quos facit unum
  unus fons, unus Spiritus, una fides.[21]

Three analogies are yet to be pointed out, analogies which make explicit the maternal traits of the Church, which in turn comes to be identified with the Woman of the Apocalypse, with Eve and with the Virgin Mary.

The vision of the twelfth chapter of the Apocalypse, showing the Woman who gives birth in heaven, is interpreted as referring to the Church. The male child whom she brings into the world is the community of believers. This is the interpretation given in the *Banquet of the Ten Virgins* of

[21] English translation by A. Swain, S.J.:
A race for heaven destined here is born
  From seed lifegiving, Spirit teeming tide.
Mother and virgin Church, the Spirit's bride,
  Here livens those who else of life were lorn.
This is the spring enlivening all our kind
  That flows from Jesu's loving, wounded Heart,
Nor suffers man from man to stand apart
  Whom water, Spirit, faith in one do bind.

Methodius of Olympus,[22] heir to a tradition that was already long, as witnessed by Hippolytus.[23]

More frequent is the theme of the new Eve, which is naturally associated with that of the new Adam. The Church was born from the open side of Christ on the Cross, as Eve was drawn from Adam's side during his sleep. As but one example, let me quote Tertullian, who writes in his treatise *De Anima*:

> Adam prefigured Christ and Adam's sleep represented the death of Christ, who had to die the sleep of death so that the Church, true mother of the living, could come from the wound in his side.[24]

Thus the image of the *Magna Mater* which dominated the Hellenistic paganism is found transposed into the Christian climate—a typical example of the boldness of Christian thought which was strong enough to seize, without contamination, everything that could serve to express it. The totality of the cosmos was included in this universal mother; everything living left her womb in order to return to it. In the same way—but with everything changed, everything renewed, everything

[22] *Sermo VIII*, c. 5 (SC, 95); cf. c. 10.
[23] *De Antichristo*, c. 60–61 (PG, 10:779–82).
[24] *De Anima*, c. 10 (CSEL, 20:372).

turned inside out, "converted"—the totality of the new cosmos is included in the Church.

Finally, other texts, equally numerous, specify that the Church is at once virgin and mother, as Saint Paul had already insinuated, and in this way the parallel mystique of the Virgin Mary is introduced. The first completely explicit reference to the maternal virginity of the Church is read in the celebrated *Letter of the Churches of Vienne and Lyons* relating the persecution in Lyons. It describes the faithful who had at first given way, then pulled themselves together:

> It was a great joy for the Virgin Mother to welcome back alive those whom she had cast out dead from her womb. It is by the living, in fact, that most of those who had apostasized will measure themselves once more; they will be conceived and brought to new life a second time.[25]

At about the same time or a little later, the author of a short treatise addressed *To Diognetus* wrote these words, which might have seemed enigmatic: "Eve is no longer seduced, but, remaining virgin, she proclaims her faith."[26] They are obviously to

[25] Eusebius, *Hist. eccles.*, l. 5, c. 1, n. 45–46 (SC, 41, G. Bardy, 18). Cf. Augustine (PL, 38:768; 40:397 and 399).
[26] *Ad Diognetum*, c. 12, n. 8 (H.-I. Marrou, SC, 33

be understood within the general framework of symbolism concerning the new Adam and the new Eve.

This maternal virginity, or this virginal maternity, which the Second Vatican Council was to bring to mind again,[27] is affirmed in many ways, notably in the works of Origen, Ambrose and Augustine. "All the Church", explains the latter, "is called virgin. The functions of her members are various, but all together they form one unique virgin. This virginity is one of thought. In what does it consist? In an upright faith, a firm hope, a sincere charity."[28]

The theme, which was developed by way of contrast with the story of the first Eve, is renewed and enriched by a parallel between the Church and the Virgin Mary.[29] Rather forgotten in recent centuries, it was to be taken up again in our own

---

bis:82–83; cf. 239–40). Cf. Justin, *Dialogue*, c. 100, n. 5 (ed. Archambault, 2 [1909], 125).

[27] *Lumen Gentium*, n. 63: "*In mysteriis enim Ecclesiae, quae et ipsa jure mater vocatur et virgo. . . .*"

[28] *In Jo.*, tract. 13, n. 12–13, with the allusion to Eve seduced and the quotation from 2 Cor 11:2–3. Likewise, *Contra Faustum*, l. 15, c. 9 (PL, 42:313–14).

[29] There are numerous documents on the subject in *Études mariales. La nouvelle Ève*, 4 v. (Lethielleux, 1954–1957). Cf. S. Tromp, *Corpus Christi quod est Ecclesia*, 2d ed. (Rome, 1946), 45–47. Alois Muller, *Ecclesia-Maria*, Paradosis, 5 (Fribourg,

times, sometimes expressed with rare success and great depth of thought, by authors as different as Paul Claudel, Pierre Teilhard de Chardin, Jules Monchanin and Hans Urs von Balthasar.[30] I would like to quote here just two examples from this abundant literature. The first is taken from a sermon by Saint Augustine:

> You to whom I am speaking, you are the members of Christ. Who has given birth to you? I hear the voice of your heart: it is the Mother Church, this holy, honored Church who, like Mary, gives birth and is virgin. She gives birth to nations, but they are the members of one alone, of him of whom she is the body and the spouse. In that, too, she bears the image of the Virgin Mary, because in this multitude, she is the mother of unity. As in Mary, we see in her perpetual integrity and incorruptible fruitfulness. What the first merited in her flesh, she has preserved in spirit. If the one gave birth to the only son, the other gives birth to numerous sons who, by this only son, are gathered into one.[31]

1952). Henri de Lubac, *Méditation sur l'Église*, 2d ed. (Aubier, 1953), chap. 7.

[30] Cf. Henri de Lubac, *Paradoxe et mystère de l'Église* (Aubier, 1967), 105–118.

[31] *Sermo* Denis 25, c. 8 (*Misc. Agost.*, 1:163). *Sermones* 192, 2; 195, 2; 213, 7 (PL, 38:1013, 1018, 1061), etc.

The second example is taken from the ancient liturgy of the Spanish Church called the Mozarabic Rite:

> The one gave salvation to the nations, the other gives the nations to the Savior. The one carried Life in her womb, the other carries it in the sacramental font. What was once accorded to Mary in the carnal order is now accorded spiritually to the Church. She conceives the Word in her unfailing faith, she gives birth to it in a spirit freed from all corruption, she holds it in a soul covered with the Virtue of the Most High.[32]

Cf. Cyprian (above, note 3). Leo, *Sermo* 63, c. 6 (PL, 54:356 BC), etc.

[32] *Liber mozarabicus sacramentorum* (PL, 162:570 BC). Cf. Guerric d'Igny, second sermon for Christmas, n. 1: "*O mater incorrupta, virgo fecunda, filius qui datus est tibi hos tibi dedit*" (SC, 66 [1970], 178).

III

CHILDBIRTH AND EDUCATION

The mystery of the Church is not a completely spiritual, celestial or interior mystery. "It is", writes Father Louis Bouyer, "the mystery of what God has accomplished, and never ceases to accomplish, on earth within a history, within the earthly history in which, by entering into it himself, he has become the principal actor."[1] It is the mystery of a social and visible Church which exists in the midst of the world, which acts through men and whose motherhood is exercised through Word and sacrament indissolubly united.[2]

A few distinct accents are noticeable within the unanimity just observed in ancient tradition with regard to this motherhood, depending on whether

[1] *L'Église de Dieu* (Cerf, 1970), 196.
[2] Augustine, *Epist.* 261, c. 2, concerning the bishop, dispenser of salvation by Word and sacrament: *"salutis illius dispensatorem per verbum et sacramentum"* (PL, 33:1077). There are numerous similar texts.

the birth of the Christian by the Church is considered in the sacrament (above all of baptism, followed by the Eucharist), or in the proclamation of the Word. But it is not necessary to see any opposition in that, or even a duality, properly speaking. In fact—as anyone with any religious instruction knows—the sacrament is never without the gift of the Word, and the Word itself is sacramental. It is the living Word announced by the Apostles, the Word of God himself, delivered, explained to men. The transmission of this Word by those who are its "servants" is not simple teaching, mere "catechesis". It is, for the one who really wants to open his heart to it, the communication of the life of Jesus Christ, Word of the Father.[3] We have seen that Saint Paul, who did not himself ordinarily baptize, nevertheless considered himself as father and mother of those whom he had raised up to the faith in order to introduce them into the Church.[4] When the *Prima*

---

[3] Bouyer, *L'Église*, 453: "The Word of God transmitted to the Church by the Apostles is not merely a Word that is entrusted to her, but the Word which gives her being, to the extent of determining forever the essence of her structure and of her mode of life. . . ."

[4] We should observe with Joseph Ratzinger, *Le nouveau peuple de Dieu*, trans. R. Givord and H. Bourboulon (Aubier, 1979), 30, that for Paul, "the Word is not hypostasized, set up

Petri celebrates the rebirth of those who receive the living Word of God,[5] it is undoubtedly a matter of both the preparatory catechesis and the baptismal formula at the same time. When Saint Irenaeus, in his *Demonstration of the Apostolic Preaching*, writes that the Apostles instituted the Church "by distributing to believers the Holy Spirit whom they had received from the Lord",[6] he is undoubtedly also thinking *per modum unius* about the concomitant distribution of the Word and the sacrament, considered as a double and unique channel through which the Spirit of the Lord is communicated. And when Paul Claudel exclaims, in the account of his conversion: "Praised be this great, majestic Mother, at whose knees I have learned everything!",[7] it is not a catechism or theology course

---

independently over against the Church; it has its place in the arrangement of mission and ministry. . . ."

[5] 1 Pet 1:23–25: ". . . *renati non ex semine corruptibili, sed incorruptibili per verbum Dei vivi. . . . Hoc est autem verbum, quod evangelizatum est in vos.*"

[6] *Demonstration*, c. 41 (SC, 62, Froidevaux, 96). *Adversus Haereses*, l. 3, c. 24, 1: "Those who do not share in the Spirit are not drawing the sustenance of life from the breasts of their Mother" (SC, 34:400). Cf. *Didache*, c. 10, n. 2.

[7] A curious parallel can be observed in Michelet, writing in his journal on August 5, 1843: "This great mother, the Church, all the more loved by me . . ." (quoted in Jean Gaulmier, *Michelet* [1968], 60).

he has in mind, nor even a sermon; it is above all the liturgy, that sacred act whose unfolding he had followed at *Notre-Dame de Paris* before participating in it.[8]

From another point of view, however, two tendencies in the way of explaining the maternal role of the Church could perhaps be distinguished. This is what Karl Delahaye has attempted, calling them the Greek tendency and the Latin tendency. For this purpose, he compares the language of the Greek Hippolytus and that of the Latin Tertullian:

> For Hippolytus, the Church is a mother through the transmission of baptism. For Tertullian, she is again mother in her care to educate afterwards. The interest of the Greek Hippolytus is directed toward the interior result. For the Latin Tertullian it is more a question of exterior—nearly juridical and disciplinary—concern for the life of believers; those who separate themselves from the Church are "without mother".[9]

[8] *L'Épée et le miroir*, 198–203. *Contacts et circonstances*, 14: "I spent all my Sundays in Notre Dame, and I went there as often as possible during the week . . ." (*Ma conversion*, 1909).

[9] *Ecclesia Mater*, 99. Tertullian, *De praescriptione haereticorum*, c. 42, n. 10: "*Plerique nec ecclesiam habent, sine matre, sine sede, sine fide, extorres quasi sibilati vagantur*" (SC, 46, Refoulé and de Labriolle, 149).

Still, antithesis should not be forced by imagining one of those dichotomies which are abused today in so many subjects, particularly this one. The Latins have never neglected the sacrament, the baptismal rebirth, the eucharistic mystery; nor have the Greeks, those who have been so interested in the *paideia*, underestimated the Church's role as educator. It is precisely Tertullian who says to us in his treatise *De Baptismo*: "You who are going to rise up again from the most holy bath of new rebirth, you who for the first time are going to stretch out your hands towards a mother and, with your brothers, ask the Father for the wealth of his charisms."[10] Like Irenaeus setting forth the vivifying faith which the Church distributes as food to her children,[11] he, too, knows that this faith is much more than a doctrine received by the intelligence thanks to the lessons of a pedagogue. The new Christian receives, he says, "the cutting of faith", borrowed from the tree which has lived and grown each day since the first communities received "the cutting from the apostolic seed".[12] As for Hippolytus, referring to the preaching of

[10] *De Baptismo*, c. 20 (SC, 35, Drouzy, 96). Cf. Faustus of Riez, *De Spiritu sancto*, l. 1, c. 2: "*Credimus Ecclesiam, quasi regenerationis matrem*" (CSEL, 21, Engelbrecht, 104).

[11] *Adversus Haereses*, l. 3, preface (SC, 34:94).

[12] *De praescriptione*, c. 20 (SC, 46:113).

the Gospel and to the slow formation of Christians, he declares: "The Church never ceases to give birth to the Word from her heart . . . and because she ceaselessly gives birth to Christ, God and man, she teaches all peoples."[13] Moreover, if Tertullian treats those who separate themselves from the Church as orphans, we have already seen above that this was equally the thought of the Greek Origen. And on the other hand, it is a Latin once again, Optatus of Milevis, who, in the same work in which he discusses schism, exalts the fraternity of Christians born of the same mother by explicitly asserting, not their community of doctrine, but the identity of the sacraments received.[14]

The early Father who best brings together these two aspects of the Church's motherhood is Origen. In uniting them, he adds a variety of harmonics which will be encountered again, in more or less scattered order, everywhere in subsequent Christian tradition, especially in the West. "With Origen, the image of the *Ecclesia mater* has a profundity never again attained. All the expressions of the

[13] *De Antichristo*, c. 61 (GCS, Hipp. vol. 1, 2:41–42).

[14] *De schismate Donatistarum*, l. 4, c. 5: "*Non enim potestis non esse fratres, quos iisdem sacramentorum visceribus una mater Ecclesia genuit, quos eodem modo adoptivos filios Deus pater excepit*" (CSEL, 26:103–4).

life of the Church are summed up in the image
of the mother who is ceaselessly giving birth.
The preaching of the Word, the administration of
baptism, prayers, various works: everything is
the activity of the Church giving birth to, developing and carrying to completion in the heart
of believers this gift from God which is eternal
life."[15]

Thus the voice of the great Origen is here the
voice of all Catholic tradition. It is particularly
valuable to listen to it today, at a time when a
number of people, giving in to that "bewilder-
ment of dissociation that invades and devastates
contemporary thought",[16] tend to loosen the bond
between Word and sacrament, or even at times to
break it. By minimizing the importance of the
second, they believe they are increasing that of
the first. In reality, they are misunderstanding the

[15] Delahaye, *Ecclesia Mater*, 120. As much could also be
said of Augustine, speaking of the Church as educator of men
and nations; thus *De moribus Ecclesiae catholicae*, l. 1, c. 10,
n. 17: "*Illi quos quasi vagientes Ecclesiae catholicae ubera sustentant
. . . pro suo quisque captu viribusque nutriuntur, perducuntque
alius sic, alius autem sic, primum in virum perfectum; deinde ad
maturitatem canitiemque sapientiae perveniunt*" (PL, 32:1318).

[16] Étienne Borne, in: *Recherches et débats*, 64 (1969), 35.
Cf. Jacques Maritain, *De l'Église du Christ, sa personne et son
personnel* (DDB, 1970), 107: "The common intelligence takes
pleasure in verbal oppositions."

one as well as the other, and all their preaching, or what still goes by that name, is not slow in showing the effects of this. Some very wrongly seek support in this matter from the recent council, under the pretext that the priest (or bishop) is designated there as minister of the Word before his sacramental duty is mentioned. This sequence is perfectly legitimate, and one might even say that it is essential, as obviously corresponding to the reality of things. Jesus did not begin by instituting Christian baptism or the Eucharist. His first apostles announced his death and Resurrection before baptizing those who believed on the weight of their testimony, and the Church, following their example, must always be missionary. But there is nothing in that to authorize the least dissociation of the two tasks, or, *a fortiori*, any contempt whatever for the second task which has been caricatured as the "sacral and worship function". The gift of the Spirit which engenders and maintains the life of Christ in us comes to us through this "great Mother" who delivers us in an incessant and many-sided activity, both Word and sacrament.[17]

We must understand, moreover, that if the Word

[17] Cf. M.-J. Le Guillou, *Le Christ et l'Église, théologie du mystère* (Centurion, 1963), 314. *Le ministère sacerdotal*, report of the theological subcommittee (Cerf, 1971), 89–90.

is already sacrament, the sacrament itself is Word. If the priest is the "messenger of the Gospel", in the name of the Church, he is still fulfilling that role, in fact eminently fulfilling it, "in the highest way in which the Word is realized, that of the eucharistic celebration, anamnesis of the death and resurrection of Jesus Christ".[18] And it is always through the Word that the priest carries out his pastoral function. He educates and guides the people entrusted to him, not as a mere master of catechetical or theological instruction, but as the father who, not without difficulty, raises his children. Just as missionary preaching was directed toward the eucharistic gathering, so the work effected by the sacramental Word is continued in pastoral preaching.[19] If, therefore, the priestly

---

F. Bourassa. *Parole et sacrement*, in: *Science et esprit*, 23 (Montreal,1971), 283–326.

[18] Karl Rahner, *L'essence du sacerdoce ministériel*, in: *Concilium*, 43:81. Pierre Grelot, *Le ministère de la nouvelle alliance*, 92, on the Word of Christ, "active power of which the proclamation of the Gospel message and the sacramental action are, in two different ways, the perceptible signs." Cf. Jean-Jacques von Allmen, *Essai sur le repas du Seigneur* (Neuchâtel, 1966), 28: "Preaching for which Holy Communion is too much, useless or in the way, is preaching that leads the Church astray instead of strengthening her."

[19] Concerning the difference between the professor of theology and the preacher of the Word, cf. Georges Chantraine,

ministry can be analyzed by distinguishing with-in it the three functions of Word, worship and government, it must not be forgotten that the reality of this ministry is one; that these three functions cannot be completely dissociated, and that each, considered separately, would inevitably be misunderstood. Finally, of course, the preceding explanations must not be taken in a narrowly sociological sense, which would too often be misleading in every respect, but as the expression of a view of faith that must govern the practice of this ministry through the most diverse situations and forms of action.[20]

If the motherhood of the Church is a reality, its analogy with physical motherhood nevertheless includes, like all true analogy, as much difference as similarity. The Church is not a mother "in the way Eve was"; she does not give birth to a people "whose birth would be a tearing away and the

---

Vraie et fausse liberté du théologien (DDB, 1969), particularly 71–97.

[20] *De sacerdotio minsteriali* (1971), 21: "*Hoc ministerium sacer-dotale . . . complectitur proclamationem verbi Dei, munus sancti-ficandi fidelium regimen. In his autem non de tribus diversisque ministeriis agitur, sed de uno atque indivisibili 'dynamismo' apos-tolico, qui promanat a ministerio Christi ministrantis atque vitam pro populo suo ponentis.*" Cf. 14: "*Sacerdotium Christi ergo semper debet considerari in tota sua novitate et in tota sua ampli-tudine, quatenus includit in se munus propheticum et munus regale.*"

source of innumerable oppositions",[21] as has been witnessed in all of history since the beginning. Quite the contrary, through childbirth, her goal is to react tirelessly against this misery that is congenital to our sinful race and to "gather into a single body the dispersed children of God".[22] That is what is expressed in a paradoxical image: whereas, in the physical order, the child leaves the womb of his mother, and, withdrawing from her, becomes increasingly independent of her protective guardianship as he grows, becomes stronger and advances in years, the Church brings us forth to the new life she bears by receiving us into her womb, and the more our divine education progresses, the more we become intimately bound to her. Saint Irenaeus was already saying "one must cling to the Church, be brought up within her womb and feed there on the Lord's Scripture."[23]

---

[21] Louis Bouyer, *Le sens de la vie monastique* (Desclée, 1950), 89–90.

[22] Jn 11:53. Cf. the *Confession helvétique postérieure* (1566): "The origin and institution of the ministries . . . were established by God himself and not by some new ordinance devised by men"—with the commentary provided for it by Jean-Jacques von Allmen, *Le saint ministère selon la conviction et la volonté des Réformés du XVIe siècle* (Neuchâtel: Delachaux and Niestlé, 1968).

[23] *Adversus Haereses*, l. 5, c. 20, n. 2 (SC, 153, Rousseau, Mercier, Doutreleau, 258–59): *"Confugere (oportet) ad Eccles-*

Saint Cyprian says in his turn: "Anyone who withdraws from the womb of the mother can no longer live and breathe alone: he loses the substance of salvation."[24] In his charity, he also expresses this wish: "If possible, let none of our brothers perish! Let our joyous mother hold enclosed within her womb the unified body of a people in full harmony!"[25]

The same idea is forcefully expressed in the *Banquet* of Methodius of Olympus when he comments upon the twelfth chapter of the Apocalypse: "The Church is with child, and she will remain in the throes of childbirth until Christ is formed and begotten in us." We recognize here the Pauline image. And again, a little farther on: "As long as all the citizens have not returned to their native country, the Church is in the throes of childbirth. She is forming 'psychics' which she brings into the world in order to make 'pneumatics' of them. This is why she is a true mother."[26]

---

iam et ejus sinu educari et dominicis Scripturis erudiri."

[24] *De Ecclesiae catholicae unitate*, c. 23 (Hartel, 1:231). A similar image in Augustine, *Confessions*, l. 4, c. 16, n. 31: *"in nido Ecclesiae tuae."*

[25] *De Ecclesiae catholicae unitate*, 230: ". . . *ut si fieri potest, nemo de fratribus pereat, et consentientis populi corpus unum gremio suo gaudens mater includat"*.

[26] *Sermo VIII*, c. 5 and 6 (SC, 95:213, 217). Cf. Optatus,

Whether it is a question of the entire history of the human race or of each of our individual lives, it can never be said that Christ is completed in any of us. In consequence, the maternal action of the Church toward us never ceases, and it is always in her womb that this action is accomplished for us. In the past, owing to historical circumstances, particularly the invasions by barbarous peoples into Western Europe, she has been able to play in certain human spheres an educative role which was one day to come to an end—but the same cannot be said of her essential role. Her mission of giving birth always remains. We do not cease to draw life from her "as children enclosed in the womb of their mother live from the substance of their mother".[27]

One consequence resulting from this is of great significance. We know Saint Paul teaches that since the fullness of time has come to pass we

---

De schismate Donatistarum, l. 7, c. 2, on the repentant sinner: "*Primo recipiendus est, deinde sustinendus pio sinu matris Ecclesiae*" (CSEL, 26:168); a closely related image, l. 1, c. 11: "*Deserta matre Catholica, impii filii . . . a radice matris Ecclesiae . . . abscedunt*", 14.

[27] Bérulle, *Discours de l'état et des grandeurs de Jésus*, 10. Cf. Bossuet, *Sermon sur la Trinité*: "Happy motherhood of the Church! . . . she conceives outside of her womb, she gives birth within her womb . . ." (Lebarcq, 2 [1891], 56). *Prima Petri*, 2:2.

are no longer children, enslaved by the elements of the world or imprisoned under custody of the Law. For us the time of pedagogues is past. According to the logic of our faith, we must become adults in Christ.[28] On the other hand, Jesus said, "If you do not become like little children, you will not enter the kingdom of heaven."[29] At first glance, these two instructions might appear contradictory. But they are not at all. Nor will we merely say that it is possible to reconcile them, that the Christian can become an adult and still preserve a childlike spirit. Such language would be completely inadequate. In reality, we must speak, not of reconciliation, but of correlation. The more the Christian becomes an adult in Christ, as Saint Paul understands this, the more also does the spirit of childhood blossom within him, as Jesus understands it. Or, if you prefer, it is in deepening this childlike spirit that the Christian advances to adulthood, penetrating ever deeper, if we can put it this way, into the womb of his mother.

"The whole task", says a modern writer, Gilbert Cesbron, "consists of becoming fully adult while

[28] Gal 3:19–29; 4:1–11.
[29] Mt 18:2–4; 19:14–15.

remaining fully a child." And he adds: "It is the secret of Christianity".[30] It is in fact a secret, and our human reasoning is powerless to discover it or to reveal it to others. Or better, as Jesus himself says: "Whoever has ears to hear, let him hear", or again: "I bless you, Father, for having hidden this from the wise and clever and for having revealed it to little ones."[31] Perhaps, however, we can try to glimpse something of it. In our natural life, in fact, each step toward adulthood is a move away from childhood; it is like a loss of paradise, a step toward old age and decrepitude. But in the spiritual life, on the contrary, all progress is, in the proper sense, a renewal. It is an increase in vitality, it is one more step taken within a substantial newness and consequently always new. He who lives by the movements of the Spirit of Christ goes, as Saint Gregory of Nyssa says, "from beginnings to

---

[30] *Ce que je crois* (Grasset, 1970), 208. On Péguy's glorification of childhood: Hans Urs von Balthasar, *De l'intégration, aspects d'une théologie de l'histoire* (DDB, 1970), 264–65: "The spheres that Péguy thereby opens to Christian piety, to the Christian sense of the world and existence are of a richness and fruitfulness not yet assimilated." Cf. Cardinal Renard, *Qu'est-ce qu'un chrétien?* chap. 2: "*Qu'est-ce qu'un chrétien adulte?*" (Beauchesne, 1971), 43–59.

[31] Mt 11:25.

beginnings" toward a new youth and toward a new spring.[32] It is also what was long ago sung so marvelously by Clement of Alexandria, that heir to an old culture in its decline, who was so keenly aware of Christianity's explosive newness. Many are familiar with the lyrical pages of his *Protrepticus* on this subject. I would like to quote some similar, lesser-known lines from his *Paedagogus*:

> Our title of "children" expresses the spring-time of our whole life. The truth that is in us does not grow old. Wisdom is always young. . . . "Like a mother consoles her son", says the Lord (Is 66:13), "I myself will also console you." The mother draws her little children into her arms and we—we seek our mother, the Church.[33]

[32] Similar passages in Irenaeus and Augustine, cf. Henri de Lubac, *La foi chrétienne, essai sur la structure du symbole des apôtres*, 2d ed. (Aubier, 1971), 365–67.

[33] L. 1, c. 5, 20–21 (SC, 70, Marrou and Harl, 147–49).

IV

MOTHERHOOD OF
THE ENTIRE CHURCH

The foregoing leads us to a specific and fundamental principle: the Church is our mother. We would not be Christians if we did not acknowledge in her this essential characteristic. Even after their secession, the Reformers of the sixteenth century explicitly acknowledged it.[1] Calvin attached such importance to it that some reproached him for setting up in that way a divine "quaternity". In our own century, Karl Barth has gone even farther; he considers that Calvin did not really understand the full significance of the thesis expressed in this image of maternity. Why, he asks, does the author of the *Christian Institute* begin to speak of the Church only in his fourth book, as one of those *externa media vel adminicula*—of the highest im-

[1] See the texts of Luther, Calvin, Bucer, Du Plessis-Mornay quoted in de Lubac, *La foi chrétienne*, 231–34.

portance without doubt, but still "exterior"—by which God invites us to and keeps us within the community of Christ?[2] Our traditional liturgies have also sung of this Mother. Witness this verse of a hymn from the Church of Paris for the Feast of the Dedication:

. . . *Christus enim, norma justitiae,*
Matrem nostram desponsat hodie
Quam de lacu traxit miseriae,
    Ecclesiam.[3]

But finally, what is this Church? Is it necessary to consider her only in her shepherds, in those who, following the first apostles, perpetuate with authority the Word and sacraments among us? In other words, is it solely a question of that Church which we call today the hierarchical Church? No, or at least not always, and never exclusively. The hymn we have just quoted shows very clearly that it is a question of all those, without distinction, whom Christ has drawn "out of the lake of

[2] *Dogmatique*, vol. 4, t. 2, fasc. 3 (Geneva, 1971), 2. Never, Barth goes on, here in agreement with Emil Brunner, "would an apostle have dreamed of considering the community as a mere 'external means' serving the salvation of individual Christians."

[3] . . . Now Christ, the model of what all may be,
Has taken Church, our mother, for his bride,
Unlocked the prison of her misery—
    His love is she. (trans. A. Swain, S.J.)

misery". And in fact it is precisely that which the most ancient patristic tradition has already declared and which all Christian centuries have repeated and which is again declared today by those who do not consider it beneath themselves to contemplate this mystery. The Woman who, in the twelfth chapter of the Apocalypse, gives birth and escapes the dragon is the entire people of God. The whole Church, the entire Christian community is mother. But she is not mother in the human way. "In carnal marriage", Saint Augustine explains to us, "the mother and child are distinct; in the Church, on the contrary, mother and child are one."[4]

That is a teaching we must analyze closely.

Considered as a "body" or as a "people", Body of Christ or People of God, the Church appears first of all as a totality. She is, if it can be put this way, the total consciousness or, better yet, the total being of believers.[5] Pastors and faithful are united in one same Church; together they form a single People, a single Body. They are all together the flock of whom Christ is the Shepherd. This is obviously Saint Irenaeus' understanding when he says, in that doctrinal summary, the *Demonstration*

[4] *In psalm.* 127, 12 (PL, 37:1684).
[5] Cf. Hans Urs von Balthasar, *Théologie de l'histoire*, 2d ed., trans. R. Givord (Fayard, 1970), 125, 136.

of the Apostolic Preaching: "The Lord has given the Church more children than he gave the Synagogue of the ancients."[6] In fact, in that previously cited *Letter of the Churches of Vienne and Lyons*, of which he is perhaps the principal writer and which in any case arose from the same milieu, concerning the two martyrs Alexander and Blandine, we read the following lines, which not a few would find strange today, but which reproduce expressions derived from Saint Paul:

> Alexander remained standing before the tribunal and, by signs, exhorted the others to confess the faith. . . ; he seemed to those who surrounded the tribunal to be experiencing the pains of childbirth. . . . As for Blandine, the last of all, like a noble mother who has exhorted her children and has sent them victorious on ahead of her to the king, she herself went through all the struggles of her children as well.

And after having completed this account, the *Letter* ends by saying that all the martyrs whose courage it has just celebrated "left behind them neither grief to their mother, nor dispute, nor hostility between their brothers, but joy, concord and charity".[7]

[6] *Demonstration*, c. 94 (L.-M. Froidevaux, SC, 62:161).
[7] In Eusebius, *Hist. eccles.*, l. 5, c. 1, n. 49 and 55: c. 2, n. 7

With Hippolytus, and even more with Origen, arises the great theme in Christian thought, resumed indefinitely ever since, of the structural analogy between the Church and the Christian soul. Origen condenses it in his concept of the *anima ecclesiastica* or of the *vir ecclesiasticus*. Saint Ambrose expresses it by saying that "it is in the saints that the Church is beautiful",[8] and Pascal is merely summarizing a long tradition when he writes to Mlle. de Roannez that "all that happens to the Church happens also to each Christian individually".[9] If, therefore, the Church is mother, each Christian also is or should be a mother. In his place, according to his own vocation, in union with all the others, he participates in the maternal function of the Church.

It is first of all in himself that, through the action of this Church, the Christian gives birth

---

(G. Bardy, SC, 41:18, 20–21, 25).

[8] *De mysteriis*, c. 7, n. 39: ". . . *In his formosa est Ecclesia*" (B. Botte, SC, 25 *bis* [1961], 176).

[9] Cf. de Lubac, *Exégèse médiévale*, 2:558–71. "The heart of every Christian", Newman will say, "should represent the Catholic Church in miniature, for the single Spirit makes the entire Church and each of her members a temple." "Connection between Personal and Public Improvement", in: *Sermons Bearing on Subjects of the Day*, new ed. (1879), 132.

and growth to the Word of God which he has received, from which he lives and which he makes bear fruit.

> The mouth of the Father has begotten a pure Word; this Word appears a second time, born of the saints. Constantly producing saints, it is also itself reproduced by its saints.[10]

Here originate the innumerable variations on the birth and growth of the Word of God in the soul that have multiplied ever since. While derived directly from Scripture, the patristic teaching on the motherhood of the Church was occasioned rather by the paschal catecheses that provided the framework for baptismal ceremonies. This new, more subtle theme is found more in the celebration of Christmas feasts. The Western Middle Ages saw, in the three Masses said at Christmas, a symbol of the three births of the Word: the first being the eternal birth in the bosom of the Father; the second, his historical birth from the womb of the Virgin as a result of his Incarnation; and the third, fruit of the second, his spiritual birth in the womb of the Christian soul.[11] Each of these three

[10] Hippolytus, *In Daniel*, l. 1, c. 10 (Bardy and Lefèvre, SC, 14:88).

[11] It is to the degree that this characteristic of the dependence of the third birth with respect to the second is

births is produced, in its way, in silence and in secret.

"The soul which has received the seed of the Word", says Origen, "forms this received Word within her until she herself gives birth to the spirit of the fear of God."[12] Saint Bernard, who drew great inspiration from Origen, also celebrates the birth of the Word in the soul, and the Cistercian school has followed his example. "Faithful soul", says Guerric d'Igny, preaching on the Annunciation, "open your breast very wide, expand your affection, fear to be confined in your heart! Conceive the one whom no creature can contain."[13] This is not, however, merely a theme of one particular school. It is encountered again everywhere. The Christian soul, affirms Rupert of Deutz, "truly becomes mother of the Word of God."[14] The Rhineland mystics, Tauler and many others, hold forth on the subject at length.[15] Bérulle sees

---

forgotten that an extra-Christian mysticism or gnosis will develop.

[12] Origen, *In Levit.*, hom. 12, c. 7 (Baehrens, 466). Cf. 1 Jn 3:9.

[13] *Sermo II in Annuntiationem* (SC, 166, Morson, Costello, Deseille [1970], 41).

[14] Rupert, *In Isaiam*, l. 2, c. 91 (PL, 167:1362 AB).

[15] Von Balthasar, *De l'intégration*, 259: "The supernatural fruitfulness of the soul arises entirely from the 'germ of God'. . . . But once the Word has been received, the co-

in the mystery of the Incarnation, without prejudice to its historical reality, "a permanent mystery and not a momentary action."[16] And Saint Francis de Sales says the same thing in another way: "It is the good Jesus to whom we must give birth and produce within ourselves."[17] This simple language is that of John XXIII in his Christmas message in 1962: "O Eternal Word of the Father, son of God and son of Mary, renew once again in the secrecy of souls the wonderful marvel of your birth!"[18]

Such a doctrine is profound. It is the common possession of both Eastern and Western spirituality. Even in our own time, the Russian Orthodox Leo Zander writes: "If the Church is and remains the body of Christ, perpetuated by the Spirit, we, her members, are all called to conceive the Lord who is born in our soul so that we might participate in the divine life." We have there,

---

operation of the soul is the indispensable condition of its growth. This explains the interweaving motifs of maternity and sonship, closely related to that of the believing soul, something which German mysticism has grasped very distinctly since Eckhart, but which Origen had already clearly seen."

[16] *Opuscules de piété*, 55, 2 (ed. Rotureau, Aubier [1943], 205).

[17] Letter of January 24, 1608.

[18] Cf. de Lubac, *Exégèse médiévale*, 4 (1964), 506–13. Jean Daniélou, *Le mystère de l'existence* (1968), 67–68.

vividly expressed, the very essence of Christian mysticism; and contrary to what might first appear to be the case, this doctrine, while interiorizing the mystery, does not in itself lead to any individualistic distortion. Still, however justified, in ecclesiology itself, this application of spiritual maternity to the soul of every Christian may be, it is undoubtedly more important and in any case more immediately consistent with patristic thought to consider this maternity as that of the entire Church, which all the faithful living the life of Christ participate in spreading. That is to say, therefore, a maternity of all, indivisibly, with respect to each one, and of each one with respect to all. The more each one, on his part, is an adult in Christ—which means, as we have seen, the more intimately he is bound to his Church—the more he exercises this maternity.[19] Clement of Alexandria understood it in this way when, after having spoken of the "perfect" ones in Christ who are all the more "little children", he went on to reunite them all in "a single virgin become mother—whom I love to call the Church".[20] This was also Newman's understanding of it when, re-

[19] Henri de Lubac, *Histoire et esprit* (Aubier, 1950), 61–63.

[20] *Paedagogus*, l. 1, c. 6, 42 (SC, 70, Marrou and Harl [1960], 186); cf. 25 and 32–34 (156 and 168–72). In the sixth *Stromaton*, c. 16, 146, Clement, referring to Exodus 20:12,

counting in his *Apologia* the impression produced in him by the assiduous reading of the Fathers, he said: in this Church of the Fathers "I recognized my spiritual Mother. . . . The renunciations of her ascetics, the patience of her martyrs, the irresistable determination of her bishops, the joyous impetus of her forward progress, exalted and confounded me at the same time."[21] We could add that it is still understood in this way even today by those Russian believers who, without being associated with any official hierarchy, edit the little mimeographed journal entitled the *Message of Salvation*: "Inestimable Mother", they say in fact, "unforgettable Mother, radiant and all beautiful, Mother of sorrows, born on the Cross, you who give birth on the Cross, Mother of innumerable children, how sweet it is to meet you!"[22]

---

will see the mother whom he must honor rather as "divine gnosis and wisdom".

[21] *Apologia pro vita sua*, trans. Michelin-Delimoges (Bloud and Gay, 1939), 62.

[22] Cf. André Martin, *Les croyants en URSS* (Fayard, 1970), 166. *Lumen Gentium*, c. 8, n. 65.

V

FATHERHOOD OF THE CLERGY

However, the complementary truth must not be forgotten. The Body of Christ is not an invisible Church or an invertebrate people. It is always owing to the immediate mediation of pastors that this maternal function of all and of each one can be exercised, whether in relation to the Word of God in the individual soul or with regard to the community as a whole. For it is through them, successors of the first apostles,[1] that the divine life continues to be transmitted, and it is they who have the responsibility of seeing to it that the "virginity" of the faith is preserved both intact and fruitful. They are the "co-workers of God" among us; they are the "dispensers of the mysteries of God" for us; they pronounce "the word of reconciliation" over us as plenipotentiaries of

[1] See below, part two, chap. 4, 242–45.

Christ.[2] This is the origin, for example, of the title *Domina mater Ecclesia* which Tertullian, inspired by the Second Letter of Saint John, gives to the "hierarchical" Church.[3] This is also the origin, as we have seen, of the title of father which Saint Paul claimed, the same title usually given to the bishop. He is truly the father of his people. The bishops joined together in council are called "the Fathers". The same holds true for those whose line extends from the beginning, assuring not only the authentic transmission of a doctrine but also the propagation of a life. The faith proclaimed at Nicea, says Saint Athanasius, "has passed from Fathers to Fathers", and it suffices for the great bishop to demonstrate that the Arian doctrine "does not come from the Fathers" to conclude that it must be rejected.[4] "Remember the holy

---

[2] 1 Cor 3:2; 4:1. 2 Cor 5:18–20. "Without doubt, the hierarchy is not the Church; but without it, there would be no Church": B. Botte, in: *Études sur le sacerdoce, Lex orandi*, 22 (Cerf, 1957), 123. The hierarchy is not the Church, but the structure of the Church is hierarchical. There are no grounds for opposing, as a current slogan does, a "pyramidal" concept of the Church against a "communal" concept; in their exclusivity, these two concepts are only caricatures, and the influence of either one upon the Church's daily life can be disastrous.

[3] *Ad martyres*, c. 1 (PL, 1:691–93).

[4] Saint Athanasius, passim (PG, 25, col. 28 BC, 465 C,

Fathers to whose hands you have been entrusted",
says Saint Gregory of Nyssa.[5] And Saint Jerome,
writing to Nepotianus: "Be obedient to your
bishop, consider him as the father of your soul."[6]

Saint Augustine shows a certain hesitation in
this matter. Arguing with the Donatist faction
about the case of the bishop Cecil, whose real
or pretended defection had been the occasion of
schism, he affects, perhaps, not to plead the cause
of a father, but to examine the cause of a brother:
"God is our father, the Church is our mother;
good or bad, Cecil is our brother. . . . Those
whom I call fathers here below, it is to honor
them, but I know no other father of my salvation
than God."[7] By that, moreover, he wants to shift
the debate, to dissociate the *causa Ecclesiae* from

---

605 C, etc.).

[5] *Epist.* 3 (PG, 46:1024 C).

[6] *Epist.* 52, c. 7 (J. Labourt, Belles-lettres, 2:182). Ed.
Schillebeeckx, *Le message de Dieu*, Fr. trans., *Foi vivante* (Cerf,
1970), 96: "In the patristic era, those who were considered
'Fathers' were very concrete personages: for the local churches,
it was their founder (Basil, *Epist.* 210, 3); for each individual
Christian, it was the bishop who had baptized him and who
had initiated him into the mystery of salvation (Basil, *Epist.*
204, 2)."

[7] *Sermo* 359, c. 6, on his discussion of Carthage: "We have
agreed to discuss this cause, but as one of a brother, not as one
of a father or mother . . ." (PL, 39:1595). Cf. *In psalm.* 86, 1.

the *causa Caeciliani*. It is clear from the long account of this long debate at Carthage (June 411) that he keeps brushing aside the urgent questions which the Donatist bishop Petilianus heaps upon him: to the point where he is accused of always giving ambiguous answers. Petilianus wants to judge the Catholic Church of Africa on the basis of Cecil's case; Augustine, for his part, appeals to Christ, who comes from God, and to the Church of Christ which has come from Jerusalem to Africa: "Neither the crimes of any man nor the calumnies of any man will separate me from this God who is father or from this Church who is mother."[8] Be that as it may, his reserve corresponds well to an habitual tendency in his thought, sometimes approaching occasionalism,[9] which makes secondary causalities disappear, as

---

[8] *Gesta collationis carthaginensis* (Mansi, vol. 4; col. 229–33). "*Petilianus episcopus: Tu quis es? Filius es Caeciliani, an non? Tenet te crimen Caeciliani, an non, si fuerit?* —*Aug.: Ego in Ecclesia sum in qua Caecilianus fuit.* —*Petil.: Unde caepisti? Quem habes patrem? etc.*" "*Petil.: Ipsa sunt illa ambigua, quibus ab hodierni diei percurrit principio. . . . Tandem aliquando expressius dicat utrum patris loco habeat Caecilianum, ex quo deducta est ista progenies.* —*Aug.: Habeo caput, sed Christus est. . . .*"

[9] Gérard Philips, *Le Christ-chef et son corps mystique*, quoted by Jacques Pintard, *Essai sur le sacerdoce selon saint Augustin*, mimeographed thesis, Paris, Faculty of Theology (1955), 128. See also Augustine, *Epist.* 232, c. 2 (PL, 33:1027).

it were, before the primary causality. He, like everyone, knows, moreover, and loves to repeat that in the work of salvation it is God who does everything: "*Ipse aedificat, ipse monet, ipse terret, ipse intellectum aperit, ipse ad fidem applicat sensum vestrum.*"[10] But he nonetheless recognizes the differences in position and function within the Church. On the other hand, the Gospel itself obliges him to maintain at one and the same time that Jesus is the only Pastor and that Peter is nonetheless pastor as well, for Jesus is "the Pastor of pastors".[11] And as for the analogous case of fatherhood, tradition was too solidly founded for him to refuse to follow it. In a sermon that dates probably from Lent of 416, he is full of wonder that a layman's son, becoming bishop, thus becomes the father of his father.[12] In another sermon, he takes the

---

[10] *In psalm.* 126, 2 (PL, 37:1668): "It is he who builds, he who warns, he who inspires (salutary) fear, he who opens the intellect, he who inspires faith in you." Cf. *Gesta collationis* (col. 233), quoting 1 Cor 3:6 and concluding: "*Patrem salutis meae non teneo nisi Deum.*" Cf. M. Jourjon in *Saint Augustin parmi nous*, 151–78.

[11] *Sermo* 285, c. 5 (PL, 38:1295–96); *Sermo* 153, c. 5 (765); *In psalm.* 126, 3 (PL, 37:1669).

[12] *In psalm.* 109, 7: ". . . *Admirabilius est quod potest contingere, ut . . . episcopus factus laici filius sit pater patris sui*" (PL, 37:1450). Cf. Pintard, *Essai*, 54, 73. *Confessions*, l. 8, c. 2, n. 3.

opportunity afforded by some words from the psalmist, "The place of your fathers, your sons shall have", to make a further refinement. He shows how bishops, taken from among the sons of the Church and not coming from outside her or from some higher caste, nevertheless become fathers for this Church which first gave birth to them:

> The apostles begot you; they preached, they are the fathers. Could they always remain among us? Will the Church be abandoned because they are gone? Not in the least. "In place of your fathers, sons have begotten you." What does that mean? The apostles were sent as fathers; to re-place those apostles, sons were born to you who were constituted bishops. Where, in fact, did these bishops come from who are all over the world today? The Church calls them fathers, she who gave birth to them, who placed them in the sees of their fathers. Do not, therefore, consider yourself abandoned because you no longer see Peter in person, or Paul, or because you no longer see those to whom you owe your birth: a fatherhood has arisen for you from your own children. . . . Such is the Catholic Church. She has given birth to sons who, through all the earth, continue the work of her first Fathers.[13]

[13] *In psalm.* 44, 32 (CCL, 38:516). Cf. *In psalm.* 28, 2.

We should note in passing that this implies a certain idea of tradition which, on the one hand, assures its normative character and, on the other, prohibits confusion with any custom, routine, or fundamentalism whatever. Tradition, according to the Fathers of the Church, is in fact just the opposite of a burden of the past: it is a vital energy, a propulsive as much as a protective force, acting within an entire community as at the heart of each of the faithful because it is none other than the very Word of God both perpetuating and renewing itself under the action of the Spirit of God; not a biblical letter in the individual hands of critics or thinkers, but the living Word entrusted to the Church and to those to whom the Church never ceases to give birth; not, moreover, a mere objective doctrine, but the whole mystery of Christ. Through this tradition, as the Second Vatican Council has just reminded us, the Church passes on to each generation "all that she herself is", all that gives her life.[14] In that very continuity, tradition is thus a perpetual principle of renewal; it ensures for the body of the Church, under the vigilance of her pastors, that perpetual youth of which Clement of Alexandria spoke to us. All generations undoubtedly do not make equal use

[14] Constitution *Dei Verbum*, c. 2, n. 8.

of it; very far from it. The phenomena of sclerosis as well as those of fatal emancipation are not rare—but the treasure of the Word is always there, at the bosom of the Church which has received the promises of life. Whatever the faults, insufficiencies or ignorance of men might be, that treasure is, as Saint Irenaeus says in inimitable language, a living deposit which in itself does not grow old; which, quite the contrary, under the action of the Spirit, is endlessly restored to youth; even more, which continuously renews the youth of the body that contains it.[15]

Here again we observe the coincidence between the teaching of the ancient Fathers and that of the last Council. Both establish the same relationship, although sometimes with different words, between the motherhood of the whole Church and the fatherhood of those who receive the mission of directing her (this is the language of the Fathers), or between the universal priesthood and the hierarchical ministry (this is the language of the

[15] *Adversus Haereses*, l. 5, c. 24, n. 1 (Sagnard, SC, 34:398–400). Cf. the very Newman-like definition given by Father Louis Bouyer, *Le sens de la vie sacerdotale*, 29: "The tradition of which we must be the repositories and the witnesses is . . . the divine Word living always in the medium proper to him, never ceasing to bathe, so to speak, in that mother-water and to dwell there alive with its original life."

Council, no less founded on tradition).[16] Those who are called to exercise this "pastoral" ministry have a share in the responsibility of Christ, the unique Mediator.[17] They are the normally indispensable instruments, chosen to communicate the life of Christ and to maintain it within the Church—which can then, in her entirety, through each of her sons, exercise her maternal function with regard to all those who have already entered or who are destined to enter into her womb.[18]

The word "mediator", sometimes applied to the clergy, should not be misinterpreted. Like the word leader, pastor or father, it is then obviously taken in an analogical or subordinate sense. And it does not mean "intermediary" any more than when it is a question of the unique Mediator, in the absolute sense. Father Louis Bouyer has explained it well in commenting on a page by Pseudo-Dionysius. Perhaps it would be useful to

[16] Constitution *Lumen Gentium*, c. 2, n. 10.

[17] Ibid., c. 3, n. 28 and 41.

[18] On the cooperation between the "fatherhood of the hierarchy" and the "motherhood of the community": Delahaye, *Ecclesia Mater*, 256–57. The reader will see for himself the nuances that distinguish our two interpretations. Cf. Saint Thomas, *Summa Theologica, Secunda secundae*, q. 183, art. 2. In *Lumen Gentium*, the title of mother is given to the Church in n. 6, 14, 42 and 63; in *Sacrosanctum Concilium*, in n. 14 and 60. Cf. de Lubac, *Paradoxe*, 59–119.

reproduce the main point of what he says:

> Even if it is through a higher creature that
> we receive the gift of God, we always receive it
> directly, and, for that reason, completely. In the
> evangelical view, mediators, whoever they may
> be, beginning with Christ himself and because all
> mediation is only an extension of his, are never
> intermediaries, who always separate as much as
> they conjoin. . . . The most humble of the faith-
> ful has needed the "hierarchy" of the Church in
> order to receive the gifts of the Father, and he can
> keep them only by maintaining respect for the
> distinction between vocations and the correspond-
> ing gifts. But it is nevertheless *the* gift of God that
> he receives, the gift in which God himself is given,
> or rather, all things considered, the gift in which
> God *gives himself* in a direct manner.[19]

"Neither Christ, nor the Church nor her hierarchy constitutes an intermediary stage between

[19] *L'Église*, 317–18. One can have many reservations, moreover, about the language as well as the thought of Dionysius;
one can also note that he used the word "hierarchy" in a
broader sense than that which has come down to us; the only
thing important to us here is to isolate the exact meaning of
Catholic doctrine in the use of the different words we are
discussing. On the subject of the influence of Dionysian
exemplarism on the concept of the priest, see the remarks of
Georges Chantraine, "*Josse Clichtove, témoin théologien de
l'humanisme parisien*", in: *Revue d'hist. ecclés.*, 66 (1971), 507–28.

man and God: in faith, the believer apprehends
directly the faith of the Church and the *fides Christi*,
which in Christ is hypostatically united with the
fides Dei."[20] Thus, to speak for a moment like
Pseudo-Dionysius, the "hierarchs", which is to
say the bishops, in no way dominate the Christian
people: they are their servants. The "hierarchy" is
a "diakonia".[21] Origen observed that he who is
called to the episcopate is called, not to a principate,
but to the service of the whole Church.[22] Optatus
of Milevis likewise contrasted the *ministerium* of
Catholic pastors to the *dominium* whose spirit he
criticized in those belonging to the "Donatist faction".[23] That is a theme often revived by Saint
Augustine. The Bishop of Hippo continually refers to himself as the servant of his people, the
servant of the members of Christ, the servant
of others in Christ. In one of his sermons, he
has one of the faithful say to him—with his own

[20] Hans Urs von Balthasar, *La Foi du Christ, Foi vivante*
(Aubier, 1968), 79.

[21] *Lumen Gentium*, c. 3, n. 24. Mt 23:11; Mk 9:35;
Lk 22:27.

[22] *In Isaiam*, hom. 6, n. 1: *"Non ad principatum vocatur, sed
ad servitutem totius Ecclesiae"* (13:239).

[23] *De schismate Donatistarum*, l. 5, c. 7: *"Nolite vobis majes-
tatis dominium vindicare. . . . Ministerium exercet turba famu-
lorum. . . . Est ergo in universis servientibus non dominium, sed
ministerium"* (CSEL, 26:136–37).

wholehearted approval—"*Servum meum te fecit, qui te suo sanguine liberum fecit*".[24] ("He has made you my slave, he who freed you by his blood.") Yet it should be noted that it is the Lord, not the people, who has placed him in this condition. If the bishops are the servants (*ministri*) of the Christian people, it is because they are, first of all, essentially the "servants of God", the "servants of Christ Jesus" among them. Thus spoke John, Paul and Ignatius, well before Augustine.[25] Paul even uses a stronger word, the very word that the Gospel of John has Jesus use to designate his apostles: they are bound to Christ as his "slaves"

[24] *Epist.* 124, n. 2: "*Populus Hipponensis cui me Dominus servum dedit*" (PL, 33:473). *Epist.* 78, address: "*Dilectissimis fratribus, clero, senioribus et universae plebi Hipponensi, cui servio in dilectione Christi, Augustinus in Domino salutem*" (267). *In psalm.* 103, *Sermo* 3, 9: "*Dicite hoc nobis, quia verum dicetis*"; he then quotes 2 Cor 4:5: "*Nos autem servos vestros per Jesum*" and adds: "*Bene diligite servos vestros, sed in Domino vestro*" (37:1366). *De oper. monach.*, c. 29, n. 37 (40:576–77), etc.

[25] Jn 12:26. 2 Cor 6:4. Phil 1:1. Col 1:7, 23. 1 Tim 4:6. 2 Tim 2:24. In 1 Th 3:2, διάκονον τοῦ θεοῦ, the last two words are perhaps a gloss to make the meaning of διάκονος more precise. Cf. Ignatius, *Ad Smyrn*, 12, 1: "Burrhos . . . is a model of service to God" (SC, 10:166). Augustine, *Epist.* 228, n. 2: "*servi Christi, ministri verbi et sacramenti ejus*"; n. 4: "*ministerium Christi*"; n. 6: "*Christi ministri*" (PL, 33:1014, 1015); but also, n. 6:"*quotidianum ministerium dominici corporis*" (1016).

(δοῦλοι).[26] They are, furthermore, as Paul says to
Titus, his "stewards".[27] They are the "ministers
of the New Covenant",[28] the "servants of the
Gospel",[29] the dispensers of the Word and sacraments through which the gift of God is communicated to the people.[30] In the first proclamation of
the Word, their service is already a "liturgy" of
a sacred nature. "I render spiritual worship to
God", wrote Paul to the Romans, "by preaching
the Gospel of his Son. . . . God has given me the
grace of being a priest of Christ Jesus among the
Gentiles, carrying out the priestly function of the
Gospel of God (ἱερουργοῦντα τὸ εὐαγγέλιον τοῦ
θεοῦ), so that they will become an acceptable
offering, sanctified in the Holy Spirit."[31]

[26] Rom 1:1. Jn 13:16.

[27] Titus 1:7. 1 Cor 4:1: "ministers of Christ and dispensers
of the mysteries of God." Augustine, *Epist.* 261, n. 1–3.

[28] 2 Cor 3:6–9.

[29] Col 1:23. Eph 3:6–7. Cf. Lk 1:2.

[30] Augustine, *De moribus Ecclesiae catholicae*, l. 1, c. 32,
n. 69: Priests and bishops are *"ministri divinorum sacramentorum"*
(PL, 32:1339). *Epist.* 259, n. 2: ". . . *in aeternae civitatis servitio
constitutus minister verbi sacramentique divini"* (33:1074). *In
psalm.* 109, 1 and 126, 2 (1445, 1668). *Contra litteras Petiliani*,
l. 3, n. 66.

[31] Rom 1:9, 15:16. Clement, *Ad. Cor.*, c. 44 (SC, 167:172–
74). Hermas, Ninth Similitude, c. 31, 4, on the members
of the hierarchy λειτουργοῦντες τῷ κυρίῳ. Numerous other

Thus, in the guidance of communities, it is a question of a service which is exercised with authority on behalf of God and which calls for obedience. This is obvious not only with Paul, whose authoritarian passages in the Second Letter to the Corinthians are famous,[32] but also in the Letter of Peter and in the Johannine writings. It is equally evident in the Letter of Clement of Rome which, written in order to remedy an anarchical situation, has been described as being "in its entirety an affirmation of unity by authority".[33] So it is, too, with Ignatius of Antioch, who wants presbyters to be obeyed "like the law of Christ", etc. In his attitude of humble service, Augustine nonetheless says to the faithful of Hippo: "Help us by your prayer and by your obedience."[34] Certainly, ministers are taken from the midst of the Christian people, and they always remain within the Church, not above her; but that does not mean that they lack real authority in the exercise of their

---

examples. Cf. Jean Colson, *Ministre de Jésus-Christ* (1966), 182–83. By contrast, Paul speaks of "ministers of Satan"; 2 Cor 11:14–15; cf. 23.

[32] 2 Cor 2:9; 4:6; 10:6; 13:10.

[33] Pierre Batiffol, *L'Église naissante et le catholicisme*, 3d ed. (Gabalda, 1909), 147.

[34] *Sermo* 340, n. 1: "*Adjuvate nos et orando et obtemperando*" (PL, 38:1484).

mission. They have been selected in a great variety of ways: acclamation by the *plebs*, election by the bishops of the province[35] or by some other constituted body, nomination by the pope at the end of various processes. Those are contingent particulars which have varied greatly from century to century and from region to region, and none of which has ever failed to arouse criticism.[36] But in no case is it from the Christian people that these ministers hold their commission, nor, consequently, the authority necessary for its achievement. They are not an emanation from the priestly consciousness of the Church. They are given to the Church by the Father, "in a movement (a 'mission') that continues the one by which he

[35] Cf. Cyprian, *Epist.* 67, c. 5. Details for the first centuries in Albano Vilela, *La condition collégiale des prêtres du IIIe siècle* (Beauchesne, 1971), 293–97. Cf. Origen, *In Levit.* hom. 6, n. 3 (Baehrens, 362–63). Pierre Batiffol, *La paix constantinienne* (Gabalda, 1914), 78–79: "When a church has lost her bishop, the neighboring bishops arrange to meet there" to elect a successor to him in the presence of the "plebs" of the place; then they impose hands on the one elected.

[36] Origen was already rejecting the election by the people: *Plebs "quae saepe clamoribus ad gratiam, aut ad pretium fortasse excitata, moveri solet"* (*In Num.* hom. 22, n. 4; Baehrens, 208). ". . . *non quos imperitum vulgus agnoscit"* (*In Gen.* hom. 3, n. 3; Baehrens, 42).

gave his Son".[37] They are not delegates of the community, but Christ's delegates within it.[38] In other words, to borrow the expressions of a Protestant theologian, "the essential ministry of the Church is of messianic, not ecclesial, origin"; it "does not come *from* the Church, it comes from Christ *to* the Church."[39] Or again, to use Father Congar's words this time, we can say that, in one respect, the hierarchical ministries are indeed instruments of the body of the Church, but that "it is necessary to see under what conditions: at least in their sacramental stages, these are instruments that Christ", in instituting the pastoral function of the apostolate, "instituted prior to the body in order to fashion the latter. They are not instruments that the body, already alive and animated by the Holy Spirit, would give itself."[40]

---

[37] J.-M. Hennaux, *Le sacerdoce, vocation ou fonction?* (NRT, 1971), 482.

[38] *Lumen Gentium*, c. 3, n. 27: "Charged with particular churches as vicars and legates of Christ, the bishops direct them, etc."

[39] Jean-Jacques von Allmen, in: *Dossier* (Lyons, 1970), 144.

[40] Yves Congar, "*Un essai de théologie sur le sacerdoce catholique*", in: *Revue des sciences religieuses* (1951), 293–94. Batiffol, *L'Église naissante*, 153: it is obvious that with Clement the pastor's authority "is not a power delegated by the assembly:

Certainly, moreover, selected as we have said from within the heart of the community of the faithful, each of the pastors represents before God the particular community of which he has been given charge, particularly in presiding over its prayer.[41] But they are also and above all the representatives of God for it.[42] More precisely, at the head of the people, gathering together their prayer and their offering, they are, like Christ, head of all of the body of the Church. Before the people, they are like Christ, coming from the Father to espouse his Church. They are the ambassadors of

it is an office . . . which those who have been invested with it pass on to their successors." For a number of people today, "the pastor is not very popular; the vertical relationship between the priest and his community appears dangerous and suspect to many"; this is undoubtedly because it is misunderstood or because certain pastors have proved to be authoritarian in things that did not concern the essence of their mission; it is also, in certain cases, perhaps because some have not known how to adopt the point of view of faith.

[41] Cyprian, *Epist.*, 67, c. 2: "*In ordinationibus sacerdotum non nisi immaculatos et integros antistites eligere debemus, qui sancte et digne sacrificia Deo offerentes, audiri in precibus possint quas faciunt pro plebis dominicae incolumitate. . . . Plura diligentia et exploratione sincera eos oportet ad sacerdotium Dei deligi quos a Deo constet audiri*" (Hartel, 2:736, 737).

[42] Cf. Pius XII, address of November 2, 1954, about those who say "that the priest acts *only* as delegated by the community" (*Doc. cath.*, November 14, 1954, 1430).

Christ and the instruments of the Holy Spirit: "As my Father has sent me, I send you".[43] "The Holy Spirit has established you to be the pastors (the guardians) of the Church of God."[44] They are therefore genuine leaders: ἡγουμένοι,[45] προήγουμένοι,[46] προϊσταμένοι.[47] All that has been written contrary to this during the past few years, by stressing only the value of the word διάκονος, is contrary to both the practice and the declara-

---

[43] Jn 20:21. Cf. Jn 7:16–17. 2 Cor 5:18–20. Maximus of Turin, *Sermo* 51: "*Ipsos Paracletus visitat et illustrat, quos mysteriis suis idoneos Salvator elegit*" (PL, 57:636 C). Cyril of Alexandria, *In Jo.* (PG, 74:708 D). Cf. Joseph Lécuyer, *Le sacerdoce dans le mystère du Christ* (Cerf, 1957), 307–11.

[44] Acts 20–28. Paul, discourse at Miletus: "*Attendite vobis et universo gregi, in quo vos Spiritus sanctus posuit episcopos regere* (ποιμαίνειν) *Ecclesiam Dei.*"

[45] Heb 13:7, 17:24. Lk 22:26. Acts 15:22; cf. 14:12. Clement, *Ad. Cor.* 1, 3; 21, 6 (SC, 167, 100, 138). Origen, *Matt. com.* 16, 8 (GCS, 40:493); *In Num.* hom. 22, 4 (GCS, 30:208).

[46] Hermas, *Visio* 2, c. 2, 6: *Visio* 3, c. 9, 7. Cf. Mt 2:6; Acts 7:10.

[47] 1 Th 5:12. Lucien Cerfaux, *La théologie de l'Église suivant saint Paul* (Cerf, 1965), 367, translates "presidents". André Lemaire, *Les ministères aux origines de l'Église* (Cerf, 1971), 79: "The *proistamenoi* thus have a doctrinal and disciplinary role strongly analogous to that of the "Elders" of the Jewish communities who possessed, in particular, the right of excommunication." Cf. 1 Cor 12:28: κυβερνήσεις.

tions of the first apostles as well as to those of their successors.[48]

It is quite possible to say, therefore, if one insists, that "the sacrament of Orders adds only a functional specification to the mission of every Christian",[49] if we wanted by doing so to underline the obvious fact that all hierarchical ministry is an "office", a "function", and this other essential truth, which is always good to remember, that there is among Christians no discrimination whatever of castes or categories in the order of the spiritual life, of the imitation of Christ and of union with God—in the order of the "common priesthood" or of "Christian dignity". Nothing in the Church resembles those radical divisions

[48] Paul was not afraid to affirm forcefully the ἐξουσία that he received from the Lord to establish the Church among the Corinthians: 2 Cor 10:8; 13:10; 7:15. There is thus no reason for opposing ἐξουσία (*potestas*) and διακονία (*ministerium*). When Hans Küng writes that "the whole New Testament intentionally avoids the secular functional terms for designating the ministers of the community" and that "instead, and by opposition, it speaks of service (διακονία)", he seems to me to exaggerate the facts for the benefit of a false doctrinal antithesis.

[49] R.-J. Bunnik, *Prêtres des temps nouveaux*, trans. from the Dutch (Casterman, 1969), 136. Cf. Henri Holstein, *Hiérarchie et peuple de Dieu* (Beauchesne, 1970), 71.

set up long ago by the Pseudo-Gnostic theorists[50] between "hylics, psychics and pneumatics". We need not fear any division between "totally committed Christians" and "second-rate Christians". All are called to the same holiness. But the phrase quoted is acceptable only on the condition of not intending the "only" to be taken in a depreciative sense, and of not misunderstanding the sacred nature of this function; on the condition of not thereby contesting the fact that, while they are taken from the heart of the community, the pastors are placed at its head and that, I repeat, it is from Christ and from his Spirit, not from the community, that they receive, along with the responsibilities of their charge, the authority which is inseparable from it.[51] But, on the other hand, the defenders of this authority cannot forget that it is itself completely subordinate to the service of the Word and sacraments to which they were called. This is a truth that is too often misunderstood or at least too often neglected, in theory as well as in practice, and one which it is perhaps particularly necessary to stress today: "the pastoral function in the Church, far from confining itself to a function of government, in-

[50] I Tim 6:20. Irenaeus, Origen, etc.

[51] Cf. A. Descamps, "*Aux origenes du ministère, la pensée de Jésus*", in: *Revue théologique de Louvain*, 2 (1971), 3–45.

cludes government only in this perspective".[52] In other words, given what we have seen above, the authority of the bishop has an essentially paternal character. If he is head, it is because he is father. And every priest charged with a ministry participates at his own level in this authority and exercises it with the same character. "Poor little priest that I am", notes the country priest depicted by Bernanos in his *Diary*, after his conversation with the lady of his village, "before this woman so superior to me . . . I understood what paternity was."[53]

Once more, in order to understand the reality without being tempted to reject either one or the other of its aspects or to make them rigid, it is necessary to take care not to oppose through a play of concepts what can be understood and justified only by union. In the examination of the

[52] Bouyer, *L'Église*, 182: "It is only as a consequence of this fundamental ministry of the Word and sacraments that the apostolic ministry implies a power of government: that is, a power to apply the Word to the whole life of the community, so that this community itself, in all the life of its members, will draw the consequences of its faith in the Word and of its participation in the sacrament." Cf. 2 Cor 10:13–18. And already, Dom Gréa, *L'Église et sa divine constitution*, new ed. by Gaston Fontaine (Casterman, 1965), l. 3, chap. 2.

[53] Georges Bernanos, *Journal d'un curé de campagne*, 199.

fundamental relationship which binds the faithful
and pastors together, we must set aside that spirit
once said by Father Yves Congar to be "inspired
by the devil", that spirit which always seeks to
"transform into a motive for opposition" what
we should be striving to maintain "in a spirit
of communion".[54] If we were not careful, our
analytical and critical epoch would furnish us with
many occasions of falling into this trap. The people of God are not cut in two. The faithful need
pastors in order to be engendered and nourished in
Christ. But that in no way signifies that pastors
are not also Christians like them, nor that they
have by themselves any superiority whatever.
They are, with them, *conservi, condiscipuli*.[55] Their
fatherhood, which is participation in the divine
Fatherhood, is, as Saint Paul says, fatherhood "in
Christ".[56] It is what could be called a wholly
"instrumental", "ministerial", or "vicarious"
fatherhood.[57] The "flock" in their keeping is not

[54] *Le Christ, Marie et l'Église* (Cerf, 1952), 32.

[55] Augustine, *Sermo* 261, c. 2 "*Simul audiamus, simul dis-
camus. Non enim quia loquor et vos auditus, ideo vobiscum non
audio. Qualis Deus Christus? Audi mecum; non, inquam, me audi,
sed audi mecum. In hac enim schola omnes sumus condiscipuli*"
(PL, 38:1203).

[56] 1 Cor 4:15. Augustine, *In psalm.* 77, 11 (CCL, 39:1077).

[57] Gutierrez, *La paternité*, 163, 235–36. To be more precise,
in order to set any possible uneasiness to rest, we should not

theirs; it is, as Saint Peter says, "the flock of God".[58]
Nor does that mean that the faithful have only a
passive role in the Church. That is a complaint
frequently heard, and it must be admitted that it
is often justified. It remains to be seen whether
for their part pastors themselves would not sometimes have to complain, and perhaps even more
so, of the passivity of the flock. In any case, let
us repeat, all the children of the *Ecclesia mater*
participate in her maternal function. All are jointly
responsible for the Gospel, all must work toward
the edification of the community, all are called
to represent to men in truth the one who came
among men to serve them. "Do you think that
we are alone, standing in the pulpit, in proclaiming Christ?" says Saint Augustine in one of his
sermons. "Of course not! The whole Church
preaches Christ."[59] And Saint Avitus of Vienne
writes to a layman: "It is not only the bishops

take this word to mean that pastors are substitutes for the
Lord who is henceforward absent from his Church, but only
to indicate the entirely subordinate character of their ministry. Cf. Vatican II constitution *Sacrum Concilium*, c. 1, n. 7:
"*Christus Ecclesiae suae semper adest, praesertim in actionibus
liturgicis.*" Mt 10:40, 18:20.

[58] 1 Pet 5:2. Cf. Acts 20:28. Augustine, *Epist.* 231, c. 6
(PL, 33:507).

[59] *In psalm.* 96, 10 (PL, 37:1243). Cf. *Sermo* 94 (38:580).

who are troubled about the state of affairs in the Church: this solicitude is common to all the faithful."[60]

The Spirit blows where he wills. And if a great part of his action, undoubtedly the most profound, is exercised in the secrecy of hearts or in breathing new life into humble everyday tasks, it is still easy to demonstrate, throughout the history of the Church, that the most active and influential members of this great body have often been laymen or priests who did not belong to the "hierarchy". What greater or more fruitful initiatives could be found, for example, than those of Benedict of Nursia, Francis of Assisi or Ignatius of Loyola?[61] (Such men did not spend their time criticizing bishops or popes, of either the present or the past, by reproaching them for not having accomplished everything.) One Church historian has been able to say that in the seventeenth century there were numerous laymen with

[60] *Epist.* 36, *viro illustri Senario: "Non ad solos sacerdotes Ecclesiae pertinet status: cunctis fidelibus sollicitudo ista communis est"* (PL, 59:253 B).

[61] And "among the lives that the Church puts forward for imitation by her faithful, that of Saint Teresa of Avila offers a particularly admirable example of what the union of the most loyal obedience to the most enterprising initiative ought to be": Yves de Montcheuil, *Problèmes de vie spirituelle*, 5th ed. (l'Épi, 1957), 89.

recognized charisms. "There are laymen at the origin of a certain number of religious orders or priestly societies." They did not proclaim that they were prophets, but they knew that they had something to say and do, and their initiatives were easily accepted by the episcopate. If the Church was not at that time called the "people of God", she was without hesitation called the "Church of the Holy Spirit", or the "Church moved by the Holy Spirit", and the hierarchy did not take offense at it, any more than the laymen ordinarily misunderstood the role and authority of the hierarchy.[62] In our own century, in doctrinal, social or spiritual matters, how many laymen —like Maurice Blondel, Louis Massignon (who late in life became a priest), Jules Zirnheld, Marius Gonin, Edmond Michelet—have played an eminent role in the life of French Catholicism! Yet pastors are nonetheless fathers.[63] It would be very wrong to reject this "concept of a paternal type of authority" as improperly derived, in order to be applied in a domain where it is inappropriate, "from the image of the authority of the father of a family in relation to his children"—or from the

[62] Cf. F. Roulier, in *Dossier* (Lyons, 1970), 208.

[63] Saint Thomas More to his judges, July 1, 1535: "It was a pope, Saint Gregory, who in sending us Saint Augustine, gave birth to us in Christ."

image of the moral authority which in times past a "person of note" could enjoy. Such is not its origin, as we have sufficiently demonstrated. In reality, to suppress the "paternal type" of authority in the Church would not only be to suppress in principle the character of respect and reciprocal affection in the relations between the faithful and pastors; it would be to destroy the only legitimate foundation of this authority. In that case, either it would be necessary to renounce all spiritual authority and preach anarchy, or the Christian would be unavoidably subjected to an authority that was abusive in its very principle, and consequently tyrannical, however benign its forms and conditions of use were originally conceived to be.

As they transmit the Word of life by "sowing" it in hearts, pastors are the guardians responsible for it. That is why, in the practical order, if it is the duty of each of the faithful, alone or in company with others, to take the initiatives to which they feel called with a view to the progress of the Church, to its social mission, to its expansion, or to its improvement, it is the duty of the pastors to examine these initiatives and to test them in order to encourage those in which the mark of the Spirit is recognized and to incorporate the fruit, so to speak, into the universal organism of the Church

in progress. This is not to say that such discernment always comes about at first sight, without
trial and error or clashes: the seal of testing is
normally necessary for any enterprise that leads to
the kingdom of God. Nor is the latest decision
always the most clearsighted. But the principal
sign that the author of an initiative is really under
the movement of the Spirit consists precisely in
his disposition to prefer in the end the good of
unity to the good he would have wished to do.[64]
Finally, as faith is the basis of all unity and the
source of all life in the Church, if it belongs to each
one, not as a right that he possesses, but as an

---

[64] It will therefore be said not only that obedience is
imperfect in the Church, but also that it is not justified if it
must lack all filial character. This is not a question of sentiment, but one of faith. Wanting to hold strictly to our subject,
we are considering here neither the collaboration of the
bishop (or priest) with laymen in the administration and
everyday life of the Church or in the establishment of various
programs of action, a necessary or desirable collaboration
according to the occasion; nor the instances when the Christian, in the very name of his faith, takes initiatives in domains
which would not be within the province of ecclesiastical
authority. We know that the problems which can arise in such
cases are complex, and that they do not always allow of an
assured solution. Nothing can replace prudential judgment or
the effort of mutual understanding. We are here concerned
only with the question of faith and of the essential discipline
of the Church.

exigency that compels him, to be, "in proportion to his lights and graces", a "witness to Jesus",[65] a witness to the faith, it belongs to the pastors alone to be the judges of the faith.[66]

[65] Rev 17:6; 20:4. In this sense, all the faithful are successors of the apostles, "the whole Church is apostolic" (Yves Congar, *Ministères et communion ecclésiale* [Cerf, 1971], 63).

[66] Cf. Bouyer, *l'Église*, 440–41. Schillebeeckx, *Le message*, 92, 93: "The subject of active tradition is undoubtedly the whole community of faith, but allowance having been made for its internal, hierarchical articulations. . . . The ecclesiastical magisterium is, in addition, the 'judge' of the tradition of faith." Cf. *Lumen Gentium*, n. 25, 2; decree *Christus Dominus*, n. 2, 2; n. 13, 1.

VI

"ECCLESIA DE TRINITATE"

The motherhood of the Church, the privileged expression of which is the fatherhood of her spiritual leaders, can be neither thoroughly understood nor unreservedly accepted by anyone concerned about the full dignity of man unless it is considered within the whole Christian mystery. For the Christian mystery is an organic whole, and one particular truth within it cannot be isolated without rendering it unintelligible or even distorting it in such a way that it then becomes a stumbling-block. Now this mystery is none other than that of our participation, through the grace of Christ, in the internal life of the Divinity. Here again, the constitution *Lumen Gentium* is the interpreter of the oldest and most profound tradition. The Church, it tells us, "is a people gathered together in the unity of the Father, the

Son and the Holy Spirit".[1] And in the decree on
ecumenism we find: "The supreme and principal
model of this sacred mystery of the unity of the
Church is, in the trinity of persons, the unity of a
single God, Father and Son in the Holy Spirit."[2]
In a similar manner, the creed which gathers us
together in the Church is essentially trinitarian.[3]
Ecclesia de Trinitate.

The Church, said Saint Irenaeus, is a body whose
head is the Word, as the Father is the head of
Christ, and the Holy Spirit, who comes from the
Father and is given by Christ, dwells in each of
the faithful.[4] A little later, Clement of Alexandria
wrote: "While heretical sects multiply, it is obvious that there is only one true Church, within
which all those drawn toward the one Lord are
united. In her, we contemplate the nature of
divine unity in its reflection, as it were."[5] But
Clement also noted that this unity of the Church
is itself the unity of a trinity:

[1] N. 4. In 1960 a document on "the divine Trinity and the
unity of the Church" was prepared at Saint Andrews by a
Commission on "Faith and Order" (*Verbum Caro*, 59 [1961],
245–79).

[2] N. 2. See also *Ad Gentes*, beginning.

[3] Cf. de Lubac, *La foi chrétienne*.

[4] *Adversus Haereses*, l. 5, c. 18, n. 2 (Ad. Rousseau, SC,
153:241 and corresponding note).

[5] *Stromates*, l. 7, c. 17 (PG, 9:552 AB).

O marvelous mystery! There is only one
Father of the universe, only one Word of the
universe and likewise only one Spirit, everywhere
the same; there is likewise only one virgin become
mother, for I love to call the Church by that name.
At once virgin and mother . . . she draws her
children to herself and nurses them with a sacred
milk, the Word of the nurselings.[6]

Soon after, Tertullian explained the matter a
little further—which is not to say that his texts are
very clear. Writing of prayer, he associated the
Church with the Father and the Son:

The title of Father expresses veneration and
power. At the same time, the Son is invoked in the
Father. . . . But mother Church is not forgotten
either. In the Father and the Son, one recognizes
the Mother, by whom the name of the Father like
that of the Son is guaranteed.[7]

He likewise introduced the Spirit into the subject of baptism:

This triad of divine names is enough to lay
the foundation for our hope. And since the testimony of faith, like the guarantee of salvation,
has the three persons as security, mention of the
Church is necessarily found added there. For

[6] *Paedagogus*, l. 1, c. 6, n. 42 (Marrou and Harl, SC, 70:187).
[7] *De oratione*, c. 2 (CSEL, 20:182).

where the three, Father, Son and Holy Spirit, are,
there also is the Church, which is the body of the
three.[8]

Having become a montanist, Tertullian again
brought the Church into relation with the Trinity,
but this was to exalt a "Church of the Spirit"
which was no longer that of the bishops.[9] It would
be irrelevant for us to dwell on this subject. Let us
simply recall that in his treatise on *The Prescription
against Heretics*, setting forth "the rule of faith
instituted by Christ", which consists essentially
in the proclamation of the Trinity, he spoke more
correctly of the *vicaria vis Spiritus sancti*. What he
thus expressed, "in a way somewhat hardened by
his juridical terminology", was "the great pattern
according to which the Father sends the Son who,
together with the Father, sends the Holy Spirit."
Now this "order of descent" is "followed by an
order of ascent, in which the Holy Spirit realizes
the work of Christ", who in his turn, when all has

---

[8] *De Baptismo*, c. 6, n. 2 (Refoulé and Drouzy, SC, 35:75).
The expression "the body of the Three" could have been
suggested by the juridical principle *"tres faciunt collegium"*
(Refoulé). Cf. *Adversus Marcionem*, l. 5, c. 19 (CSEL, 13:645).

[9] *De Pudicitia*, c. 21, n. 16–17 (CSEL, 20:271). Cf. *De Fuga*,
c. 14; *De exhortatione castitatis*, c. 7. Cf. A. d'Alès, *La théologie
de Tertullien* (Beauchesne, 1905), 215–16.

been subjected to him, as Saint Paul proclaims,[10] "will pay homage to the one who has subjected all things to him."[11]

Such is the pattern we must have in mind if we are to understand the Church and the role of her pastors. God the Father is the original source of life. Jesus, incarnate Word, is author of this life for us. He communicates it to us by communicating the Spirit of the Father to us.[12] The hierarchical Church is "pneumatic" as well: it is the Spirit sent by Jesus who animates her, and it is in the Spirit that she makes Christ known to us so that, always in the Spirit, each of us interiorizes him in ourselves. Only then can we reascend with confidence, in a filial spirit, to the source, to the mystery of the Father.[13] "During the whole of

[10] I Cor 15:28.

[11] Yves Congar, *Esquisses du mystère de l'Église*, new ed. (Cerf, 1953), 142; cf. 50. Tertullian, *De praescriptione*, c. 13, n. 1–6 (Refoulé and de Labriolle, SC, 46:106).

[12] Acts 3:15; cf. 5:31. Cf. Eusebius, *Hist. eccles.*, l. 5, c. 1 (SC, 41:14), etc.

[13] Gréa, *L'Église*, 67–68, 82–88. Bossuet, *Quatrième lettre à une demoiselle de Metz*, n. 7: "In the unity of the Church appears the Trinity in unity: the Father, as the origin to which we are reunited; the Son, as the medium in which we are reunited; the Holy Spirit as the bond by which we are reunited; and all that is one. Amen to God." Cf. Origen, *Conversation with Heraclitus* (Scherer, SC, 67:62–65).

Christian antiquity", writes Father Louis Bouyer
—and we would add that Christian antiquity is
normative here—"no creature could come into
direct relationship with the Father. It is always
through the Son and in the Spirit that we are
bound to him. The very idea of any relationship
with him whatever that would have to be considered as anterior—even merely logically anterior—
to our relationships with the Son and the Spirit is
unthinkable. According to the remarkable but so
profound expression of Saint Irenaeus, the Father
meets and touches us only through his two infinitely holy hands which are the Son and the
Spirit."[14] Now, it is, as it were, through the
two maternal arms of the Church that these two
hands of the Father come to us. And it is then,
having received the Spirit who opens us to the
understanding of Christ,[15] that, according to the
liturgical expression, "we dare to say: Our Father"

[14] Irenaeus, *Adversus Haereses*, l. 4, praef., n. 4 and c. 28,
n. 1 (SC, 100:390 and 626), etc. Louis Bouyer, *Le trône de la
Sagesse* (Cerf, 1957), 256; *l'Église*, 375; *Le sens de la vie
sacerdotale*, 12. Cf. Jules Lebreton, *Histoire du dogme de la
Trinité*, 2 (Beauchesne, 1928), 579–82.

[15] Rom 8; 1 Cor 2:16. On the Trinity at work in the
Church, see also Rom 15:16; 1 Cor 12:4–6; 2 Cor 13:13; 1 Pet
1:2.

—in adoring the unfathomable mystery of the Divinity.[16]

It is only in this broad perspective, brought once again to the fore by Vatican II,[17] that the motherhood of the Church and, more particularly, the fatherhood of her pastors find their proper place and assume their full significance.

Ecclesia mater: as we said in the beginning, these two words express a reality, the very reality of Christian life. People generally speak of "Christianity" as they do of "Catholicism". There is obviously nothing to condemn in this usage, which is as justified as it is old. It is nevertheless regrettable that it too often suggests the idea of one doctrine among others, or of one society among others, even if perfect adherence is accorded this doctrine or this society. In and of themselves, these two words do not lead us much beyond this. Such an idea would not be false, but it would be

[16] According to Rom 8:14–17: "All those moved by the Spirit of God are sons of God. . . . You have received a spirit of adopted sons which makes us cry out: Abba, Father!"

[17] *Lumen Gentium*, c. 3, n. 28, 1; c. 5, n. 39, 1; c. 7, n. 51, 1. Cf. G. Martelet in *l'Église de Vatican II*, 2:532. Hennaux, *Le sacerdoce*, 478–79: "It is only by abstraction that we can speak of the Church as a self-contained entity, without considering her outside of actual birth from Jesus, without considering the Trinitarian movement which constitutes her." Cf. Irenaeus, *Adversus Haereses*, l. 3, c. 24, n. 1 (PG, 7:966 B).

entirely incomplete and superficial. It is a question
of a life, of the divine life to which we are called.
Into this life, the Church, the *Catholica mater*,
gives us birth. Her whole mission is to give birth
to the new humanity in Christ—or, to borrow the
more concrete language of Saint Paul again, to
give birth to the new man, which is to say Christ
in his fullness. [18]

It follows from this that the fatherhood of her
pastors, sublime in its origin, but which can never
be anything but a derivative fatherhood, must
always be exercised in the humble consciousness
of this derivation. The authority which it contains
does not properly belong to them, any more than
the efficacy of the Word and sacraments which
they are commissioned to administer comes from
themselves. "It is the sign and the instrument of
the authority (*exousia*) of Christ." [19] There is a

[18] On this fullness, or "pleroma", of Christ according to
Saint Paul: Bouyer, *l'Église*, 310–14. Cf. Eph 1:23; Col 1:24.
Father Bouyer's interpretation corroborates that of Father
Teilhard de Chardin.

[19] Note on the "ordained ministry" of the Commission
"Faith and Order" (Louvain, 1971). Cf. John Chrysostom, *In
2 Tim. 2*: "All comes from grace. The priest's task is only to
open his mouth. But it is God who effects all. The priest
achieves only the sign. The oblation is the same whether it is
offered by Peter or by Paul" (PG, 62:612). Augustine, *In Jo.*
tract. 5, n. 15 (CCL, 36:50). 1 Cor 3:9: the apostle is the

grandeur in the hierarchical ministry which must not be downgraded; but "it is also necessary always to keep in mind that this grandeur is nothing other than an essential reference to the ministry of Christ", who is the representative of the Father, and that it "consequently demands, in the ministerial body as a whole as well as in the person of each minister, an attitude of contemplative humility with respect to him who is the permanent source as well as the sole *raison d'être*" of their fatherhood.[20]

This fatherhood of our pastors is nonetheless real, since it derives precisely from the one divine Fatherhood. Catholic tradition has drawn an inference from this by an argument which assumes its full weight only if the soul is open to this mystery. It will naturally be rejected, or at least found to be inconsequential, by a kind of theology that would like to define itself solely as "the critical function in the Church"—while claiming at times to exercise a kind of doctrinal dictatorship in her. But in the light of faith, such a theology condemns itself. It may not be useless, but in

"fellow-worker with God"; Christians are the "field of God, the building of God".

[20] Jorge Medina Estevez, commentary on the Propositions on the priesthood of the International Theological Commission (1970).

creating a rupture,[21] it has renounced its better part, which is the exploration of the mystery.

All those who have a part in the hierarchical ministry of the Church continue in the service of their contemporaries the work inaugurated by the appointment of the first Apostles, a work which must not cease until the "Parousia of the Lord". Each according to his gifts and according to his attributes takes up this apostolic task such as Saint Paul defined it in speaking of himself, and also as Saint John understood it when he heralded that "eternal life" manifested in Jesus Christ, and when he called all men to enter into communion with his witnesses; and again as Saint Peter carried it out in addressing the "shepherds" whose "chief shepherd" is Christ.[22] *Mutatis mutandis*—for they were no longer founders—it is in this same way that those whom the Apostles appointed and those who succeeded them, those men whom we so rightly call the "Fathers of the Church", under-

[21] The Orthodox theologian Georges Florovsky has drawn attention to the "strange rupture between theological knowledge and contemplative prayer, between the theological school and the ecclesial life" whose effects were as disastrous in the East as in the West. Cf. Yves-Noël Lelouvier, *Perspectives russes sur l'Église* (Centurion, 1968), 120–21. See also Hans Urs von Balthasar, *Retour au centre* (DDB, 1971). It is here a question of a more radical break.

[22] I Jn 1:1–4. I Pet 5:1–5.

stood their task.[23] Now, "the apostle does not merely proclaim good news to men, he brings them a new life, a new existence. By the proclamation of the Word, the celebration of the Eucharist and pastoral care, the apostle creates new men, among whom he continues to exercise a maternal function. Like a father, he has begotten them; like a faithful mother, he nourishes them. It is this total, true and profound motherhood that prompts the apostle to renounce a limited and circumscribed fatherhood."[24]

[23] They also conceived their ministry as the original founders conceived it. "At the beginning of the third century, in the *Tradition* of Hippolytus, we see that the New Testament doctrine and practice of ordination have not changed; the continuity is evident": Max Thurian, *Sacerdoce et ministère* (Taizé, 1970), 229. Cf. the prayer for the consecration of bishops, in chap. 3 (Botte, SC, 11 *bis*:42–47): it is structured according to the Trinitarian scheme. "The power of the Spirit given to the Son by the Father, for the sake of his messianic mission, then transmitted by Christ to the apostles for the sake of their evangelical mission throughout the world; the new bishop receives it in his turn through the imposition of hands" (Thurian, 235). This prayer has recently been revived for the ordination of bishops; cf. the apostolic constitution *Pontificalis Romani Recognitio* of June 18, 1968. See below, note 54.

[24] Olegario Gonzales de Cardedal, *Le célibat ecclésiastique*, report to the Theological Commission, 1970. Cf. *Presby-*

These lines from a contemporary Spanish theologian do not set forth a wholly personal opinion.
Following the conciliar decree on the ministry and
life of priests, they bring out one of the lines of
force that originated in the Gospel and, earlier
than customarily admitted today, established the
practice of continence in the Church, followed by
the institution of priestly celibacy.[25] Not that this
institution is due to any arguments that might
have been formulated with varying success in one
era or another. Just like juridical organization,
theological reflection is always only subsequent
to the unfailing instinct that guides the tradition
of the Church and makes her discern, with eyes
fixed on Jesus, what best agrees with the spirit

---

terorum Ordinis, c. 3, n. 16: "*Missio enim sacerdotis integra
dedicatur servitio novae humanitatis. . . .*"

[25] "The practice of continence was at first a custom which
spread among the clergy, with varying speed according to the
different churches, but even in the Eastern churches, and
which assumed from before the fourth century on . . . the
aspect and strictness of a law. Besides, if it had been otherwise, the canonical edicts that categorically decree it, beginning with that of the Council of Elvira (which dates from the
beginning of the fourth century) would be inexplicable." This
is what the thesis of Father Christian Cochini (Faculty of
Theology of Paris, 1969) has "demonstrated, with documen-
tary evidence": G. Courtade, *Nouvelles de l'Institut catholique
de Paris* (1970), 59.

of the New Covenant.[26] But even if theological reflection invents nothing, it can bring to light and justify some of the motivations behind the practice. Another of our contemporaries, Heinrich Schlier, who is not only an exegete of the first order, but also a profound Christian thinker, comes to the same conclusion by a slightly different route:

> The controversy about ministry in the Church has not ceased, and it can no longer be said that its end is in sight. . . . But if we want to begin again to consider these matters in depth, we should not forget that the divine decision which, through the power of the Spirit, gave rise to the official ministry, continues to act in it. It acts in the consecration of the one who is called to the ministry; it also acts insofar as the minister enters upon a state of life, i.e., the vocation of such a service. He is not simply taking on a profession, he is not just exercising (external) functions. Rather, he is entering into the celibacy demanded by the call of God for such a ministry.
>
> It is around precisely this point that the controversy is violently waged. And it is here that we must, in my opinion, maintain the principle of divine decision in order to respond adequately to

[26] Jean Galot, S.J., *Célibat sacerdotal et célibat du Christ*, Doc. cath., 67 (1970), 31–34.

its unparalleled grandeur, which is of the eschatological order. Celibacy is certainly a charism, but
it is also a decision, and it alone offers the objective
possibility of corresponding existentially to the
divine decision in a state of life. It is also the
objective condition of God. . . . By celibacy, the
divine decision which puts an end to the whole
dialectic of natural life goes so far that, in the state
of life of its official ministers, it constitutes the
sign that this dialectic has ended.[27]

Such is the eschatological anticipation, within
the temporal order itself, of that kingdom of God
proclaimed and established by the Gospel. It remains true in every century. It is thoroughly consistent with the paternal mission of pastors that for
them the dialectic of carnal life, always precarious
and limited, gives way to the dialectic of eternal
life which it is their mission to spread. There is no
ground for seeing in this "any depreciation of the
divine gift of life", but it is necessary to recognize
in it "a higher love for the new life which springs
from the paschal mystery."[28] These are not, let

[27] *Le catholicisme comme décision*, in: *Catholica*, 14 (1970); Fr.
trans. in *Axes*, 3 (November 1970), 15–16. (The word
"decision" recurs frequently in this text, alluding to its frequent use in Bultmann.)
[28] Encyclical *Sacerdotalis Coelibatus*, June 24, 1967 (*Doc.
cath.*, 64 [1967], col. 1254).

us repeat, merely the views of a handful of contemporary theologians. Without doubt, one does
find in different eras an argument in favor of
the celibacy of priests which is quite similar at
first glance and not without value, but which
remains on a pragmatic level. Thus Clement of
Alexandria observed that the first apostles had
lived in continence in order to consecrate themselves "undividedly" and "without impediment"
—as Saint Paul said under totally different circumstances but in the same spirit[29]—to the service
of the Word.[30] Likewise, for Saint Ephrem, the
various ministers must observe continence in order
to attend more freely to the service of God "in the
exercise of the spiritual functions of the divine
priesthood";[31] and Polycrates of Ephesus wrote
to Pope Victor that, thanks to celibacy, Melito,
Bishop of Sardes, had been able to live "entirely in
the Holy Spirit".[32] It was this type of argument
that Cardinal Suhard, among others, was to take
up again in his pastoral letter of 1949 on *Le Prêtre
dans la cité*: "By detaching the apostle from one

[29] 1 Cor 7:35: ἀπερισπάστως. Paul was speaking in this
instance of the prayer of spouses.

[30] *Stromates*, l. 4, c. 15 (Stählin, 2:291). Cf. l. 3, c. 10
(226–27).

[31] *Adversus Haereses*, c. 59, n. 4.

[32] In Eusebius, *Hist. eccles.*, l. 5, c. 24, n. 5 (SC, 41:68).

restricted home, voluntary chastity binds him to all without distinction and without reserve."[33] And that is again one of the points that the encyclical *Sacerdotalis Coelibatus* set forth in 1967. It is legitimate to think, with Heinz Schürmann,[34] that this is an accurate interpretation of the word spoken by Jesus when he suggests to his disciples that they renounce marriage "for the sake of the kingdom of heaven".[35] The expression does indeed seem to mean: so that the proclamation of the kingdom and action for the sake of the coming of the kingdom be neither hindered nor divided. However that may be, and whatever the social conditions in which the ministry is exercised may be, it will always be true, as Olier expressed it in his *Traité des Saints Ordres*, that a priest "freed from everything is ready to do everything and to undertake everything for God."[36]

Others, however, following the same line of reasoning enter perhaps, if not more deeply at least explicitly, into a reflection upon the ministry of the New Covenant and into the very thought of Jesus. Thus Eusebius of Caesarea, in extending the

---

[33] *Le prêtre dans la cité*, 81.

[34] *Le groupe des disciples de Jésus*, in: *Christus*, 50 (1966), 202.

[35] Mt 19:10–12.

[36] Part two, chap. 1 (ed. de la Colombe, 146).

suggestions of Origen, wrote in his *Demonstratio evangelica*:[37]

> We must consider ourselves fortunate if the doctors and preachers of the Word are equal to the task by being totally detached from the goods of life and from all kinds of cares in this life. It is in fact necessary, now, that the latter, especially, hasten to renounce marriage so as to devote themselves to higher tasks. They are engaged in a work of divine and spiritual generation. It is not one or two children, it is an innumerable multitude whom they have the mission to raise, to form according to the divine teachings and to direct in the other arenas of life.[38]

This was also the thought emphasized, in his vivid style, in another passage by Saint Ephrem, addressing one of his poems to his compatriot Abraham, newly elected to the episcopal seat of Nisibis. And it was also that of Saint Augustine introducing a new bishop to the people:[39] "Aided

[37] *Homiliae in Leviticum*, hom. 4, 6 and 6, 6 (Baehrens, 323–25 and 367–70). Cf. Henri Crouzel, *Mariage et virginité selon Origène*, 109. *In Num.*; hom. 20, 2 (188).

[38] *Demonstratio evangelica*, l. 1, c. 9 (PG, 22:77–81). This text properly applies to clergymen and not to monks as some have thought: Henri Crouzel, in: J. Coppens, *Sacerdoce et célibat* (1971), 336–37.

[39] *Miscellanea agost.*, 1:563–64. It is the occasion that makes

by the grace of Christ, he did not want to have
children according to the flesh so as to have many
of them according to the spirit." And again, it was
the thought of Saint Gregory the Great in his
commentary on the First Book of Kings. To the
priests of the Old Covenant, who begot children
according to the flesh, Gregory compared and
opposed those of the New Law, who "bear the
fruit of a spiritual lineage all the more abundant as
their chastity cannot even be impaired by what is
in fact something good, marriage."[40] It is the
thought we see expressed today as well by the
bishops of the United States, who in a pastoral
letter (November 13, 1969), after having said that
"priestly celibacy is revealed to be profoundly
appropriate to the man completely at the disposal
of the kingdom", add that the priest, by his
consecration to celibacy, "is set apart in order

Augustine speak here of a bishop. It is known that the
canonical legislation of Africa (as that of Spain and Rome)
required continence at that time for all priests. The ordinance
of one of the councils of Carthage (June 16, 390) gave as the
reason for the obligation *"ut quod Apostoli docuerunt, et ipsa
servavit antiquitas, nos quoque custodiamus."*

[40] *In I Reg.* 2, 18 (1, 2, n. 9; PL, 79:94–95). This refers to
Samuel clothed in linen: *"Nam in comparatione legalis vitae nova
Evangelii conversatio lini subtilitas est"* (*subtilitas* = spiritual
gentleness).

to engender the Body of Christ which is the Church."[41]

It is indeed certain that in practice such a consecration demands on the part of the priest who wants to remain faithful to it a discipline of life enjoined by the consciousness of both the gift he has received and the responsibility he has simultaneously had to assume.[42] "The fidelity which this implies cannot last without a perpetually renewed adherence to Christ in prayer and work." I believe that it also makes a community organization of the priestly life very desirable. Throughout the history of the Church, and especially during periods of reform and spiritual renewal, we find a flowering of various institutions created for this

[41] *Doc. cath.*, 67 (1970), 322. The bishops began by recalling (320) that the bond between priesthood and celibacy "is not just the result of theological reasoning or a law, it is firmly rooted in the vital experience of the Church"; it has "survived a number of grave crises and has received the general support of the faithful. It is this maturing of faith and Christian love, rather than theoretical arguments, which will continue to guide the Church in its current consideration."

[42] Botte, *Études sur le sacerdoce*, 33. Jules Monchanin, *Biologie et morale sexuelle*, in: *Questions relatives à la sexualité* (Lyons, n.d.), 93: "It is indeed evident that the man who has chosen to be chaste must impose a strict physical, intellectual and affective discipline on himself" (*Le ministère sacerdotal* [1971], 100–107 and 115–21).

purpose, one of the prototypes of which is the ecclesiastical community at Hippo (*monasterium clericorum*) gathered around Bishop Augustine.[43] Our century owes it to itself not to disregard this long collective experience and the wisdom it contains. But what is more, this consecration through celibacy is understood and justified only if the very idea of Christian ministry is received in faith and retained in its proper originality instead of being equated with profane pagan or Jewish models; only if it is not miserably truncated, if Word and sacrament are not arbitrarily dissociated[44] so that by the rejection of the sacrament, the Word which one wants to retain is falsified in its very essence, if what is actually the specific expression of the Christian faith and life, as recognized by more than one Protestant theologian, is not treated, on the contrary, as a "fragment of paganism",[45] if we do not undertake a criticism

[43] *Sermo* 355, c. I, n. 2 (PL, 39:1570).

[44] Or again, as has been done, "proclamation of the Word" and "sacral and cult⁻ function"; or yet again, dissociation of the "pastor", likened to an official "bureaucrat", and the "preacher of the Word".

[45] The connection between the Gospel and the Eucharist is admirably shown by von Allmen, *Essai*. Cf. Philippe-H. Menoud, *"La définition du sacrement selon le Nouveau Testament"*, in: *Revue de théologie et de philosophie* (Lausanne, 1950), 147. Heinrich Schlier, *Le temps de l'Église*, trans. Father Corin

—which only wants to consider the abuses or to exaggerate certain features by emphasizing certain accents to the point of caricature—of what in a fever of secularism is denounced as the "sacerdotalisation of the ministry",[46] if we do not claim to assign, in defiance of all serious history, a "post-tridentine"—or "medieval", or "post-Constantinian", or, finally, "sub-apostolic"—

(Casterman, 1961), 249–68. Yves Congar, *Les deux formes du pain de vie dans l'Évangile et dans la Tradition*, in: *Parole de Dieu et sacerdoce* (Desclée, 1962), 21–58.

[46] Pierre Grelot, *Serviteurs du Christ*, in: *Christus*, 50 (1966), 252–53: "At the time when the New Testament achieved its final form, the pastorate, presbyterate and episcopate were in no way considered as more or less temporary functions exercised in the name of the Christian people in virtue of the 'royal priesthood' common to all the baptized. They were carried out in the name of Christ for the good of the Christian people in virtue of the special charism which was linked to the mission received and conferred through the imposition of hands. The sacramentality of Holy Orders thus asserted itself forcefully without there yet being any need to theorize about it. And if the evangelical innovation deliberately avoided the technical vocabulary of the Jewish or pagan priesthood in defining this unparalleled situation, the consciousness of serving the priesthood of Christ was already establishing, in the very Gospel, the first landmarks of a theological interpretation that would find its full development in subsequent reflection." Similarly: *Le ministre de la nouvelle alliance*, 123–40: "*L'interprétation sacerdotale du ministère*". On this priestly aspect of the ministry in the New Testament (von Allmen,

origin to the most fundamental elements of the
New Covenant;[47] in short, only if we keep alive
the holy reverence for the Eucharist which was
evident from the beginning at the center of every
Christian community and which is the very heart
of the Church.[48]

Essai, 147), see: A. Vanhoye, *Situation du Christ: Épitre aux
Hébreux, 1 et 2* (Cerf, 1969), 359–87. On the sacrificial color-
ing derived from the "Servant of Yahweh", see: Colson,
Ministre, 187.

[47] In fact, the priestly vocabulary adopted from the beginning of the second century has its origin in the typological
interpretation of the Old Testament. More precisely, "the
priests of the Old Testament, whose ministry found its fulfillment in Christ, have been recognized as the prefiguration
of bishops and priests" (M. Jourjon, Dossier [Lyons, 1970],
83). Cf. Thurian, *Sacerdoce*, 229–30: "It should be emphasized
that this continuity (with the Old Testament), according to
Hippolytus, resides in the merciful design of God and not in
the nature and function of the ministry." According to the
post-ordination prayers, bishop and priest would be "nothing like the Roman '*sacerdos*', the official of public worship
who must merely carry out certain rites. And they would not
have much more in common with the priest of the Old
Testament. . . . In spite of the typology, the Christian priesthood is of another order" (Botte, *Études sur le sacerdoce*,
33–34). And it is again shown in the Roman Pontifical, fruit
of theological elaboration, that we find in the Christian priesthood "the humble service of Christ the Priest, unique mediator between God and men" (Grelot).

[48] Grelot, *Le ministère*, 95: "The joining of the Eucharist

As the tradition of the Church teaches and Vatican II has reaffirmed,[49] the episcopal or priestly ministry is, as its very name implies, an office, a responsibility, a function.[50] But this function is not to be taken in an inner-worldly sense. It is a sacred function: it proceeds from the call of the Lord,[51] which manifests itself, at one and the same time, by interior vocation and, in a decisive way, by the external call of the Church. It is, in the end, consecrated by the gift of the Spirit: "Revive the gift of God which is in you thanks to the imposition of my hands",[52] wrote Saint Paul to

---

and the functions of authority in each local church appears as an unvarying practice whose apostolic origin cannot be contested." On the Eucharist in Acts: Philippe-H. Menoud, *La vie de l'Église naissante* (Delachaux and Niestlé, 1952), 35–43.

[49] *Presbyterium Ordinis*, n. 2: "The Lord, wishing to make a single body of Christians in which 'all the members have not the same function' (Rom 12:4) established ministers among them. . . ."

[50] Augustine, *In psalm.* 126, 3: "*Custodimus enim vos ex officio dispensationis*" (PL, 37:1669), etc. Jean Colson, *Les fonctions ecclésiales aux deux premiers siècles* (DDB, 1956), 350: "The episcopate and presbyterate are specialized functions," etc. See above, chap. 5, 103–5.

[51] Mk 3:13. Jn 15:16. Cf. Hennaux, *Le sacerdoce*, 473–88. Hans Urs von Balthasar, *Personne et fonction*, in: *Parole de Dieu et sacerdoce*, *Mélanges offerts à Mgr. Weber* (Desclée, 1962), 59:77.

[52] 2 Tim 1:6. Cf. 1 Tim 4:14; 5:22. Chrysostom, *Hom. 16*

his beloved Timothy, and he described his own function as a "ministry of the Spirit".[53] The oldest prayers known to us for the ordination of bishops or priests make just as explicit mention of this gift of the Spirit, the "sovereign" Spirit, the "indefectible" Spirit, which, from Jesus Christ and from his first Apostles, must flow out over all those who are designated to continue their work.[54]

Such a function thus has no earthly counterpart.

---

in Tim. (PG, 62:587).

[53] 2 Cor 3:8: ἡ διακονία τοῦ πνεύματος. Cf. 1 Th 1:5.

[54] *The Tradition of Hippolytus*: "You who were pleased . . . to be glorified in those whom you chose, now again pour forth the power that proceeds from you, that of the sovereign Spirit which you gave to your beloved child Jesus Christ, which he has granted to your holy apostles." "Lord, grant the Spirit of your grace while keeping it indefectible in us . . ." (Botte, SC, 11 *bis*: 45 and 59).—This is the origin of what the Greek Fathers call the ϲφραγίς and scholastic theology, the "character". This is the basis for the dogmatic decision of the Council of Trent. Cf. *Lumen Gentium*, n. 21. Previously, Augustine, *De bono conjugali*, c. 24, n. 32: "*Si fiat ordinatio ad plebem congregandam, etiamsi plebis congregatio non subsequatur, manet tamen in illis ordinatis sacramentum ordinationis; et si aliqua culpa quisquam ab officio removeatur, sacramento Domini semel imposito non carebit, quamvis ad judicium permanente*" (PL, 40:394). See the recent study of J.-M. Garrigues, M.-J. Le Guillou, A. Riou: *Le caractère sacerdotal dans la tradition des Pères grecs* (*Nouvelle revue théologique*, 1971), 801–20.

The ministerial priesthood is a priestly ministry[55] which engages one's whole life.[56] The bishop or priest is ordained for the community, and the oversight or negligence of this truth in practice is the source of more than one abuse noted in the course of history. This community, however, is not any gathering whatever: it must be, as we said above, a new humanity, a "new man" in Christ. And the oversight or negligence in practice of this

[55] It will be observed that the two expressions are used interchangeably in the preliminary document of the 1971 Synod, *De Sacerdotio Ministeriali*. These terms, like others, have been criticized in recent times for various reasons. But this came from overlooking the fact that the language of theology is always inadequate and analogical; it is deficient by nature. Theology can "put the new wealth brought to the world by Christ into concepts only by using old words which it borrows from human language and whose inadequacy becomes evident in proportion as it makes that language express truths of a higher order" (Ratzinger, in G. Barauna, *L'Église de Vatican II* [Cerf, 1966], 766). This is so particularly with respect to the "priesthood".

[56] "Liturgical tradition is unanimous in considering the gift of the Spirit, at the time of ordination, to engage totally the entire life of priests which is essentially conformed to the life of Christ, pastor and servant" (*Le sacerdoce ministériel* [1971], conclusion). Cf. Vatican II, *Presb. Ordinis*, n. 2. On the relationship between celibacy, permanent commitment and ministry, see: André Manaranche, "*Au Synode: le ministère sacerdotal*", in: *Cahiers de l'actualité religieuse et sociale*, 1. 10 (1971), 531:40.

other truth—to which we must always return—would not be less injurious. Clearly, the profound appropriateness of celibacy would be illusory to one who no longer wished to see in the ministry of the New Covenant, in this service which represents and makes real the service of him who was the suffering Servant, anything but an external, completely "sociological" function, a mere profession, perhaps a temporary one, similar to human trades or social tasks, even the most noble ones.[57] This institution would no longer be seen as anything but an arbitrary law and not as the expression of an evangelical exigency, the best response to both the call and the example of Jesus.[58] Even more, there would then be no shortage of arguments for denouncing the celibacy of the priest as an obstacle to his work and the law which imposes it upon him as a violation of his natural rights. But besides the fact that all au-

---

[57] Preaching leads to the Eucharist which consecrates all of Christian existence so that, says Saint Augustine, "*tota redempta civitas, hoc est congregatio societasque sanctorum, universale sacrificium offeratur Deo per Sacerdotem magnum*" (*De Civitate Dei*, l. 10, c. 6, PL, 41:284).

[58] Cf. *Presb. Ordinis*, c. 3, n. 16: "*Coelibatus vero multimodam convenientiam cum sacerdotio habet. . . .*" Cf. François Francou, *La foi d'un prêtre* (Centurion, 1971), 150–69. André Manaranche, *Prêtres à la manière des apôtres* (1967). Cf. Mt 4:22; 9:9–10; 19:12. 1 Cor 7:32–35, etc.

thority recognized in his ministry would in this case have lost its foundation, this would not only deny Catholic tradition but in actual fact repudiate the very reality of the Church by emptying the Christian mystery.

VII

THE IMPERSONAL WORLD

Before concluding, I would like to give some attention to another more general but no less real consideration.

Jesus called distinctly each of those whom he formed into the "Twelve", referring to them by name, sometimes even giving them a new name.[1] Thus each of those who come to the Church, presented by a sponsor, receives a personal name, an external sign of a new and profound reality; a perceptible sign of the "dignity of the Christian" which itself inheres in the "dignity of man", just as grace presupposes and elevates "nature". The Christian community, the gathering of the children of a common mother, is the place par excellence of personal relationships.[2] Even in the form of

[1] Cf. Jn 1:42.
[2] Bouyer, *L'Église*, 601: "The Church is the interpersonal society par excellence."

government that results from the necessary distinction between the religious society and the civil and political society, respect for persons asserts itself when faith in the personal God who is revealed in Jesus Christ, such as it is lived by the first of these two societies, is also the faith of the second. It still asserts itself naturally in a secularized society when at least some effect of this faith remains in the consciousness of the leaders. The need of each person to breathe freely, spiritually, resounds in the depths of souls, and this is more or less echoed both in legislation and in customs. Whatever the number and gravity of the attacks on this respect for persons, it is, in the history of civilizations, an undeniable fact. We know that this was not so in ancient societies. We also know that it is not always so in our own century.

It would be pointless to recall at length, after so many others have done so, the features that characterize totalitarian forms of government—and that "concentration-camp universe" to which they lead: the reduction of man to a thing, his manipulation by propaganda and still worse. But the very ones who would reject such regimes with horror, do they not often prepare the way for them when the sense of the values of interior life, which we owe to the Gospel, grows dim within them? We have one indication of this, among others, in the banishment of the very word soul. The criticism of a dualism termed Platonic or Cartesian is readily invoked at this point, but in reality it is a matter of something else entirely. "It is no longer the soul that is spoken of today", writes Pierre Emmanuel, "but 'subjectivity', that pejorative word by which objectivity, become maniacal, repudiates all experience of the heart, all interior comprehension of reality, all communion which escapes the criteria of would-be scientific agreement",[3] in other words, the whole order of personal intimacy and truly personal relationships with others. A desire for generalized objectification "reduces us to our one immediate social role."[4]

These observations by a man who combines rational reflection with the intuition of the poet should be a salutary warning to us.[5] There are,

[3] *Le bonheur et l'imaginaire*, in: *Recherches et Débats*, 69 (1970), 52.

[4] Pierre Emmanuel, *Choses dites* (DDB, 1970), 259. Cf. 55: "We are living today in the most enormous collectivities that man has ever known, and we no longer know what a true community is."

[5] On the criticism of the "universal totalitarian state" in the Apocalypse, see: Heinrich Schlier, *Jésus-Christ et l'histoire d'après l'Apocalypse*, in: *Essais sur le Nouveau Testament*, Fr. trans. (Cerf, 1968), 349–56.

however, some cases where the course of events is inescapable. There are certain evils for which the primary responsibility does not belong to any philosophical, social or political theory, even if one or another theory, grafting itself onto them, arises to legitimatize and aggravate them. It is thus that we witness today the growth, nearly everywhere in the world, of a vast phenomenon, the phenomenon of social depersonalization. Like a shadow, it accompanies an occurrence which is in itself a step forward and which in any case no human force could stop: the extraordinary development of science and technology. The consequences of this, which multiply before our eyes, are inescapable. We have arrived at that time foretold by Cournot around 1860, at that "era of mechanization in which man would be little by little absorbed by the very force of the products of reason."[6] Numerous observers have already depicted this for us. It is an "exaggerated development of the collective impersonal engendered by

[6] Similarly, Pierre Leroux wrote as early as 1846, in his *Discours aux philosophes*, 20: "The misery of the man left to his own devices in the solitude of this society becomes distressing and frightful. On all the great mysteries that encompass human life as on all the duties of this life, the silent society abandons him to himself: not one lesson, no advice, no support. . . ."

the contemporary world because of accelerated urbanization, industrial concentration, more and more rapid communication." It is an "administrative universe" being constructed on the model of the machine and the number, extending its anonymous tyranny over all citizens. It is a universal "rationalization" in view of greater efficiency, ignoring all gratuitousness. It is, owing to the force of circumstances, a "technocracy", whose leaders, caught in its wheels, are no longer able to examine the human condition and the essential needs of man, hypnotized as they are by the problems of profit and loss. It is thus "into this order of what is or can be systematically organized that they try to lock us today." It is a "mass mentality" toward the human species which, far from bringing men closer together by fraternal bonds, ends ordinarily in the psychological isolation of the individual: the latter is no longer integrated, but absorbed and lost. And then, to the very degree that he is clearsighted, he is in danger of despair.[7]

[7] See, for example, C. Jung, *Présent et avenir*, 178. Bertrand Russell, *Ma conception du monde*, 172. Gabriel Marcel, *"L'éclipse des valeurs fondamentales"*, in: *La France catholique* (November 13, 1970). Pie Régamey, in: *Vie consacrée*, 42 (1970), 214. Manuel de Diéguez, *De l'idolâtrie* (Gallimard, 1969), 170–72; and *Science et nescience* (1970), passim., etc. Edgard Morin calls to mind, in *Journal de Californie* (Seuil, 1970), the

This portrait is not overly somber. Everyday experience verifies many of its features and even shows it becoming more rapidly entrenched. The simple phenomenon of urbanization, which proceeds everywhere, swallows up the person. For modern towns have no soul. They are the artificial product of a world "entirely dedicated to the production of the useful", that world which Paul Claudel, through a character in his play *le Père humilié*, symbolized by the double image of a "phosphorous works" and a "railway restaurant".[8] The large housing developments that have proliferated around older towns have a double irremediable fault: they have no history, and nothing in them is organized around principles of truly human life. Far from uniting their residents in their diversity, such developments juxtapose and blind them to the point where all distinctiveness is lost. Man becomes as anonymous there as his apartment and house.[9] The large modern communities are both "fragmented and agglomerated" at one and the same time.

"tragedy of organization", of that economic-social organization that alters and dries up what is human, engendering in many the despair of feeling the unexpressed or repressed depths of their being.

[8] *Le Père humilié*, act 3, scene 2 (the pope).

[9] Francou, *La foi*, 69–70.

Entertainment itself, the only kind they can offer to this formless mass of individuals, can scarcely be other than a "symphony of instincts" producing "a group unity that favors anonymity and even depersonalization".[10]

One of those who have best diagnosed this illness in our modern societies is Father Teilhard de Chardin. Many of his admirers—as also many of his detractors—have not echoed this aspect of his thought. He did write, however, and repeat with insistence, that "man's real menace is not the earth's cooling, but a glacial, interiorly impersonal world."[11] And again, showing the threat to be already largely realized: "If there is a universal complaint today in the world, is it not that of the human person suffocated by the collective monsters which a pitiless necessity of life forces us to sustain around us everywhere? The big towns, big industry, big economic organizations . . . heartless, faceless Molochs."[12] A "mechanization of the earth" is taking place in our time, noted this great traveler and perspicacious observer. "As long as it absorbs or seems to absorb the per-

[10] Emmanuel, *Choses dites*, 238, 259.

[11] Letter of January 3, 1948; *Accomplir l'homme* (Grasset, 1969), 217.

[12] *Esquisse d'un Univers personnel* (1936; *Oeuvres*, Seuil, 6:99).

son, the 'Collective' is essentially unlovable. . . . Common sense is right: it is impossible to devote oneself to the anonymous Number".[13] Without doubt, our era has experienced great progress in many things. Some achievements are admirable, and even more admirable is the vigorous spirit that produces them. There can be no question of restraining this spirit; besides, such an attempt would be in vain. If Teilhard reacted harshly and continuously against the religions of progress, this was not done in the name of any nostalgia for the past. But, as Father René d'Ouince recently said in summarizing his thought and coloring it somewhat according to the present situation, "no progress is worthy of man unless it tries to deliver him from the double evil of anonymity and solitude".[14] But "this new civilization that our generation is so intent on building, without taking into account the future that such a civilization will bring about for it, is openly utilitarian and covertly oppressive. Increased production becomes the supreme imperative, the absolute value, with its train of consequences: growing rationalization, the preeminence of efficiency, the sovereignty of social planners. . . . The rigidity

[13] *Le phénomène humain* (Seuil, 1956), 297.

[14] *Le Père Teilhard de Chardin et l'avenir de la pensée chrétienne* (Aubier, 1970), 94.

of structures paralyzes personal initiative, the bureaucratic hierarchy stifles creative initiative."[15]

In its general features, such a diagnosis applies equally to regimes quite opposed to each other. André Malraux noted this earlier in *la Tentation de l'Occident*: "There is a hopeless conflict", he said, "at the heart of our Western world. It teaches the conscience to disappear and prepares us for metallic kingdoms of absurdity." But above all, adds Teilhard—and he does so insistently in opposition to all the "devotees of Progress"—this modern society, which promises us in various forms an illusory and foolish "golden age", in reality offers no "way out" to our desire: refusing to know God, insensible to his revelation, it imprisons us in a closed world without love and without hope—and we are in danger of dying there, suffocated.[16]

---

[15] Ibid., 83–84. Cardinal Suenens recently made a similar statement, adding to the picture a feature that grows larger every day: "The dictatorship of anonymous forces that threaten the human person, to wit: an excessive mechanization of human work, an all-powerful technocracy, the anonymity of a public opinion formed by demagogy." Mariological Congress of Zagreb, August 1971.

[16] Henri de Lubac, *Teilhard missionnaire et apologiste* (Toulouse, 1966), 93–100. Teilhard de Chardin, *Trois choses que je vois* (typewritten, 1948), 11: "Without Christianity, the world becomes unbreathable twice over. Unbreathable first

"The personal depth of the individual has its source in the 'eternal', and all culture, all society, all civilization that fails to admit this is a threat to man. If the optimism of progress celebrated by a technician's civilization makes so much noise today, it is because it is obliged to cover up the cries of agony made by the oppressed person."[17]

A complete remedy for this collective evil is not possible. Earthly existence will never be an idyll. We can even expect, again with Teilhard, that humanity will come to "interior conflicts more violent still than those we now know", for a universe "in the process of conscious concentration", such as ours, is perhaps one that is called to suffer more.[18] All our progress, all our conquests seem to be in league against us and to catch us in nets of finer and finer mesh. The utopias that then

---

of all because the way in front of it is hopelessly closed, facing a total death. Unbreathable also because there is no longer any living warmth there to enliven its frightening mechanism." *Réflexions sur le bonheur* (1943): To be happy, it is necessary to dedicate oneself completely; but "to succeed in complete dedication, it is necessary to be able to love. But how can one love a collective, impersonal—in certain respects, monstrous —reality such as the world or even humanity!"

[17] Von Balthasar, *De l'intégration*, 63.

[18] *Esquisse*, 105. This is again one of Teilhard's recurrent themes.

abound are only imaginary compensations. When Christians allow themselves to be lulled into acquiescence by this, when, in order to color them with a mystical flame, they distort the gift of God, they do not perceive the spiritual misery into which they are sinking and do not suspect the severity of the future they are helping to prepare. Let us listen rather to this cry: "My Lord and my God! You have given me a soul anguished by the annihilation of the human person in irresponsibility, its burial in anonymity. . . ." But is this truly a cry of distress? Is this the mere echo of the stifled cry of so many souls? Is it not, rather, at the same time, the thanksgiving of a Christian soul who has received from his Lord this gift of sympathy, this privilege of living, at the very heart of his faith, the great anguish of the men of his time? It is his own way to make up today, according to Saint Paul's expression, "what is still lacking in the Passion of Christ."[19]

[19] Cf. Jacques Ellul, *L'Impossible prière* (Centurion, 1971), 91–92: According to some theoreticians, "there is no neighbor in the relationship of language; there are only two factors of a structure which functions. If this very negative analysis has an appearance of accuracy, that proceeds from the factual situation: the absence of encounter in our society, the absence of the I and the Thou, because man tends to reify himself in the universe of objects in which he finds himself placed."

VIII

THE CHURCH AND THE PERSON

This being so, what unparalleled benefit we receive from our Church for our earthly existence itself, if only we dreamed it, if only we took our faith seriously!

It is right that she be, as it were, personified by this title of "mother". Christian revelation, which she has kept alive through the centuries—at the price of what battles, against so many misunderstandings and lukewarmness or "explanations" and "hermeneutics" of higher pretensions—bears inseparably on God and on man. It is the revelation of our destiny, which is divine destiny. In other words, it is at the same time and inseparably theology and anthropology. It is by calling man that the God who manifested himself in biblical history and who finally reveals himself in Jesus Christ, giving us a glimpse of the mystery of his interior life, at the same stroke reveals man to himself. It is in his divine vocation that man learns to know himself. God reveals himself to him in a more and more sharply contoured personal form, but also one that is more and more mysterious, whose correlative is the increasing personalization of the one who receives his revelation. God, as Teilhard says very well, is "Personality personalizing". Henceforward, man, adorer of the divine Trinity within which he has been inserted, knows he exists with an existence that participates in God's absoluteness. He is no longer completely immersed in earthly society or in the cosmos. This complicates human problems and accounts for the impatience of so many theoreticians and the hostility of so many authorities before this strange Church whose position has not been anticipated in their calculations and which frustrates the simplicity of their plans—but man is infinitely ennobled by it. If we fail to recognize this historical fact, this great fact unique in history, this Jewish fact prolonged and expanded into the Christian fact, we close ourselves off from the understanding of what is most fundamental in history, and we are no longer able to discern—even apart from faith itself—what is today the legitimate heritage of Christianity and what would amount to pagan regression. Like those philosophers of religion or those theoreticians of spirituality, to cite only one example, who, ignoring the specificity of their subjects, mix all religious phenomena scattered through time and space into common relativism like so many "cultural facts", in which only some emancipated minds like their own would be capable of perceiving the unique design.

The Christian has received a name. "You have called me by my name!" cries Paul Claudel in the joy of his deliverance.[1] and Charles Péguy, through the voice of little Hauviette in *le Mystère de la charité*: "The good God has named all the world. . . . We belong to his family. He has called us all by our name, which is our baptismal name."[2] "It is the profound Christian idea that the names are not erased from God's ledger."[3] There is a rich symbolism in this idea of the "name", "which forms an important part of New Testament theology. God's personal relationship to the Christian is expressed in the fact that the Christian possesses a new name by which Christ calls him, which is written in the book of life and which Christ acknowledges before his Father."[4]

[1] *Magnificat*, in *Cinq grandes Odes*, 80.

[2] *Le mystère de la charité de Jeanne d'Arc*, ed. A. Béguin, 39. Cf. *Clio* (Prose, Gallimard, 2:433).

[3] Péguy, *Clio*.

[4] Paul Hacker, *The Christian Attitude Toward Non-Christian Religions*, in: *Zeitschrift für Missionswissenschaft und Religions-*

In the Gospel of John, the Good Shepherd calls each of his sheep by name.[5] In the Apocalypse, it is again said that the "victor" will receive a white stone upon which his name, a new name, will be written.[6] In proportion to our faith, the Church, this "family" into which baptism has introduced us, preserves the consciousness of our personal identity with this symbolic name. She furnishes us with the environment in which this consciousness can flourish. She maintains among us those things that are so endangered: respect for life and death, the sense of fidelity in love, the sacred character of the family; she maintains them as only a mother can. From birth to the grave, she envelops our life in her vast sacramentary structure. Through her, we learn that something in us, what is most ourselves, escapes all deterioration as it does all constraint. Through her, owing to the demands she reveals to us on behalf of the Lord, we obtain and strengthen the sense of our own responsibility. And we do so first of all by "recognizing that we are sinners": in fact, nothing testifies to the essential dignity of our existence more than this recognition of our sinfulness. Through her,

---

wissenschaft (Muenster, 1971), 90. Lk 10:20. Rev 3:5; 13:8; 17:8.

[5] Jn 10:3.

[6] Rev 2:17.

in her, we have fathers and brothers—we have a mother! Through her, a dizzying opening that is obscure but unfailing raises us up to a Father, "our Father in heaven". We are taken into this community of life as into a net. But, contrary to the one woven by a mechanized society, the more closely this web is woven, the more it allows us to expand. In it we breathe, we exist! This is the mystery of the communion of saints.[7] And what we thus live in mystery, but with the assurance of faith, helps us to endure the social constraints which bruise us, to overcome that gregarious solitude in which, as Teilhard says, we are on the point of suffocating.[8]

All of that is independent of appearances, which

---

[7] Cf. Moehler, quoted by Bouyer, *L'Église*, 131–32 and 195–99.

[8] Cf. Cesbron, *Ce que je crois*, 202: "The more the century dechristianizes itself, the more it seems that Christianity alone would enable us to live humanly. We can no longer even breathe. How much more beautiful the cities would be, and life itself, if love ruled there. In truth, without love, they become more suffocating day by day. It alone could put an end to this mire of our souls. The communion of saints is the only remedy to the life of the concentration camp. . . . The only way to make the world livable would be through absolute respect for each person, an adult freedom, profound equality, brotherhood, the spirit of childhood, the spirit of detachment, the foolishness of love—in brief, all that Christ came to

are so changeable because of the differences among men. The motherhood of the Church, as I have said from the beginning of this study, is not connected with any sensible experience. It is, nevertheless, a reality which engenders an experience. It would be most unjust if, because we have met with some indifference or lack of understanding in our relations within the Church or because we have been able to verify some abuse here or there, we were not willing to recognize so many facts, so many attitudes, so many institutions, so many emotions, so many initiatives of all kinds which have created over the centuries, and which so often continue to maintain under difficult circumstances, a spiritual climate ignored by one who is not Christian or who has not really drawn near the Church. Does not the very scandal provoked when this climate is, on occasions, absent testify to this fact? Besides, it is not the satisfaction of a certain sentimentality nor encouragement for an easy life which we are to expect from the Church. A truly loving mother, she saves our personal life, not by flattering our instincts, but by calling us back to both the gentleness and the strictness of the Gospel. We must place ourselves, not

---

embody, to prescribe, or rather to restore, to seal with the red mark of his blood."

on the psychological level, but on the spiritual ("pneumatic") level in order to judge this. It is at the moment when her countenance seems perhaps austere to us that she is best fulfilling her maternal function.

Today, as in the past, everything in the faith of the Church summons us to the most personal life. Everything in her liturgy speaks of it to us and furnishes its realization in us in the most concrete union. Today, as yesterday and since the beginning,[9] she resists all attempts—which are so consistent with one of the inclinations of our intelligence, but so destructive for our personal existence itself—to transform the faith addressed to the person of Jesus Christ into a clever gnosis, an impersonal gnosis. It is indeed supremely desirable that the consciousness of this personalizing force which was given to her forever not be blunted by contact with the depersonalizing forces which are at work everywhere around her. Father Teilhard de Chardin observed once that the Christian sometimes needs courage to "overcome the antipersonalist complex" which paralyzes so many of our contemporaries by preventing them from attributing "a face and a heart" to the divinity.[10]

[9] 2 Pet 1:16–17.
[10] Teilhard de Chardin, *Le Phénomène humain*, 297.

More insidiously, perhaps, and without our even being on our guard against it, something similar is insinuating itself into our lives today: "The abstraction which is rife everywhere", observes Pierre Emmanuel, "has already conquered Christian thought, whose faith is weakening in its symbols, in religious sensibility, in visionary power."[11] The very ones who suppose that they can reach a more personal faith by excluding from Christian life all that they disdainfully term "religion" tend, on the contrary, toward an abstract, dry faith without traditional roots, a secularized faith which would soon lose, to say nothing more, its power to unify and liberate.

Along the same lines, there is another more immediate, if not more real, danger. Does the charitable simplicity of personal relationships founded on the evangelical concept of neighbor not very often risk giving way to the organization of collective charity, which is so necessary in other respects?[12] The latter will never replace the former.

[11] *Le bonheur*, 57.

[12] Bouyer, *L'Église*, 339–40: "That realism essential to New Testament spirituality, and thus to the Church which we see born there, finds its touchstone in the evangelical idea of the 'neighbor'. . . . If we do not even love our brother, whom we see, neither can we love God, whom we do not see. According to this Johannine formula, it can be said that we

Do we not need today an increase in faith in order to discover, "without losing contact with the concrete reality of the individuals who surround us, the means of embracing them altogether in an attitude which, despite its enormous expansion, preserves the warmth of human affection"?[13] For lack of this increase, "agape, which no longer claims to be the proof and the fruit of the love of God", is changed from love for neighbor into sympathy for those who are remote.

> Of course, this too is a duty, but it can also be an evasion. . . . It is appalling to see how the neighbor, the Lazarus, is neglected—not only the one in front of the door but also the one inside the house. With love for "man" or "men", who trouble me and make demands on me much less than the neighbor, love in the Christian sense loses the concrete character which belongs to its essence. If love for God is absorbed into love for neighbor, and love for neighbor weakened into love for "man", it is not surprising that the principal concern of the Church and of Christianity gradually, but already visibly, tends to search for ways to satisfy men and to secure their well-being. That is also a task which has its time and place. But this is

---

will never love 'men' if we do not love concretely this or that man with whom Providence brings us into contact."

[13] Teilhard de Chardin, *Esquisse*, 104.

not the true response to God's love. And the danger is already perceptible: God's decision, as well as the height and the depth of the world revealed by it, falls into oblivion, and man then shrivels up, so to speak, because the Christian is undoubtedly now open to the world, but the world no longer discerns anything in him and through him but the obscurity of its own existence. It is not in vain that Saint Paul said "Do not let your charity be feigned."[14]

These reflections of Heinrich Schlier, which result from a clearsighted analysis of the present situation, cannot be pondered too deeply.

Discernment is imperative with respect to the groups of all kinds that are being formed at present within the Church herself, on the fringes of her essential structures. Some of these groups are, as in other eras, a flowering, as it were, of her vitality, a new and serene flowering. But in others we find, despite first appearances, a new instance of that "depersonalization" through which the Church would lose her own character, or rather through which her children would no longer be able to recognize her and would no longer receive any benefit from her. Do even the best entirely escape the deformation of gregariousness, of the

[14] Rom 12:9. Schlier, *Essais*, 20–21.

"impersonal collective" so opposed to that personalizing unity, to that real "communion" toward
which the force of the Spirit of God tends to
direct us within the great Church. What diverse
realities, for example, are referred to today by
the same term "basic communities" or "small
communities"! It might be good to recall on this
subject that in the early days of the Church, particular groups, or "conventicles" that were in
danger of turning into a sect, were distrusted. All
were, as much as possible, to join together in a
single place for the liturgical assembly.[15] Ignatius
of Antioch made repeated denunciations in this
connection.[16] These instructions are not necessarily always to be taken literally, but we must at
least catch their spirit.

Is depersonalization not overtaking some sec-
tors of Christian thought? We will not dwell on a
plan such as the insane one that would consist,
with a view to obtaining a better hearing in the
present world, in "replacing the personalist categories in which our faith has been expressed up to
the present time, with objective categories."[17] An

[15] I Cor 11:20. Cf. Oscar Cullmann, *Le culte dans l'Église
primitive* (1944), 9.

[16] Ignatius, *Eph.* 5, 2. *Magn.* 7, 1. *Trall.* 7, 2. *Philad.* 4.
Smyrn. 8, 1; 9, 1.

[17] It was a matter of replacing faith in a personal God and

all too real plan, but one which does not proceed from Catholic theologians. Are we not ourselves, however, sometimes overcome by this malady of faith which transforms it in our minds into a sort of ideology? We have greatly reproached the old scholasticism for its objectivism and its abstract manner. Have we not come to the point of going farther along that route than scholasticism when, in order to organize theology into a "coherent discourse", we move farther away from its living sources? Cardinal Suenens recently related a very significant remark that had come straight from the mouth of Father Karl Rahner: "I asked Father Rahner how he explained the decrease of Marian piety in the Church. His reply is worthy of attention. Too many Christians, he said to me, whatever their religious obedience, have a tendency to make an ideology, an abstraction, out of Christianity. And abstractions have no need of a mother."[18] Here again, what is said of Mary applies to the Church. The motherhood of the Church no longer means anything to our systems —but we, in order to free ourselves from their abstraction, need to return to our mother.

There has been, if we dare say so, yet another

---

in the person of Jesus Christ by democratic ideals.

[18] Conference at the Sixth Mariological Congress, Zagreb, August 1971.

factor of impersonalism at work for some time. It concerns the pastors of the Church and occasionally penetrates to the pastors themselves. Do we not in fact see here and there a rather inaccurate interpretation spreading of episcopal collegiality, so opportunely recalled by Vatican II?[19] In my opinion, that cannot occur without some rather serious practical consequences.

On the one hand, a certain number of theoreticians tend to make a vast new category out of this collegiality, as if to align the Church with the most questionable forms of temporal societies. The mysterious depth of Christian life as well as the paternal character of the authority that gov-

[19] Thus, after each council, a kind of integralism can be seen developing in one part of the body of the Church, pushing one particular point of doctrine to an extreme and in a unilateral way, falsifying it by this very process, tearing away from it the vital significance which it had within the synthesis. After Trent, for example, there is the famous theory of the "two sources" (much less universal than is often reported), dissociating Scripture and tradition; after Vatican I there are the excesses of a curialist "papalism"; after Vatican II, there is now (among other deformations) an integralism of (false) collegiality, pushed in the direction of a democratic collectivism. Each time, the council is betrayed by those who claim to be its only true interpreters and who call themselves the vanguard of the Church. The phenomenon assumes an exceptional gravity today from the fact that it is amplified and sustained by certain aspects of a universal crisis.

erns it are thereby misunderstood. This changes
the nature of the Church of Christ, of her tradition, of her most recent conciliar teaching. At the
same time, on the other hand, there is a practice
becoming established which, without endorsing
such a theory, would inevitably, nevertheless,
predispose our minds to it in the long run. In fact,
collegiality, which greatly increases rather than
reduces the personal responsibility and, consequently, the personal obligation of each pastor,
sometimes seems to be confused with a sort of
government of assemblies, commissions and com-
mittees. This results in an excess of bureaucratic
organization, withdrawing the pastor from his
people, in many cases paralyzing his activity and
favoring abstraction.[20] If we are not careful, there
is a sort of fatal inclination involved in this; but if
we are aware of it, a resolute will can remedy it.
But it is necessary first to be convinced of it.
Nothing would be more dangerous for the spiritual well-being of the Christian community than
to have this tendency come to prevail. Nothing
would contribute more to concealing the fatherly
character of episcopal authority and, consequently,
the maternal countenance of the Church. Have
some not already come to speak with an all too

[20] See below, part two, chap. 5, 266–69.

significant mimicry of the "machinery of the episcopate"?

We must, however, have confidence and remain assured that this is merely a passing threat—
each era has its own—which human experience as
well as divine light will not delay dispelling. We
will then undoubtedly see better what today is
obscured in our vision by the effect of theories
which have been inadequately criticized. The relationship of father to son, which is deeply rooted
in the gift that has come from the Father, which is
maintained in the *Ecclesia Mater* and established
within her fraternal relationships across time and
space, is in itself very different from what any
psychological investigation would reveal in it.[21]
Neither is it just some obsolete relic of a paternalis-
tic age studied by historical sociology. It provides
us with the necessary, blessed and irreplaceable
expression of the mysterious reality which constitutes the dignity of the Christian just as it contributes today even to saving the dignity of man.[22]

[21] See the sound reflections on this subject by A. Vergote,
"*Le nom du Père et l'écart de la topographie symbolique*", in:
L'analyse du langage théologique, le nom de Dieu (Aubier, 1969),
263–64. Cf. Jacques Guillet, *Jésus devant sa vie et sa mort*
(Aubier, 1971), 111–16.

[22] Cf. the pages by Ferdinand Ulrich, *Atheismus und Mensch-
werdung* (Einsiedeln: Johannes Verlag, 1966), 8: "*Die Kirche*

The day is coming when we will all be able to recognize in this motherhood of our Church an image, or even an effective symbol, of that Love which the poet was not afraid to call the motherhood of God:

> Have pity on me, Lord,
> Through your maternal compassion, for I know your love for me
> Is like that of a mother who has just given birth.[23]

---

als personale Gestalt der befreiten Endlichkeit: Virgo-Mater", 65–69. Thomas More and Erasmus stressed the necessary paternal character of authority in the Church. "It is a vision of faith that is on trial, not a sentiment." Germain Marc'hadour, *Thomas More* (Seghers, 1971), 104. Cf. Ellul, *L'Impossible prière*, 131–32, 165–69.

[23] Paul Claudel, *La Ville*, first version, last act, Pleiade (Gallimard, Théâtre), 2:407. Although the words *Ecclesia Mater* express the nature of the Church in all truth, as I have just tried to demonstrate, all ecclesiology could clearly not be gathered somehow under this title. The reader will remember to place the preceding pages in their proper context and not ascribe too much ambition to them. More than one of the questions entered into here are discussed from only a limited point of view.

PART TWO

PARTICULAR CHURCHES
IN THE
UNIVERSAL CHURCH

I

QUESTIONS OF TERMINOLOGY

From the beginning, as we know, the Christian language spoke of the Church, in the singular, and of the churches, in the plural. The Church of God is unique: there is only a single Body of Christ, a single Spouse of Christ, a single fold, a single flock under a single Shepherd; there is only a single new Israel, that holy people whom the Apostle Paul designated as the "Israel of God",[1] that "Church of God" against which he had at first fought.[2] Nevertheless, from the first Christian community, the mother church of Jerusalem,[3] other communities were founded, other churches which were as numerous as the cities into which the unique Church was in that way introduced. It

[1] Gal 6:16. Cf. Firmilian: "*Sponsa Christi una est*" (in Cyprian, *Epist.* 75, c. 13; Hartel, 2:819).

[2] Gal 1:13. 1 Cor 15:9. Phil 3:6.

[3] Rom 15:19, etc. Cf. Acts 15:4.

is thus that the Acts of the Apostles show us Paul, accompanied by Silas, traveling through Syria and Cilicia to visit the churches there and to strengthen them in the faith.[4] Again in recent times, at the Second Vatican Council, the constitution *Lumen Gentium* reminds us: "This Church of Christ is truly present in all the legitimate local groups of the faithful, which, united to their pastors, also receive the name of churches in the New Testament."[5]

The Church of Christ is universal: she is "catholic". These two adjectives are very close in their etymology; they could almost be called synonyms. "*Universitas*" was defined by Isidore of Seville as a reality in which all elements converge toward unity.[6] In traditional mathematical speculation, a universal number is the number that expresses and symbolizes the idea of totality.[7] Even today, in Claudel's *Art poétique*, we can read that universe

---

[4] Acts 15:41; 16:5.

[5] Cap. 3, no. 26, 1: "*Haec Christi Ecclesia vere adest in omnibus legitimis fidelium congregationibus localibus, quae, pastoribus suis adhaerentes, et ipsae in Novo Testamento Ecclesiae vocantur.*" Cf. Hilary, *In psalm.* 14:3 (PL, 9:301 A).

[6] *Etymologiae*, l. 8, c. 1, n. 2:"*Universitas ab uno cognominata est, propter quod in unitatem colligitur*" (PL, 82:295 A).

[7] Cf. Robert Grosseteste, *De Luce*, ed. Baur, 58; cited by Pierre Michaud-Quantin, Universitas, *Expressiones du mouvement communautaire dans le moyen âge latin* (Vrin, 1970), 34.

is "the total word" which expresses a "turning toward unity".[8] On the other hand, it is certain that from classical antiquity the word "*catholicos*" was often taken, like "universal", in the simple sense of "general", and that it was often taken this way in Christian antiquity itself. From which, again, arises the first definition by Isidore of Seville: "*Catholicus universalis sive generalis interpretatur*"; if it is immediately followed by another, more adequate definition—"*Quasi ἀπὸ τοῦ καθ' ὅλον, id est secundum totum*"—the commentary given brings us back again to the former: the Catholic Church "*per totum orbem terrarum diffunditur*".[9] The words are not always taken in all the fullness and strictness of their meaning.

Connected at the beginning, "universal" and "catholic" have ended by diverging considerably. In current language, they no longer have quite the same meaning today, nor, above all, the same resonance. All things considered, these two adjectives even orient thought in two opposite directions: the first evokes on the whole a spreading out, the second, a gathering together. "Universal" in modern English usually suggests the idea of a reality prevalent everywhere: we speak, for

[8] *Art poétique*, 149.
[9] *Etymologiae*, l. 7, c. 4, n. 14; l. 8, c. 1, n. 1 (PL, 82:293–94).

example, of universal use or of a universal celebrity. "Catholic" says something more and different: it suggests the idea of an organic whole, of a cohesion, of a firm synthesis, of a reality which is not scattered but, on the contrary, turned toward a center which assures its unity, whatever the expanse in area or the internal differentiation might be. It means, notes Barth, "all-embracing; it speaks of an identity, a continuity, a universality sovereignly asserting itself within all the diversities".[10] The word thus implies an active, dynamic and intensive emphasis, while "universal" is rather passive, static and extensive. A quality intrinsic to the Church, catholicity is expressed in a universal apostolic enthusiasm; it is the active force of this fertile olive tree that is the new Israel.[11] It is, in principle and in development, the unity of fullness; not totalitarian but totalizing, as expressed perfectly by the constitution *Lumen Gentium*: "The Catholic Church tends toward the recapitulation of all humanity, with all the goods that it contains, under Christ the Head, in the unity of his Spirit. In virtue of this catholicity, each part contributes the benefit of its own gifts to the others and to the whole Church,

[10] *Kirchliche Dogmatik*, vol. 4, t. 1, 783.
[11] Lucien Cerfaux, *La théologie de l'Église suivant saint Paul* (Cerf, 1965), 376–77.

so that the whole and each of the parts are increased by a mutual exchange and by a common effort toward a fullness in unity."[12] We can also see through that how the two notions of unity and universality converge into that of uniqueness and can then understand how this same word "catholic" could very soon serve to designate both the universality of the Church and the orthodoxy of her faith.[13]

This is why it would not be possible, without serious doctrinal detriment, to renounce this word "catholic" in the creeds and professions of faith. As early as the dawn of the second century, it served to designate the Church, since it is found already in the letters of Saint Ignatius of Antioch[14] and a little later in the account of Saint Polycarp's martyrdom.[15] Saint Cyprian, who uses the two

[12] *Lumen Gentium*, c. 2, n. 13, 2 and 3.

[13] Cf. J. N. D. Kelly, *"Catholique" et "apostolique" aux premiers siècles*, in: *Istina* (1969), 34–39. Could "catholic faith" really be replaced by "universal faith"? Could the *"catholica professio"* (Gregory the Great, *Epist.* 6, n. 32) be transformed into "universal profession"? Could "catholic sense" become "universal sense"?

[14] Cf. P.-Th. Camelot, edition of the *Letters* of Ignatius, SC, 10:58.

[15] *Martyrium Polycarpi*, c. 8, n. 1; c. 19, n. 2; and the same title: ". . . and to all the communities of the holy Catholic Church . . ." SC, 10:242, 252, 268.

formulas by turns, *"Ecclesia catholica quae una est"* and *"Ecclesia quae catholica una est"*, makes it signify in a vital way "the real presence of the origin in each Church and in all."[16] Saint Cyril of Jerusalem, who gives a synthetic definition of it to the future baptized, deems it "the proper name of the holy Church".[17] Saint Hilary applies it, in the same passage, to both the Church and the truth.[18] If Optatus of Milevis[19] and, following him, Saint Augustine[20] use it readily in a geographical sense because of their fight against Donatism, which was a local and particularist schism, they do not abandon the recognition of a more complete meaning

[16] Adrien Demoustier, S.J., *"L'ontologie de l'Église selon saint Cyprien"*, in: *Recherches de science religieuse*, 52 (1964), 367–69. Cyprian, *Epist.* 65, c. 4 (Hartel, 2:725), etc.

[17] *Catechesis XVIII*, c. 23 and 26 (PG, 32:1044, 1048 B).

[18] *In Matt.* l. 10, c. 9: *"Ecclesia, quae catholica dicitur"*, preceded by *"veritatem catholicam"* (PL, 9:969 C). And many other texts.

[19] L. 2, c. 1: The Donatists are *"in particula Africae, in angulo parvae regionis"*, while the Catholic Church is *"rationabilis et ubique diffusa"*; c. 2: *"eam esse ecclesiam catholicam, quae sit in toto terrarum orbe diffusa"* (C. Ziwsa, CSEL, 26:33 and 36).

[20] *Contra Cresconium*, l. 1, c. 32, n. 38: *"Hoc per universam Catholicam, quae toto diffunditur observari placuit quod tenemus,* etc." (PL, 43:465), etc.

to it.[21] Augustine, who recalls its antiquity,[22] frequently uses it as a noun.

The word was very well chosen. Nothing could better characterize the originality of a Church which is made up of particular churches and is whole in all of them, as will be explained in the following chapter. Orthodox theologians attach great importance to it.[23] The first Reformers and their disciples felt no scruples at all about it and showed none of the reticence observed afterwards: it is regularly encountered in Calvin; it appears in the Protestant professions of faith; and the Protestant theologians of the seventeenth century use it readily.[24] It is noteworthy that the word is retained even today by the joint commission constituted in 1967 "between the Ecumenical

---

[21] Optatus, l. 3, n. 2: ". . . *in toto orbe terrarum, in quo est una Ecclesia*" (71), etc.

[22] *De unitate Ecclesiae*, c. 2: "*Ecclesia . . . utique una est, quam Majores Catholicam nominarunt*" (PL, 43:391–92).

[23] Thus J. D. Zizioulas, "*La communauté eucharistique et la catholicité de l'Église*", in: *Istina* (1969), 70–72. If it is an exaggeration to say (67) that "during at least the first three centuries, the term 'Catholic Church' was used only for the local church" (see 32, n. 2), it was nevertheless enough for the difference from "universal" to become apparent.

[24] Cf. Jean Bosc, "*La catholicité de l'Église*", in: *Istina* (1969), 89. Jean-Jacques von Allmen, *Prophétisme sacramentel* (1964), 29–30.

Council of Churches and the Roman Catholic Church", a commission which has the very title of "Catholicity and Apostolicity".[25] If we wanted to abandon it today in order to adopt the expression "universal Church", we would almost inevitably be suggesting the idea of a "Church" entirely different from that which Jesus Christ instituted on the foundation of the Apostles and which has lasted ever since that time in history: it would be the idea of a "Church" without structure, invisible and diffuse, after the manner of the first Lutheran ecclesiology,[26] which most theologians, even Protestants, justly consider inconsistent and false. Even more, in a quite understandable, wider sense, fostered by the "atmosphere of the times", we would be encouraging, whether we liked it or not, a kind of "religious universalism" by which all religious people of the world would secretly form, without even knowing it, one vast community, with questions of organization, worship, discipline, even of beliefs, being of little importance. The Christian faith would thus be emptied of its content. Now that would not constitute merely a logical, even abstract, consequence and a

[25] Cf. *Irenikon* (1970), 163–71.

[26] ". . . *multitudinem quamdam nescio quam, insensilem et mathematicam, Platonis ideis cognatam*", said Saint Thomas More, *Responsio ad Lutherum*, Yale ed. (1968), 167.

distant threat. The thing is in fact established: such is very much the sense frequently given to universalism and to the very expression of universal Church in the language of our day.[27]

Within the limited context which is ours in the present study, we will nonetheless speak, with Vatican II, of the "universal Church", intending by that the whole of the Church, just as we will speak of the "churches" which constitute this

[27] This is why the five French members of the International Theological Commission constituted at the request of the Episcopal Synod addressed a letter to the bishops of France in October 1970, later published, in which they said: "We are unanimous on this point in particular: that it is impossible to replace the words 'Catholic Church' by the words 'universal Church'. To do so would inevitably give the faithful the impression that it is no longer a question of confessing our faith in a Church founded by Christ and destined to be the Church in which all Christians are one in faith and in the authentic sacraments, as in fidelity to legitimate pastors, but only a vague faith in some invisible church in which all Christians could remain in spiritual unity despite all the divisions. On the contrary, the word '*catholica*', from its first introduction in the *Credo*, was intended precisely to distinguish the Church visibly as one and unique in authenticity of faith, of the sacraments and of the hierarchy in contradistinction to all the communities which do not comply with these requirements. To abandon the word catholic for the word universal would thus amount to renouncing the very affirmation in view of which this article of the *Credo* was conceived." (*Doc. cath.*, January 17, 1971; 68:80.)

whole. For it is *within the Catholic Church* that these two correlative terms will be considered. How must we understand the relation that exists between the whole Church and the diverse local or particular churches: such is the problem we are concerned to resolve in principle.

Here again are two adjectives, "local" and "particular", which are often joined like synonyms or indiscriminately taken one for the other. A quick examination—whether it be of historical writings or theological writings of our century, whether more particularly of the commentaries provoked by the last council, or finally of episcopal texts (again at the Roman Synod of 1969)—shows that both are habitually used.

In 1909, in his description of *l'Église naissante*, Monsignor Pierre Batiffol wrote: "For the historian, Catholicism is, at first glance, a scattering of local churches."[28] In 1947, Maurice Goguel spoke, with Saint Paul, of a solidarity and an organic unity "among all the local churches".[29] In 1957, M. A.-G. Martimort wrote: "There is in each local church only one bishop."[30] In 1970, Father Louis Bouyer likewise wrote that "the one and

[28] Pierre Batiffol, *L'Église naissante et le catholicisme*, 3d ed. (Gabalda, 1909), 1.

[29] *L'Église primitive* (Payot, 1947), 42.

[30] *L'Évêque* (Cerf), 47.

universal Church . . . has concrete existence, properly speaking, only in the local churches" and that, on the other hand, "every local church is nothing but the manifestation of that Body of Christ which is equally present, the same in every place, in all the others."[31] It is in the same sense that, in October 1969, Cardinal Cooke urged the synod to describe the functions of the "local bishop" in the Church.[32] The other adjective is preferred by Dr. Perler in the study in which he shows how Saint Ignatius of Antioch foresaw "the problem of the relations between the individual bishop and the assembly of bishops", which is to say "between the particular church and the universal Church".[33] Dom Emmanuel Lanne also writes that "the universal Church exists only because there are particular churches".[34] Similarly,

[31] *L'Église de Dieu* (Cerf, 1970), 488. See below, 201–9.

[32] ". . . *Quomodo debemus describere munera episcopi localis in Ecclesia et quomodo afficitur munus ejus a relatione sua cum Collegio et cum Romano Pontifice.*"

[33] O. Perler, *Ignatius von Antiochien und die römische Christengemeinde*, in *Divus Thomas*, 22 (Freiburg, 1944); cited by B.-D. Dupuy in: *L'Épiscopat et l'Église universelle* (Cerf, 1962), 40.

[34] "*Les rapports entre l'Église universelle et les Églises particulières du point de vue missionaire*", in: *Omnis Terra* (April 1971), 285. Likewise, in *Istina* (1969), 189: ". . . The local church, that which the New Delhi text calls the 'fully engaged

while for M. Cyrille Vogel "the bishop is the head and the pastor of the local community,"[35] Monsignor Elchinger sets forth "the doctrinal mission of the bishop in the particular church",[36] and while D.-H. Maret speaks of "the local church of Rome" of which the bishop of Rome is the head, T.-J. Jimenez Urresti says that "the pope, as the bishop of Rome, is the bishop of a particular church."[37] Other authors—or sometimes the same ones—are eclectic and pass from one adjective to the other. Thus we have Dom Burkhard Neunheuser writing: "the particular, that is, the local church",[38] or B. Bazatole: "the Church, without ceasing to be fully catholic, becomes particular, local."[39] Thus again, Father B.-D. Dupuy, showing the bishop to be the "center of the local

---

community' (1961) and which Vatican II names 'particular church', and again 'the local church in her sacramental life' . . ." (*La primauté romaine et les Églises orientales*).

[35] In: *L'Épiscopat et l'Église universelle*, 594.

[36] Ibid., 361.

[37] *La collégialité episcopale* (Cerf, 1965), 94, 98 and 261.

[38] *Église universelle et Église locale*, in G. Barauna, *L'Église de Vatican II*, 2 (Cerf, 1966), 610; cf. 616, etc.

[39] B. Bazatole, *L'Évêque et la vie chrétienne au sein de l'Église locale*, in: *L'Épiscopat et l'Église universelle*, 332; 337: "The mystery of the universal Church in the local church". Bouyer, *L'Église*, 215–16: "According to the New Testament, the universal Church is present in the particular community. In

church" and the one who ensures "the connection of this particular church with the Church",[40] etc.

There is nothing unnatural or not entirely legitimate in that—all the more so because ordinarily the general context or the very phrase which contains one or the other adjective supplies the necessary information.[41] All the examples we have just cited clearly show that, whether designated as local or particular, the church in question is always a group of Christ's faithful brought together around a bishop, who is their guide and head, in order to receive "the Word and the sacrament" from him. Nevertheless, because of the wider sense increasingly given today to the concept of the local church, it might be of benefit, at least in certain cases, to adopt a stricter terminology. In fact, as opposed to the term "universal Church", we are sometimes led, according to the questions treated, to speak of "the churches" in two senses that are quite distinctly diverse. This becomes a source of ambiguity. For example, at the Roman Synod of 1969, Cardinal François

---

each of the local churches, it is *the one* people of God who appear."

[40] *Vers une théologie de l'épiscopat*, in: *L'Épiscopat*, 23.

[41] The historian will speak rather of *local* church; thus, Louis Duchesne, *Origines du culte chrétien*, 2d ed. (1909), in his first chapter on the "ecclesiastical circumscriptions".

Marty, Archbishop of Paris, declared: "The bishops wish to recall the value, the importance and the role of the particular churches for which they bear pastoral responsibility." But what must be rightly understood by these "particular churches"? One could wonder. Was it a question of the same reality as that which Monsignor McGrath, Archbishop of Panama, had in view at the same synod, noting that in the initial report the particular church was inadequately considered?[42] This seems doubtful. Thus, before any attempt at evaluation or doctrinal judgment, an effort to clarify seems opportune.

One good way to provide this—one which is obviously not imperative, but which can be convenient—would be to differentiate the two meanings in question by turns through the respective use of the two adjectives. We would then speak, in a first instance, of particular churches and would reserve for the other instance the designation of local churches.

Now that it is precisely what the Second Vatican Council did habitually, although not at all systematically, and, moreover, without any didactic intent. If we take the whole body of promul-

[42] "*Parum consideratur Ecclesia particularis.*"

gated documents, it must be recognized that its
terminology is not "entirely coherent".[43] We
can nevertheless discern several constants, and
more particularly in the document which is for us
the fundamental doctrinal text, to wit, the third
chapter of the constitution *Lumen Gentium*, devoted to "the hierarchical constitution of the
Church and especially the episcopate".

On four successive occasions, this chapter clearly
designates under the name of particular church the
community ruled by its bishop:

> *Collegialis unio etiam in mutuis relationibus singulorum
> episcoporum cum particularibus Ecclesiis Ecclesiasque
> universali apparet.*[44]

> *Episcopi autem singuli visibile principium et funda-
> mentum sunt unitatis in suis Ecclesiis particularibus.*[45]

> *Singuli episcopi, qui particularibus Ecclesiis praeficiun-
> tur. . . .*[46]

[43] Lanne, *"Les rapports"*, 283.

[44] C. 3, n. 23, 1: "Collegial unity also appears in the
mutual relations of each of the bishops with the particular
churches and with the universal Church."

[45] Ibid.: "The bishops are, each individually, the principle
and foundation of unity in their particular churches."

[46] C. 3, n. 23, 2: "The individual bishops, placed at the
head of each of the particular churches. . . ."

*Episcopi Ecclesias particulares sibi commissas . . . re-
gunt.*[47]

On the other hand, it speaks, in the same constitution and still in the same chapter, of certain
groups of (particular) churches, groups that were
"organically joined together", "willed by Providence", which "without detriment to the unity of
the faith . . . have their own discipline". And
these groups, constituted "in the course of time",
receive the name local churches.[48]

The same habitual terminology is found in the
decree *Christus Dominus* on the pastoral responsibility of bishops, whose second chapter bears the
title: "*De episcopis, quoad Ecclesias particulares seu
Dioeceses*"; we read there in no. 11: "*Dioecesis . . .
episcopo . . . concreditur, ita ut . . . Ecclesiam par-
ticularem constituat*"; and again: "*Singuli episcopi,
quibus Ecclesiae particularis cura commissa est, etc.*"
Similarly, in no. 22, 3, with regard to the diocese:
"*Officia, instituta et opera ne desint, quae Ecclesiae
particularis propria sunt, etc.*"[49]

---

[47] C. 3, n. 27, 1: "Entrusted with particular churches, the
bishops direct them. . . ."

[48] C. 3, n. 23, 4: "Divine Providence intended the diverse
churches, . . . in the course of time, to gather together into
several groups. . . . This variety of local churches. . . ."

[49] "The diocese is a portion of the people of God entrusted

We likewise read in the decree *Ad Gentes*, on the missionary activity of the Church, in the third chapter which treats precisely *de Ecclesiis particularibus*: "*Cum Ecclesia particularis universalem Ecclesiam quam perfectissime repraesentare videatur . . .*" (20, 1); and again: "*Ut hoc missionale Ecclesiae particularis perfici possit, etc.*" (20, 7).[50]

Similarly, again, if the decree *Unitatis Redintegratio* on ecumenism, in its third chapter, recalls that "there are several particular or local churches in the East", we can consider that this is not a simple pleonasm, but that the second adjective is related to the words that follow: "the foremost of which are the particular churches. . . ."[51]

---

to a bishop . . . so that it thus constitutes a particular church . . ."; —"Each bishop to whom the care of a particular church has been entrusted . . ."; —"Let the services, institutions and works which are proper to the particular church not be lacking."

[50] "The particular church being held to represent the universal Church as perfectly as possible. . . ." —"So that this missionary work of a particular church might be carried to many. . . ."

[51] *Unitatis Redintegratio*, n. 14: ". . . *plures in Oriente florere particulares seu locales Ecclesias, inter quas primum locum tenent Ecclesiae Patriarchales, et ex quibus non paucae ab ipsis Apostolis ortum habere gloriantur.*" In the volume published by Éditions du Vitrail, 623, the translation omits the *et* before "*ex quibus*", which somewhat alters the meaning.

Some arbitrariness, of course, enters into the choice of words here. It is in fact clear that the particular church, gathered together around its bishop, is also a local reality. As *Lumen Gentium* says, it is a *congregatio localis* (26, 1); "it is in diverse places that churches have been founded by the Apostles and their successors"[52] and where they are still founded today. This local aspect is emphasized by the name "diocese". It can also be noted that the two types of churches that we distinguish by the two adjectives are not always as distinct as we seem to suppose; intermediate types exist, as will be seen in the following chapter. On the other hand, while it is said, in the second chapter of the same constitution on the Church, "that there legitimately exist, in the ecclesial communion, particular churches enjoying their own traditions",[53] the context really seems to show that this one expression takes in both "particular churches" and "local churches" at the same time, such as the third chapter, as we have seen, at-

---

[52] "*Variae variis in locis ab Apostolis eorumque successoribus institutae (sunt) Ecclesiae.*" That remains true even in the exceptional cases where an ecclesial community is scattered and not incorporated into a single territory.

[53] "*In ecclesiastica communione legitime adsunt Ecclesiae particulares propriis traditionibus fruentes. . . .*" We will come across this passage again further on.

tempts to distinguish them. This is because in this second chapter it is still only a question of an undifferentiated description of the "People of God"; the analysis of its diverse organs will begin with the third chapter. Finally, we must observe that the decree on the Eastern Catholic Churches uses a different terminology. In its second section, entitled, curiously enough, *De Ecclesiis Particularibus Seu Ritibus*, this decree understands by particular church an "internally autonomous, hierarchical community" although always "in perfect communion with the other churches and with the universal Church";[54] in actual fact, it is there above all a question of the patriarchates, whose ancient patrimony must be safeguarded (sections 3 and 4). It was difficult to give it a concrete definition equally applicable to all. Besides, such terminology is acknowledged as less than adequate for several reasons.[55]

Notwithstanding these few exceptions or these few imprecisions in language, we can, for the sake of clarity and without attaching any other than practical importance to it, retain the Council's more usual manner of speaking, reserving the

[54] Monsignor Neophytos Edelby, in *Vatican II. Les Églises orientales catholiques* (Cerf, 1970), 143.

[55] Ibid., 99, 140–43, 157. We cannot go into those details here.

name of particular church for the church presided over by a bishop. This is what was done, for example, at the Roman Synod of October 1969 by Cardinal Poma, Archbishop of Bologna, or Cardinal Suenens, Archbishop of Malines. "The particular churches", the first said, "which is to say, those which each bishop directs and represents";[56] and the second: "It is necessary to bring clearly to light the nature and importance of the particular church, in which its own bishop is the pastor of the people entrusted to him."[57] We note that such was already the terminology adopted by Dom Adrien Gréa, whose celebrated book on the *Église et sa divine constitution*, republished in 1965, anticipates on several fundamental points the ecclesiology of Vatican II. "The bishop", wrote Dom Gréa, "is the head of the particular church", and "the particular church is in substance all that the universal Church is."[58]

---

[56] "*Ecclesiae particulares, quas singuli episcopi regunt et repraesentant. . . .*"

[57] "*Requiritur ut in clara luce ponatur natura et momentum Ecclesiae particularis, in qua episcopus proprius est pastor populi sibi commissi.*"

[58] Dom Gréa, *L'Église et sa divine constitution*, new ed. by Gaston Fontaine (Casterman, 1965), 69 and 79; cf. 289.

II

PARTICULAR CHURCH
AND LOCAL CHURCH

Of the two realities thus distinguished by means of the two adjectives, the most fundamental is, without any possible doubt, that which the constitution *Lumen Gentium* has in mind when it speaks of the *Ecclesia particularis*.

In their doctrinal exposition of the relation between "the Church" and "the churches", the authors usually refer, as did the Council itself, to the classical texts of Saint Ignatius of Antioch. Monsignor Gilbert Ramanantoanina, Archbishop of Fianarantsoa (Madagascar), did so again at the Roman Synod of 1969. "The figure of the particular church, as it appears in the letters of Saint Ignatius", he explains, "represents the bishop who, holding the place of Christ himself, presides visibly over this particular church."[1] What consti-

---

[1] *"Figura Ecclesiae particularis ut apparet in litteris sancti Ignatii*

tutes this church is thus the coming together of baptized people around the bishop who teaches the faith and celebrates the Eucharist. It is, as *Lumen Gentium* says in brief, in no. 26, 1, the "altar community under the sacred ministry of the bishop";[2] or, according to the more explicit formula of the decree on the pastoral charge of bishops, in no. 11, "The diocese, bound to its pastor and, through him, gathered together in the Holy Spirit, thanks to the Gospel and to the Eucharist, constitutes a particular church." Saint Ignatius of Antioch made many allusions to this unity, at once visible and mystical, as it is realized in the celebration of the Eucharist. Father Camelot brought the principal ones together in the following lines:

> The Eucharist is celebrated "to the glory of God". It is a liturgical meal in which the bishop (or his delegate) reproduces the gestures of Jesus "giving thanks" and "breaking bread". . . . This meal is a sacrifice; the mention of Christ's blood, the repeated allusions to the altar, demonstrate this sufficiently; a sacrifice which gathers the believers together around the bishop as around a

---

. . . *repraesentat episcopum qui praesidet visibiliter loco ipsius Christi Ecclesiae particulari.* . . ."

[2] "*Communitas altaris sub episcopi sacro ministerio.*"

single altar, the visible symbol of the one Church grouped around the one Christ, Son of the one Father; it is in the Eucharist that unity is best revealed.[3]

It is all too clear that faith is never sufficiently alive in the hearts of all the members of a church for her to respond completely to what is thus given to her from above. But such is indeed the reality which is given to her. Insofar as she becomes aware of it, this church "knows that the solidarity which binds her to Jesus and to those who invoke and confess his name henceforward outweighs all other solidarity, be it familial, social, racial, political, cultural or professional, and that this new solidarity has such priority that to defend it can even cost one's life."[4] Although she always exists in a given place and brings together men attracted by all sorts of human interests, the particular church is not therefore determined as such by topography or by any other factor whether of the natural order or of the human order. She is determined by "the mystery of faith". We would

[3] SC, 10:53. Ignatius, *Eph.* 5, 2; 20, 2; *Smyrn.* 8, 1; *Magn.* 7, 2; *Trall.* 7, 2; *Philad.* 4, 1.

[4] Jean-Jacques von Allmen, "*L'Église locale parmi les autres Églises locales*", in *Irenikon* (1970), 515–16.

say, in a word, that her criterion is of an essentially *theological* order.[5]

Now this is not entirely the case for the groups of churches of which the Council speaks in no. 23, 4, and which it names "local churches". Although "willed by Providence", these more or less extensive, varied groups have something contingent in their very structure, and the factors which have contributed to their formation are, at the very least in part, of the merely human order. "They enjoy", according to circumstance, "their own discipline, their own liturgical usage, their theological and spiritual heritage", and this is entirely legitimate; because (that is, insofar as) all that exists is organized and developed "without prejudice to the unity of faith and to the unique constitution of the universal Church."[6] For more than one reason, several of these groups are considered particularly vulnerable: they are "the ancient patriarchal churches"; but it is possible to form others; others, of diverse types, have always been formed in the course of the ages, according to the vicissitudes of history. We would say, following the conciliar

[5] See, for example, H.-M. Legrand, in *La charge pastorale des évêques*, Unam Sanctam, 71 (Cerf, 1969), 104–113.

[6] ". . . *Salva fidei unitate et unica divina constitutione universalis Ecclesiae, gaudent propria disciplina, proprio liturgico usu, theologico spiritualique patrimonio.*"

decree *Ad Gentes*, that in large part, their criterion is of the *socio-cultural* order.[7]

We are not, for all that, losing sight of the fact that so categorical a distinction is inevitably over-simplified. This one is even doubly so. On the one hand, in fact, all that is said here or will be said below of the local church considered as a group of particular churches can be applied just as well to each particular church if she is considered no longer as such (as "gathered together by her pastor in the Holy Spirit thanks to the Gospel and to the Eucharist"), but insofar as she also has her local characteristics whether or not she is grouped with others. But even more, on the other hand, the existence of several kinds of groups of churches, of diverse origin and nature, are to be noted in history. As early as the apostolic age, a number of churches in Asia grouped themselves together, subject, it seems, to Ephesus where Saint John, their founder, resided. It was the same for the churches of Crete of which Titus, sent by Saint Paul, had charge—a little, says Heinrich Schlier, in the manner of an apostolic delegate or a metro-politan bishop.[8] After the death of the founder or

[7] *Ad Gentes*, c. 3, n. 22, 2: "*Necesse est, ut in unoquoque magno territorio socio-culturali . . .*"; "*. . . intra limites uniuscu-jusque magni territorii socio-culturalis. . . .*"

[8] 2 Jn. Titus 1:5, etc. Pierre Benoit, "*Les origines de*

after his departure—once he had "laid the foundations of the faith and established pastors"[9]—this situation might remain. We see an analogous example in the fourth century—the young church of Armenia subject to Caesarea of Cappadocia because it was at Caesarea that her founder had been baptized.[10] Or else the strong personality of a head of a particular church can create a kind of bond between the surrounding churches to which his influence extends: this was the case with Ignatius of Antioch, who could introduce himself to the Romans as "Bishop of Syria", with Polycarp of Smyrna, "Doctor of Asia",[11] with Dionysius of Corinth, whose "Catholic letters" were received over a vast territory, with Cyprian of Carthage, with Dionysius of Alexandria.[12] Or again, when a

---

l'épiscopat", in: *Exégèse et théologie*, 2 (Cerf, 1961), 243–44. Jean Colson, *Les fonctions ecclésiales aux deux premiers siècles* (DDB, 1956), 199–200. André Lemaire, *Les ministères aux origines de l'Église* (Cerf, 1971), 118, 138. Schlier, *Essais*, 213; obviously rough analogies.

[9] Eusebius, *Hist. eccles.*, l. 3, c. 31, n. 3 (SC, Bardy, 31:151).

[10] Cf. J.-R. Palanque, in Fliche and Martin, *Histoire de l'Église*, 3 (Bloud and Gay, 1936), 490–92. Louis Duchesne, *Origines du culte chrétien*, 3d ed. (1903), 28–29.

[11] Ignatius, *Rom.* 2, 2; *Martyr. Polyc.* 12, 2 (SC, Camelot, 10:128 and 258).

[12] Colson, *Les fonctions*, 243–48. Pierre Batiffol, *Cathedra*

church that has grown larger happens to split up, the new group thus formed remains, naturally enough, under the authority of the mother church.

The socio-cultural factor does not come into play, at least not in the foreground, in any of these cases.[13] The case of the church of Armenia is typical. It was a wholly religious factor which kept her paradoxically bound at first to the episcopal seat of Cappadocia, and it was, on the contrary, the determining action of geography and politics which finally separated her from it at the end of a century and a half. But much more numerous are the opposite cases in which we see groups formed under the influence of a few large cities or according to administrative divisions or natural regions,[14] or, as nearly everywhere today,

---

Petri (Cerf, 1939), 12.

[13] The Council speaks in very general terms of the patriarchates. According to whether they can more or less claim an apostolic origin or to whether they owe their formation to political developments, they would be classified in one or the other of the two categories we are distinguishing here. It is a question of the first case in *Lumen Gentium*, chap. 3, n. 23, 4: ". . . *Antiquae Patriarchales Ecclesiae, veluti matrices fidei, alias pepererunt quasi filios. . . .*" Cf. Monsignor Gérard Philips, *L'Église et son mystère au second concile du Vatican*, 1 (Desclée, 1967), 313–15.

[14] Dom Emmanuel Lanne, *"Pluralisme et unité"*, in: *Istina*

in the image and on the scale of nations. It nevertheless remains true that each church, local or
particular, always has more or less its own physi-
ognomy composed of traits in which the worldly
and the religious mingle, and the description we
read from the pen of Jean-Jacques von Allmen can,
in varying degrees, be applied to each one:

> The inevitable and good local adaptations to a
> particular culture and milieu, the history lived by
> the local church, the battles she has had to wage to
> keep her faith and her life pure, the persecutions
> which she has been able to endure, the doctrinal
> reflections she has been able or obliged to carry
> forward in some particular direction, the thought
> patterns of those of whom she is composed, the
> internal conflicts between people which she has
> not been able to avoid, etc., have fashioned her
> ecclesial "personality" in such a way that the
> Church of God as she is at Corinth is not im-
> mediately congruent with, superimposable upon
> the church of the Thessalonians which is in God
> the Father and in Our Lord Jesus Christ.[15]

The distinction proposed here nonetheless remains useful, sometimes even necessary. Although
oversimplified, it is a distinction sufficiently

_____

(1969), 177–78.

[15] *L'Église locale parmi les autres Églises locales*, in: *Irenikon*
(1970), 517.

grounded in fact and one whose sharpness has increased today. Supposing that they could be placed in opposition to each other *in the abstract*, by taking into consideration the single difference in their two aspects, the particular church and the local church, such as we have defined them respectively, would each be animated, so to speak, by an opposite movement. In any case, let us say in more concrete terms that since the local church is always formed from particular churches (or even sometimes from a single one), this twofold movement, centripetal and (more or less) centrifugal, exists in every church.

Taken as such, the particular church is always universalist and centripetal. Consequently it is unnecessary to state with reference to her, as the conciliar text does for the groups given the name of local churches, that she exists "without prejudice to unity. . . ." Such a statement would be absurd. The particular church, in fact, "is not merely an administrative division of the total Church"; she does not "result from a partition which would fragment the expanse of the universal Church, but from a concentration of the Church exercising her own capacity for fulfillment."[16] She is not a section of a vaster adminis-

---

[16] Karl Rahner, *Quelques réflexions sur les principes constitu-*

trative body, one part fitted to other parts in order
to form a larger whole, each of these parts remaining exterior to the others, in the way the
French provinces, for example, are fitted to each
other in order to form, grouped or not into more
important divisions, the administrative body of
the State. It is for this reason that some would
even have wished to proscribe from ecclesiastical
language the word "diocese", which can by its origins evoke the idea of a circumscription analogous
to the ancient dioceses of the Roman Empire. The
scruple was without doubt excessive; it was also
inspired by inaccurate historical views and failed
to recognize one aspect, as legitimate as it is necessary, of the reality involved. To begin with,
Christianity has had to forge its own language
from existing words, and it was often less in-
convenient to transform the meaning of words
taken from secular usage than to use a sacred
vocabulary borrowed from paganism or even
from the religion of Israel. And then, the dioceses
of the Catholic Church never covered the territory
of the imperial dioceses, although the general bor-
ders of Christianity were gradually drawn, especially in the East, "under the same geographical

---

tionnels de l'Église, in: *L'Épiscopat et l'Église universelle* (1962),
549, 555.

and historical influences that had determined those of the Empire."[17] Finally, since the Church is formed by men living on earth, it must indeed be admitted that each church exists on a territory which is not that of her neighbors, that her members are not the members of these other churches, that her pastor exercises a jurisdiction over her that he does not exercise over the others: that is what can be called the canonical aspect of the particular church, and it is to this aspect above all that the name "diocese" corresponds. Nevertheless, the scruple we raised proceeded from a legitimate concern, and it can in fact be noted that the decree *Christus Dominus* on the pastoral charge of bishops, without proscribing the word, pushed it into the background. Its second chapter, which deals nevertheless with canonical questions, received the title "Bishops in Relation to Particular Churches or Dioceses".[18]

Between the particular church and the universality of the Church "there is, as it were, a mutual interiority".[19] At the heart of each (particular)

[17] Duchesne, *Origines*, 21–22. Cf. p. 19: Up to the end of the third century, we still see "no trace of a tendency to model ecclesiastical provinces on civil provinces".

[18] "*De episcopis, quoad Ecclesia particulares seu dioceses.*" Cf. the details given by Lanne, "*Pluralisme*", 57.

[19] Yves Congar, *La collégialité de l'épiscopat*, 1: "*Avant le*

church, all the (universal) Church is thus present in principle. Each one is, qualitatively, the Church. Each one is a living cell "in which the whole vital mystery of the one Body of the Church is present, each one is open on all sides through the bonds of communion and preserves her existence as Church only through this openness."[20] The language of Saint Paul had already expressed this when the Apostle addressed himself, not precisely to the church at Corinth, but "to the Church of God established at Corinth", or when he spoke to the Romans of "the Church which is at Cenchreae"[21]—this same Church of God which is established at Corinth and at Cenchreae as she is in other cities. Ignatius of Antioch likewise addressed himself to "the Church of God which is at Philadelphia of Asia",[22] at Magnesia, Tralles, Smyrna, etc. Origen used these formulas again.[23] *The Martyrdom of Polycarp* contains a similar, more

---

milieu du IVe siècle".

[20] Joseph Ratzinger, in: *Concilium*, 1 (1965), 37–38.

[21] 1 Cor 1:2. 2 Cor 1:1. Rom 16:1. We know that Paul often designates the particular community by *Ecclesia*; whence the use of the plural; but more than once the word designates the universal Church.

[22] *Ad. Philad.*, SC, 10:141, etc.

[23] *Contra Celsum*, l. 3, c. 29–30, speaking of "the Church of God which is at Athens",—"which is at Alexandria". Koetschau, 1:227.

explicit greeting: "The Church of God which resides at Smyrna, to the Church of God which resides at Philomelium and to all the residences everywhere of the holy and Catholic Church."[24]

Since there is a mutual interiority or inclusion, there is a radical correlation, so that it is not enough to say that the particular churches have to be inserted into the universal Church: they are so by their very existence. The universal Church is therefore not one of a "federative" unity—as if particular churches were at first able to establish themselves, each one separately, and then were free to join together: she is the Spouse of Christ. Her unity is "organic and mystical".[25] The People of God are a single people, "not because they are composed of numerous particular churches, but because each particular community is for its part only a form in which this *one* People of God occurs".[26] The ancient affirmation of the Roman

[24] SC, 10:242.

[25] Charles Journet, *Primauté de Pierre* (Alsatia, 1953), 76. Cf. Paul Evdokimov, in: *Concilium*, 64:111. "It is only in agreement or communion with others that a church identifies herself with the Church of God, for the unity is that of the Church, not of the churches."

[26] Heinrich Schlier. Saint Irenaeus on several occasions stresses this unique and universal character of the Church founded by the Apostles: *Adversus Haereses*, l. 1, c. 10, n. 1–2 (PG, 7:550 A); l. 3, c. 12, n. 7 (SC, 34, Sagnard, 228).

Creed, stressing the unity of the Church, is significant.

The weakness of an ecclesiology too narrowly (or rather we should say too incompletely) "eucharistic" would be in privileging the "dimension" of the particular church by seeming to forget this radical correlation.[27] Fuller attention to the nature of the episcopacy and to the mystery of the Eucharist avoids this partiality. The episcopacy is in fact one: "it is not possessed in part". Whatever the method by which he has been chosen, whether by election or not, and whoever the electors might be, a Christian becomes bishop only through his admission to this undivided body of the epis-

[27] Alexander Schmemann was conscious of this possible partiality; it is necessary to "assert energetically", he writes, "that in no way does the (eucharistic ecclesiology) make of the local church a monad closed in on herself. . . . The organic unity of the universal Church is no less real and, so to speak, 'palpable' than the unity of the local church." He says further that "the identity of this fullness (of the local church) with that of the one Church of God is attested by the consecration of the bishop elected by other bishops." (In *La primauté de Pierre dans l'Église orthodoxe* [Neuchâtel: Delachaux and Niestlé, 1960], 131–32, 135.) We would say more explicitly: ". . . is realized and attested. . . ." —On eucharistic ecclesiology in its relation to the problem of union: Nicolas Afanasieff, *Una Sancta*, in: *Irenikon*, 36 (1963), 436–75. Florovsky, in Yves-Noël Lelouvier, *Perspectives russes sur l'Église* (Centurion, 1968), 36–37.

copacy. The whole Church is affected by it. Consequently it is the whole Church, in her undivided episcopacy, which makes him a bishop. That is the reason why the action of several bishops has always been required for his consecration (his *ordinatio*). The rule generally accepted from of old, sanctioned by the Council of Nicea, requires at least three of them.[28] In the ancient church of Africa at the time of Saint Augustine, canonical legislation, confirming a tradition already long attested by Saint Cyprian,[29] required the symbolic number of twelve *ordinatores*.[30] Now since the episcopacy is complete in each one, "the universal Church is complete in each of the churches"; thus,

[28] In principle, all the bishops of the province must concur; those who are prevented from doing so must send their written consent.

[29] *Epist.* 67, c. 4 and 5, citing Acts 6:2 (Hartel, 2:738, 739).

[30] Augustine, *Contra Cresconium*, l. 3, c. 52–54 (PL, 43:527–30); p. 4, c. 4–6 (549–52). Thirty-ninth canon of the third Council of Carthage, in 397. Cf. Jacques Pintard, *Essai sur le sacerdoce selon saint Augustin*, mimeographed thesis (Faculty of Theology, Paris, 1955), 21: "At the beginning of the Donatist schism, the fact that Caecilianus had only been consecrated by three bishops aroused nearly as many protests as the presence of the 'traitor' Felix of Apthunga among those three." See also Paul Zmire in *Recherches augustiniennes*, 8 (1971), 18–20. For the election and without doubt the ordination of Cornelius at Rome, there were sixteen bishops.

"the unity of the hierarchy makes the particular church one and the same thing as the universal Church".[31] Similarly, it is not merely the unity of the people gathered around him which is realized in the Eucharist celebrated by the bishop, as we said above: what is realized at one and the same time, indivisibly, is the unity of this people with all others who, in other places around their bishop, participate in the same mystery.

This communion among the churches also received its symbolic expression in a certain number of rites which have regrettably fallen into disuse or have atrophied without being renewed. In the ancient Roman liturgy, at the papal Mass, a particle of the consecrated host was set aside to be saved until the following Mass; the sub-deacon then carried it to the altar, and it was placed in the chalice at the moment of the "breaking"; it was the rite of the *Sancta*. Through an analogous rite, the *fermentum*, other particles were sent to all the priests who were celebrating in the various districts. In this way, through these inevitably partial exchanges, the truth was signified that everywhere and always, in all the liturgical assemblies, it is "the same sacrifice, the same Eucharist,

[31] Gréa, *L'Église*, 68–70, 289. Dom Botte, in *Études sur le sacrement de l'Ordre* (Cerf, 1957), 99, 108–114. Bouyer, *L'Église*, 488.

the same communion".[32] The letter which Saint Irenaeus addressed to Pope Victor on the subject of Easter attests the existence as early as the twelfth century of an analogous usage of even wider extent.[33] "One in all the universe", wrote Peter the Venerable in the twelfth century, "is the Christian sacrifice: for the Christian people who offer it are one, one is the God to whom it is offered, one is the faith through which it is offered, one that which is offered."[34]

Just as the universal Church does not result, in a second "moment", from an addition of particular churches or from their federation, neither could these churches be considered the result of the division of a universal Church alleged to be anterior to them. They all proceed from a prior, particular, concrete church, that of Jerusalem; they came from her, "as it were, by cutting and planting".[35] An anterior universal Church, or one

[32] Duchesne, *Origines*, 5th ed. (1925), 196. Pierre Batiffol, *Leçons sur la messe* (1919), 76–77 and 90–92. *Liber Pontificales*, ed. Duchesne, 1 (1886), 168, 216.

[33] In Eusebius, *Hist. eccles.*, l. 5, c. 24, n. 15 (Bardy, SC, 41:70–71). On these practices in the Greek liturgy: Erik Peterson, "*Meris, Hostien-Partikel und Offer-Anteil*", in: *Ephemerides liturgicae*, 61 (1947), 3–12.

[34] *Tractatus Contra Petrobusianos* (PL, 189: 796).

[35] Bouyer, *L'Église*, 337; cf. 174. Rom 15:19–20. On the "transfer" of Jerusalem to Rome, according to the informa-

alleged to be existing on her own, apart from all others, is only a creation of the mind. The bishop "is not primarily the representative of the whole Church or the representative of his church: he is their bond and their very mediation".[36] It is he who, through all his activity, seeks to insure that the unifying reality of the eucharistic mystery over which he presides produces its effect everywhere. The two principal documents which remain with us as witnesses of the life of the primitive Church, the letter of Clement of Rome and the letters of Ignatius of Antioch, likewise show him to us in his role of promoter of unanimity, ὁμονοία.[37]

Insofar as she is comprised of particular churches, in a hierarchical order or not, it is very clear that what we have just said about these churches applies equally to the church which we are here calling "local". But insofar as she constitutes a characteristic grouping, this local church is distinguished by a series of original traits, behavior

---

tion from Paul and Luke: von Allmen, "*L'Église locale*", 528–29.

[36] H.-M. Legrand, "*Inverser Babel*", in: *Spiritus*, 43 (1970), 336–38.

[37] The word appears about fifteen times in Clement (cf. A. Jaubert, SC, 167:34–35). Ignatius, *Eph.* 4:1 (SC, 10:712).

and "proper" usages[38] which individualize her, differentiate and set her apart from others, and which she demands, if necessary, in defiance of the lack of understanding of other groupings or against imprudent, or what are judged to be imprudent, attempts at unification.[39]

Once again, nothing is more legitimate in principle. We must not attach any pejorative nuance to it. Quite the contrary. Firmilian of Caesarea once wrote to Cyprian of Carthage: "In most of the countries there is some difference (in the detail of the holy ceremonies); nevertheless, the peace and unity of the Catholic Church have never been troubled by it."[40] If in fact "everything through which the characteristic spirit of the people is

[38] This is the word that constantly returns in the texts of Vatican II on this subject.

[39] It is indeed normal, for example, for young churches, newly formed "in territories culturally different from the old churches", to appear sometimes somewhat "jealous of their cultural originality". Cf. Jean Vankrunkelsven, in: *Spiritus* 43:393.

[40] In Cyprian, *Epist.* 75, c. 25 (Hartel, 2:826). An unquestionable principle, despite the questionable application that Firmilian made of it. We can recall here the famous examples of the conciliatory discussion between Polycarp and Anicetus in Eusebius, *Hist. eccles.*, l. 5, c. 24, n. 16–17 (Bardy, SC, 41:71).

expressed is a contribution to all of humanity",[41] that must be equally true for the Church. Assuredly, only the church we are here calling particular belongs to the fundamental structure of the universal Church (the latter being realized only in the former); but the local church, with her singular traits, is nonetheless something useful, or even indispensible *ad bonum Ecclesiae*. J. J. von Allmen writes on this subject: "God does not save anthropological abstractions" which would be the same everywhere, "but men and women of flesh and blood".[42] Christ came to save all: his Church must assume all. It is the law of the Incarnation—prelude and permanent support for the law of redemption. The large cultural areas are also—actually or potentially, in fact or in hope—the large areas into which what might be called the human geography of the Church is divided. The word "divided" is here less inadequate than in the case of the particular churches, although the vitality of the diverse cultures always more or less presupposes their interpenetration. "It is in the creation of differentiated cultures that the originality" of persons or peoples "is manifested par excellence", but "it is also through constant con-

[41] Cardinal Jean Daniélou, *"Resserrer l'unité"*, in: *France catholique* (February 6, 1970).

[42] In *"L'Église locale"*, 516.

frontation and exchange with others that each culture increases and develops by assimilating in its own way and according to its designs the elements coming from outside, while a culture which is isolated is doomed to decline and death."[43]

[43] Ch. Couturier, "*Églises particulières et originalité des cultures*", in: *Mission de l'Église* (February-March), 12.

III

PLURALISM OR HARMONY?

Far from failing to recognize or wishing to extenuate the cultural diversities within the Church, the last council vigorously affirmed the duty to respect them. It brought out their necessary and beneficial role—very particularly in the second chapter of *Lumen Gentium* and in the third chapter of *Ad Gentes*. "Each of the parts", says *Lumen Gentium*, "brings to the others and to the whole Church the benefit of its own gifts so that the whole and each of its parts are increased by a mutual universal exchange and by a common effort toward a fullness in unity." That is why it is good that diverse groups who "each enjoy their own traditions" exist "within the communion of the Church".[1] Regarding "young churches", the decree *Ad Gentes* becomes more insistent in order

[1] *Lumen Gentium*, c. 2, n. 13. Cf. Leo XIII, apostolic letter, *Praeclara Gratulationis* of June 20, 1894, etc.

to advocate the concrete application of the principle set down by *Lumen Gentium*:

> As in the economy of the Incarnation, the young churches, rooted in Christ and built on the foundation of the Apostles, take over, for a marvelous exchange, all the riches of the nations which have been given to Christ as an inheritance. They borrow from the customs and traditions of their people, from their wisdom, their science, their arts, their teaching, all that can contribute to confessing the glory of the Creator, to manifesting the grace of the Savior and to the right ordering of Christian life. —To obtain this result, it is necessary that theological reflection be encouraged in each socio-cultural region, as they are called. . . . In this way, all appearance of syncretism and false particularism will be put aside; Christian life will be adapted to the spirit and charter of each culture; particular traditions of each family of nations, with their own special qualities, illumined by the light of the Gospel, will be assumed into Catholic unity. . . .[2]

These teachings of the Council were called to mind again at the Roman Synod of 1969. They constitute, as it were, the character of missionary theology. The way for them had been prepared by the great missionary encyclicals of Benedict XV

---

[2] *Ad Gentes*, c. 3, n. 22, 1–2; cf. n. 3.

and Pius XI, encyclicals which were not always received wholeheartedly. Among the older documents, it is appropriate to cite at least the famous instructions of the "Propaganda" addressed in 1659 "to the apostolic vicars of the kingdoms of Tonkin and Cochin-China",[3] as well as those of Saint Gregory to Saint Augustine of Canterbury at the time when he sent him with a handful of Roman monks to the Angles and the similar instructions of his successor, Vitalian, to the Greek monk Theodore, who was to be the second founder of the Church in England.[4]

Putting these teachings into practice, however, can pose many problems. Many an example of this is seen as far back as the earliest periods of Christian expansion. What history seems to show, first of all, is that "the great missionary churches have been churches who brought the Christian culture of their origin along with the Gospel: Alexandria into Ethiopia, Syria into China, Constantinople to the Slavs, Rome into all the West. Churches of weak autonomous Christian culture have not been very evangelistic".[5] The

[3] Bernard Jacqueline, in the documents *Omnis Terra*, Rome (May 1971), 330–44.

[4] Cf. Duchesne, *Origines*, 3d ed., 99.

[5] The latter should be taken, however, with some slight nuances. Thus, examination of the celebrated stele of Si-ngan-fou (781) shows, on the part of the Syrian missionaries,

cultural contribution which is inevitably (and, for that matter, fortunately) a part of the work of evangelization should not stifle the culture of the people to whom the Gospel is brought. On the contrary, it should be instrumental in vivifying and deepening that culture by christianizing it. For this purpose, a constant effort of moderation and spiritual discernment, proceeding from both human wisdom and disinterested charity, is therefore necessary.

On the other hand, "ever since the dynamism of Pentecost, the very fabric of numerous cultures" has become the fabric of as many groups of churches. We can speak in this sense, in a broad way, of the Syriac, Greek, Latin, Coptic, Armenian, Ethiopian, Indian (in Malabar) church, etc. They are not copies of a "uniform model which they have more or less adapted". Their originality is something more radical. Each one has blossomed, so to speak, on her own ground, giving herself "a liturgy, a hymnography, a theology, a legal system, in profound symbiosis"with the human milieu she christianized.[6] It is in fact im-

---

a concern for the sinicization in the presentation of the Christian faith. Cf. Édouard Duperray, *Ambassadeurs de Dieu à la Chine* (Casterman, 1956), 23–25.

[6] Legrand, "*Inverser Babel*", 331.

possible entirely to separate liturgical and disciplinary elements, which appear more exterior and contingent, from doctrinal elements, which one would hope to recognize everywhere in a nearly identical form.[7] And it is no less impossible for the same mind, whether individual or collective, to separate radically Christian faith and human culture as some theorists teach today in search of a "secularization" from which they think a perfect purity of faith would result: that would indeed be its extinction by asphyxiation instead. These adversaries of all "Christian culture" could no more provide for the missionary apostolate than they could support a living faith within a Christian environment; they do not know what they are talking about.

Though the Christian faith is unique, human culture varies according to time and place. This is the reason for the socio-cultural originality, at times very marked, of each local church. This is a benefit for catholicity as a whole. A rich element of human variety is joined with the element of divine unity brought by the first founders, all moved by the one Spirit, as a message through which the personality of each of them is already

[7] This was the illusion of some "uniate" solutions. Cf. Lanne, *"Pluralisme"*, 183–84.

reflected. Thus is brought about that union of the supernatural and "nature" (which is to say, here, of the human, of culture), by which all that is authentically Catholic is recognized. Father Yves de Montcheuil observed in 1939, following Moehler and in reaction against a tendency which was then asserting itself to enclose all Christian thought within the bonds of a single system, that "there is nothing more contrary to true Christian unity than the search for unification: the latter always consists in the desire to render a particular form universal, to confine life to one of its expressions".[8] The concrete and living unity of the Church is not a uniformity. It is, if we can say it like this, a "pluriformity".[9] It is a concert, a harmony.[10] The image Saint Ignatius of Antioch applied to each particular church can be applied to the universal

[8] "*Verité et diversité dans l'Église*", in: Pierre Chaillet, *L'Église est une, hommage à Moehler* (Bloud and Gay, 1939), 252.

[9] Dom Burkhard Neunheuser, in: *L'Église de Vatican II* (Unam Sanctam, 51 b), 637.

[10] Henri de Lubac, *Catholicisme* (Cerf, 1938), chap. 9. Jules Monchanin, "*Christianisation des cultures orientales*", in his *Écrits spirituels*, introduced by Édouard Duperray (Centurion, 1965). Jacques-Albert Cuttat, *Expérience chrétienne et spiritualité orientale* (DDB, 1967). Monsignor Wicquart, *La foi chrétienne dans la variété et la variation des cultures*, documents *Omnis Terra* (February 1971).

Church: "it is like a great lyre, all of whose sounds, while remaining different, must harmonize for a hymn in praise of the Father."[11]

And yet, in order to realize this harmony, all diversity must be taken up into the essential movement toward unity. The diffusion of the Spirit at Pentecost brought about this movement: at that time, says Saint Irenaeus, "in the harmony of all the languages, they sang a hymn to God, the Spirit bringing distant races back to unity and offering to the Father the first fruits of all the nations".[12] And this is not merely a "yearning for unity" which is observed in the first century;[13] it is, in the first place, a consciousness of the unity given by God;

[11] *Ad Eph.* c. 4 (SC, 10:72). All of this, which concerns the life of the churches, could receive a more general application in keeping with the attitude of modern minds. Hans Urs von Balthasar thinks "there is today perhaps a more acute sense of the impossibility of a rigid intellectual unity in the interpretation of ever-imperfect formulas of faith. This is not serious if there is really a passing beyond into Love, toward that always-greater Love which is God's and not that love which we fabricate together." A deep affection for the living tradition of the Church will always overcome conceptual diversities by orienting them all into the sense of unity.

[12] *Adversus Haereses*, l. 3, c. 17, n. 2 (Sagnard, SC, 34:305). On the unity of the Church and of her faith notwithstanding diverse languages: l. 1, c. 10, n. 1–2 (PG, 7:549–54).

[13] Étienne Trocmé, in *Lumière et vie*, 103 (1971), 10.

it is a concern to maintain it, an aspiration to be faithful to it, despite the pulling, the conflicts, whether personal or collective, which were certainly no more lacking in the beginning than at any other time. Christ's tunic was "of a single piece, of one fabric"; Saint Cyprian sees in it a symbol of the Church's unity,[14] and Saint Ignatius of Antioch invited all the members of Christ to "remain in this immaculate unity in order to participate in God himself".[15] Now the local church would obviously no longer play her role or merit her name if she checked the movement of unity which is the proper dynamism of the particular churches she groups together. This can nevertheless happen, and it is what does inevitably happen when this dynamism, which is that of the faith, decreases. Then they are so preoccupied with expressing the original life of the group to which they belong "at one moment of history and in one specific place" that they neglect or tolerate with impatience and seek even to strain the double

[14] *De Ecclesiae catholicae unitate*, c. 7: The *unitas Ecclesiae* is a "*concordia cohaerens*" (Hartel, 1:215–16).

[15] *Ad Eph.*, c. 4, n. 2: ἐν ἀμώμῳ ἑνότητι. Camelot translates: "inseparable". Bailly gives: "irreproachable". We are borrowing from Batiffol, *L'Église naissante*, 159, "immaculate", which is very consonant with the idea of the "immaculate faith" frequently found in the Fathers.

bond of unity, that "uninterrupted bond with the apostolic tradition of the one Church through time" which is at the same time the "bond of communion in all places".[16] Then they become passionately fond of the human differences they represent, more than of the supernatural unity in which they participate. This is a source of all kinds of partitioning, clashes, incomprehension, contempt, hostilities. It also risks multiple deformations and a loss of the Catholic heritage: whoever isolates himself from others is impoverished. They are giving in to a centrifugal movement instead of dominating it. What was to be convergence and harmony is transformed into dissonance and divergence. The ecclesial sense slackens.[17]

They even go so far as to construct a theory out of this state of affairs. Then the legitimate fact of a certain diversity, that is, of a varied plurality—this fact which is always imposed, more or less forcefully, by the realities of geography, soil, climate, temperament, work, history, social evolution, etc., this fact which is in itself good and "providential"—takes a back seat to something

[16] Lanne, *"Pluralisme"*, 287.
[17] Cf. the homily of Paul VI, *Holy Thursday*, April 3, 1969. *Doc. cath.* (1969), 356–57.

totally different, the unilateral and immoderate exaltation of a doctrinal pluralism.

At the very moment it encouraged the originality of local churches, the Council did not fail to warn them against this danger. In each instance, it recalled the fundamental necessity of the movement toward fullness and unity. We can also note in the passage cited above from the text of the decree *Ad Gentes* the recommendation for a rather rigorous "theological reflection" so that the very appearance of "syncretism" or "false particularism" might be avoided. The Roman Synod of 1969, in its turn, also attended to this. The statements on this subject made at that time can be summarized by the opposition of the two words we have borrowed from them: the opposition between a plurality, which is to be recognized and even promoted, and doctrinal pluralism, which is to be rejected.[18]

[18] We are here using the word to express an ideology, a system, or at least a synthetic bent of mind. The proposed distinction is analogous to those which can be set up, for example, between dogmatics and dogmatism, or between secularity and secularism. Nothing prevents us from using the word in a less pejorative sense, in which case it would then be advisable to find another word for the thing here described. With terminologies sometimes varying according to the authors, or even within a single work, we could seem here to be in disagreement with one or another when it is merely a

Of legitimate plurality, Cardinal Meouchi, Patriarch of the Maronites, said with good reason, referring to the texts of Vatican II: "This plurality, within the very strong unity of communion, has always been the tradition of apostolic churches."[19] The very word communion, moreover, implies it. This is what Cardinal Wojtyla, Archbishop of Cracow, observed at the same synod: "Communion in fact designates unity in its dynamic aspect. It is this kind of unity that is obtained between diverse members by a communication that tends always to be more profound and abundant. Consequently, plurality, even diversity itself, is to be understood in relation to communion, with the tendency toward unity."[20]

---

question of words. Thus, Dom Emmanuel Lanne sometimes uses "pluralism" as a synonym for "diversity"; he himself forcefully points out nonetheless that "in the New Testament, the unity in Christ is stressed, not the diversity, even if this latter is deep-seated. The miracle of the languages at Pentecost signifies the gathering together of all into the same Gospel as a result of the one Spirit who is given. . . . The accent does not in the first place rest on the diversity of the cultures to whom the message is announced, but on the unicity of this message . . ." (*"Pluralisme"*, 175).

[19] *"Illa pluralitas (secundum Vaticanum II) in unitate arctissima communionis semper fuit traditio Ecclesiarum apostolicarum."*

[20] *"Communio et enim unitatem designat sub aspectu dynamico, quae inter plures et diversos obtineri valet per viam communicationis*

We see this tendency toward unity, founded on faith in the unity of Christ, so strong in the beginning that it allowed the blossoming of profound diversities everywhere as though they were so many riches. Is the collection of writings in the New Testament not a manifest sign of this? The claim that appears at the present time to see hardly more in it than a collection of "disparate writings of christology", coming after exegetical discoveries of many, often valuable, details, but after a spiritual darkening besides, does not do it justice. Such a claim ultimately makes us blind to its true character and deaf to "its one voice".[21] Through a series of diverse perspectives and conceptualizations, which are impossible to organize into a system but which all converge on the same mystery, it is always the same faith in the same Christ that is expressed. We are entitled to consider that, at least in some measure, the same is true today.[22] It is necessary to have a great re-

---

semper profundius et abundantius. Pluralitas ergo, immo et diversitas per respectum ad communionem semper cum tendentia ad unitatem est recipienda."

[21] Cf. the reflections of Dr. Visser't Hooft, Report to the Central Committee of the Ecumenical Council of Churches (February 1966) at Geneva (*Istina*, 11:149–80).

[22] Father Yves Congar recalls on this subject the doctrine of Saint Thomas on the "*intentio mentis*" and his definition of the article of faith: "*perceptio divinae veritatis tendens in ipsam*"

spect for such diversities, which contribute to true Catholic unity. But, in contrast, such a unity would be compromised by the advent of a doctrinal pluralism. Instead of the one universal Church appearing all the more one as her unity is one of fullness— *circumdata varietate*—we would then see a Church pulled in different directions and threatened by reciprocal dislocations. History offers more than one example of it. It has been observed that "the map of successive schisms which have split the Christian Church" has "constantly and nearly perfectly coincided with that of great cultural areas". This is because "the sociological dynamisms constitutive of all culture normally carry it along toward an exclusivism"[23] to which it can succumb. Then, in periods of decline, there are always a few minds to be found to set the fact down as principle. It also happens sometimes, more simply, that generous minds, especially when they see things from the outside, tend to confine a local church within her own culture in the belief that they are thus fostering her own life—as others tend to confine the working world within a

---

(*In 3 Sent.*, dist. 25 A. 1, a. 1, q° 1, objectis 4). *Ministères et communion ecclésiale* (Cerf, 1971), 243.

[23] Legrand, *"Inverser Babel"*, 336. In which the author notes "the opposite temptation, that of considering catholicity as uniformity."

"working culture". This is to forget that all true culture, despite the "sociological dynamisms" which it was necessary for us to recall, has an open and universalizing character. If it becomes static and isolationist, the pluralism thus promoted and practiced is no more favorable to human development than to Catholic unity.

The age of great schisms, such as those to which we have just alluded, can undoubtedly be considered completed. We would have to be blind, however, to persuade ourselves that all analogous danger has become fanciful. It was precisely the authorized representative of a very vast "local church", the president of CELAM (the group of all Latin American churches), who, at the Synod of October 1969, characterized this danger most forcefully as present in new forms. "All through history", said Monsignor Brandao, Archbishop of Bahia and primate of Brazil, "a certain theological and pastoral pluralism[24] has always existed. But, alas, such a pluralism is too often today exalted before the People of God, creating, as it were, an irreducible abyss between what is called left and right, or progressives and conservatives".[25]

[24] See above, 222, note 18.

[25] "*In decursu historiae Ecclesiae, quasi fructus legis vitae, semper exstitit quidam pluralismus theologicus et pastoralis. Talis pluralismus hodie, proh dolor, saepe saepius falso extollitur coram*

Just as the ancient wars between nations have today become wars that are at once civil and international, so also the religious particularism of old tends to come to life again by becoming more ideological than local. Its nationalist form is not dead, however, and other bishops at the same synod denounced it as being still too present a reality. Father Ange Anton, S.J., Secretary, pointed out the necessity of studying more closely the socio-cultural reality of the churches and its pastoral implications precisely in order to avoid more successfully the danger of "nationalist" excesses,[26] a request with which most of the bishops were in agreement. And Cardinal Zungrana, Archbishop of Uagadugu (Upper Volta), expressed this complaint: "sometimes one encounters a certain nationalism which is in truth anti-catholic. Whereas the Apostle Paul speaks rather of the Church which is at Corinth or at Rome, etc., always and everywhere the same, today we have men who,

---

populo Dei tanquam irreductibilis abyssus inter sic dictam alam dexteram et sinistram, vel inter progressistas et conservatores. . . ."

[26] ". . . *ut notio Ecclesiae particularis tam in ordine theologico quam in ordine juridico necnon et sociologico-culturali, cum omnibus suis postulatis exhauriatur, neque tamen in nimios 'nationalismos' incidat, longa restat via." Responsiones P. Angeli Anton*, I, 5 (7).

on the contrary, oppose the church of one nation to the church of another region."[27]

Such an ecclesial nationalism would improperly seek to justify its claims of autonomy with what Vatican II teaches us, whether about the particular church or the local church. The sociological considerations it pleads sometimes make it forget that "natural sociology cannot be determinative in theology".[28] Nevertheless, its pretensions are sometimes greater. Paradoxically, but conforming to the laws of a logic of the passions, its claim of local autonomy can be paralleled by propaganda tending to align the universal Church with its own particularities. The somewhat arrogant conviction of having attained a degree of culture superior to those of other human groups, more particularly to that which reigns at the center of the Church, thus provokes a kind of fever of religious imperialism. In this case, it is not merely a local church which risks becoming atrophied and losing its Christian vitality in some variety of

[27] "*Quidam aliquoties invenitur 'nationalismus' revera anti-catholicus. Dum potius Paulus apostolus loquitur de Ecclesia Dei quae est Corinthis, Romae . . . semper et ubique eadem, isti homines e contra Ecclesiam unius nationis opponunt Ecclesiae aliae regionis.*" Cf. Philips, *L'Église et son mystère*, 1:301.

[28] Monsignor André Charue, Bishop of Namur, preface to *L'Épiscopat et l'Église universelle* (Cerf, 1962), 14.

syncretism—from voodoo worship, for example, to the profession of an Aryan Christianity or to some other more recent invention—it is the entire Church that would risk being contaminated if pastors and faithful, in a burst of faith coming from the Holy Spirit, did not resist such psychological action.

This is obviously a question of extreme cases—although the facts are there to dissuade us from believing that such cases are merely imaginary evils. History shows us others which were also not without gravity and which continue to burden our age. It is unquestionable that the rise of nationalism in the West toward the end of the Middle Ages created a situation favorable to the formation, in the sixteenth century, of territorial churches separated from catholicity. And then again, if the importance of local communities has not always been sufficiently recognized in the Latin Church, in the Eastern Churches, on the other hand, while the idea of "autocephaly" prevailed, it was not without an often immediate danger of "destroying the feeling of adherence to the universal Church".[29] Orthodox theologians are not always the last to denounce this evil—

[29] Joseph Ratzinger, in Barauna, *L'Église*, 3:775. See some refinements on the Eastern model of collegiality by André de Halleux, *Revue théologique de Louvain*, 2 (1971), 76–87.

theologians such as Alexander Schmemann, who contrasts it with the situation in the primitive Church. The latter, he says, had "the sense of being the 'third race', that in which there was neither Jew nor Greek; she was conscious of carrying the true life within her: without denying the natural characteristics of each people, she transcended and transfigured them by thus giving them fullness and catholicity".[30] Would it not be dangerous to allow the introduction today of those very "customs of autocephalous churches"[31] which they are trying to remedy in Orthodoxy itself?[32]

Ecclesiastical nationalism also assumes more benign forms in which this sense of catholicity, of which the Christian tradition offers us so much living evidence, is at the very least reduced.[33] These are perhaps the ones against which we most need to protect ourselves today. It is assuredly legitimate, and for more than one good reason, to speak of a "church of England", of a "church of France", and of a "church of Spain", etc., just as

---

[30] In *La primauté*, 146.

[31] Legrand, "*Inverser Babel*", 342.

[32] Cf. Paul Evdokimov and Olivier Clément, "*Vers le concile, appel à l'Église*", in: *Contacts*, a French Orthodox journal, 23 (1971), 191–210.

[33] I cited several of them in *Catholicisme*.

we speak of "the church of Latin America" or sometimes even of "the church of Africa". Such expressions have only a practical value of designation; they are justifiable in doctrine, although they must not be pressed too far, as the language of Saint Paul warns us: in fact, when he came to name the groups of churches that owed their existence to him, he did not say: the church of Galatia or the church of Asia, but "the churches of Galatia", "the churches of Asia".[34] Nevertheless, if another, nearly identical expression were to spread in an insistent or somewhat systematic way, if people began to speak of a "French church", etc., it would be difficult for us to see that as an auspicious sign. While this would not oblige us to consider this church already on the path to schism, we would doubtless not be wrong to discern in such language a diminished understanding of the mystical reality of both the particular and the universal Church. But, provided that care is taken, all organization and all initiative tending to create and develop the internal vitality of each local church is always to be encouraged.

Dr. A. M. Ramsey, Archbishop of Canterbury, seems to have indicated very well both the importance of the local church and the conditions she

[34] I Cor 16:1 and 19.

must satisfy when he wrote: "A local church can claim the loyalty of the Christian with respect to herself only by leading him beyond herself to the universal family she represents. The Catholic structure is therefore not a hierarchical tyranny but a means of deliverance through an incorporation into the Gospel of God, of the Church of all times."[35]

[35] *The Gospel and the Catholic Church*, 135; cited by D. W. Allen and A. M. Allchin, in: *Irenikon* (1964), 186.

IV

THE EPISCOPAL COLLEGE

The collegial bond of bishops, which is a universal bond, constitutes the permanent remedy for the danger of withdrawal, which, in diverse and more or less renewed forms, always exists. "The episcopacy is one and indivisible."[1] The Church is one in the unity of her episcopacy.

"The idea of episcopal collegiality", noted Father Yves Congar in 1962, "has, within a few months, won over theological opinion."[2] From the time John XXIII announced the Council, in fact, ex-

[1] Saint Cyprian, *De Ecclesiae catholicae unitate*, c. 5: "*. . . quam unitatem tenere firmiter et vindicare debemus, maxime episcopi qui in Ecclesia praesidemus, ut episcopatum quoque ipsum unum atque indivisum probemus.*" (G. Hartel [Vienna, 1868], 213; CSEL, 3:1.) *Epist.* 66, c. 8: "*. . . quando Ecclesia . . . sit utique conexa et cohaerentium sibi invicem sacerdotum glutino copulata*" (Hartel [1871], 733; CSEL, 3:2).

[2] Preface to Jean Colson, *L'Épiscopat catholique*, Unam Sanctam, 43 (Cerf, 1963).

pectations and resolutions alike were crystallized, as it were, around the question of the episcopacy. This was simultaneously a spontaneous reaction against a centralization which in excess is harmful to the life of the churches and the culmination of a vast historical and theological effort pursued for the last century. It was not, in any case, a matter of innovation. "It is obvious that Vatican II did not create collegiality any more than Vatican I created primacy."[3] Roman theologians of recent centuries were even the principal ones among those who systematized its doctrine, as Giuseppe Alberigo had the credit of recalling in 1964.[4] And, by placing it on the Council's program, were we not resuming, under better conditions, the plan of Vatican I which external circumstances had prevented from being realized?

We do in fact know that the constitution *Pastor Aeternus*, devoted to the Roman Pontiff, is entitled *"Constitutio Dogmatica Prima de Ecclesia Christi"* and that the perspectives of the schema prepared by Kleutgen for the *"Constitutio Secunda"*, according to the suggestions of the Fathers of the Council,

[3] Hervé Coathalem, *Un horizon de Vatican II* (NRT, 92, 1970), 1014.

[4] G. Alberigo, *Lo sviluppo della dottrina sui poteri nella Chiesa universale. Momenti essenziali tra il 16 e il 19 secolo* (Herder, 1964).

prefigure precisely what is today designated by "episcopal collegiality".[5] From that time on, the idea had matured. But even if it was imperative and if most minds welcomed it, for many its contours remained vague. The Council, as was proper, gave it an eminent place. It recalled its essential nature. In order to avoid the misunderstandings which did not fail to confuse the discussions, it even entered into several detailed explanations on the subject that some found excessively emphatic. The idea is appealed to again and again today, not only in theological circles, but in all manner of discussions. But can we be sure that it is always well understood? Far from it!

It would be naive to be overly surprised by this. In the sudden intensity of its revival, the doctrine of episcopal collegiality risked becoming distorted by conforming, in many minds, to ready-made models taken from the history of human societies or from the situations or ideas of our times. This is the risk that has threatened all ecclesiological doctrines for nineteen centuries. It is the danger they

[5] J.-P. Torrell, *La théologie de l'épiscopat au premier concile du Vatican* (Cerf, 1961), 87, 276. Cf. Henri Rondet, *Vatican I* (Lethielleux, 1962), 161–62, 191–207. What would have been the result had this been carried through? Vatican I "is only an unfinished cathedral, and it is useless to extrapolate from it" (F. Roulier, *Dossier* [Lyons, 1970], 212).

run into when, forgetting the unique and mysterious character of the Church of Christ, they give in to an inclination to facile analogies. The results are then always deceptive: as was, in antiquity, the theory of Eusebius of Caesarea on the relations of the Church and the Empire; as were, toward the end of our Middle Ages, the conciliarist theories; and, closer to our own time, the theory of Joseph de Maistre on the papacy. . . .[6] There are certainly analogous applications or extensions of the concept of collegiality within the Church, the principal one being that which concerns the relations of the bishop and his *"presbyterium"*,[7] and they could be set forth if this

[6] Cf. Coathalem, *Un horizon*, 1017–18. Henri de Lubac, *Paradoxe et mystère de l'Église* (Aubier, 1967), 38–42. Joseph Ratzinger, *Le nouveau peuple de Dieu*, trans. R. Givord and H. Bourboulon (Aubier, 1971), 99 (with regard to the Council): "All the errors proceed, in the end, from having applied a pattern of secular society to the Church, thus obscuring her unique character, which she bears within her because of her divine origin." Von Allmen, *Prophétisme*, 40–41.

[7] Cf. the sixth Proposition issued by the International Theological Commission in October 1970: "The ministry of the new covenant has, in analogous ways, a collegial dimension, whether we consider the bishops around the pope in the universal Church or the priests around their bishop in the local church." *Lumen Gentium*, c. 3, n. 28; *Presb. Ordinis*, c. 2,

were the place for it; but they presuppose that the uniqueness of this concept has been precisely grasped. There are also what one could, with Father Congar, call the "substructures" of episcopal collegiality,[8] which are to be explored in the fundamentally organic and indivisible nature of the People of God, or in "the communion of the faithful of Christ taken in their totality", as the report on the doctrinal part of the Roman Synod of 1969 puts it, which is to say again, within the original unity of the Church such as we have tried to outline it. That is a fundamental point. The collegiality of bishops "can develop in all its pastoral fruitfulness only when it appears connected to the fundamental idea of those who, from the 'First-born' of the Father on, have mutually become brothers. . . . It achieves its meaning only if the particular bishop truly represents his church and if, because of him, a part of the ecclesial

---

n. 8. Cf. Albano Vilela, *La condition collégiale des prêtres au IIIe siècle* (Beauchesne, 1971).

[8] Introduction to *La collégialité épiscopale* (Cerf, 1965), 8. Cf. *Lumen Gentium*, n. 12. E.-L. Mascall, *Théologie de l'avenir*, Fr. trans. (1970), 133. G. Thils, *L'infaillibilité du peuple chrétien in credendo* (Paris-Louvain, 1964). Joseph Ratzinger, *La collégialité épiscopale, développement théologique*, in Barauna, *L'Église*, 763–90.

fullness is truly gathered into the oneness of the whole."[9]

Consequently, this doctrine of episcopal collegiality, taken in literal and precise terms, comprises traits which are not capable of being transposed just as they are. Now, despite the care taken by the Council to prevent confusion, this doctrine gave rise not only to unwarranted extrapolations, but also—just like the doctrine of religious freedom or that of Scripture and tradition, or that of the universal priesthood and the People of God[10]—to aberrant interpretations. That these interpretations are sometimes presented as defining the spirit of the Council beyond a letter which one must "transcend" does nothing to change the fact that they are misinterpretations.[11] Before wishing to "transcend", it is necessary to seek to understand.

The abstract noun *collegialitas* is modern (it does not even figure in the texts of Vatican II)—as is

[9] Ratzinger, *Le nouveau peuple*, 112, 118.

[10] Ratzinger, *Le nouveau peuple*, 15, protests "against the misuse (which has only increased since the end of the Council) of a concept of the people of God totally detached from its origins".

[11] From which arise, in repercussion, unending hostilities. Cf. Alexis Ourvers, in *Itinéraires* (January 1970), 156: "Collegiality is a modern invention, pure legend, nonsense, a theological hoax. . . . The word, like the thing itself, has never existed."

papatus as well.[12] The idea of episcopal collegiality has nonetheless been expressed from antiquity on, not, of course, in a systematized theory, but in fact and through "formulas of perfect clarity",[13] notably by a certain number of popes, the foremost of whom was Celestine I. "You have parted from our college", or "from the universality of the college", Celestine wrote, for example, to Nestorius.[14] This word "college" was already found in Saint Cyprian. The Latin liturgy uses it for the Apostles, for example, in celebrating Saint Andrew bound to his brother Peter, among other things, *apostolicae collegio dignitatis*.[15] But we note, as the Council itself frequently called to mind, that the word is to be taken in the sense which ecclesiastical tradition attributes to it based on the realities of primitive Christianity.[16] The most per-

[12] Ducange cites Léon d'Ostie as the first witness to its use at the beginning of the twelfth century. Batiffol, *Cathedra*, 96.

[13] Joseph Lécuyer, *Études sur la collégialité épiscopale* (Mappus, Le Puy, 1964), 56.

[14] PL, 50:477 A and 483 B. Or to the bishops of Gaul about some who were "*de laicorum consortio in collegium nostrum admissi*" (529 B). Likewise, Nicholas I, John IX, Benedict IV, John XV (Lécuyer, *Études*, 56–59).

[15] *Sacramentaire léonien* (L.-C. Mohlberg, 156). The word often has a more restricted meaning, too, applicable to any group or gathering of bishops.

[16] Philips, *L'Église et son mystère*, 1:231–33. This is the basic

sistent objections derived from a failure to understand this, and it was necessary to cut them short.
We will not enter here into a long analysis of
vocabulary, many elements of which would be
furnished by the fourteen columns of the *Thesaurus
linguae latinae*. Let us simply say that *collegium*, in
the language of the Church, does not have the
meaning given it by the Roman law codified by
Ulpian and still retained today by most of our
encyclopedias according to common and current
usage.[17] Nor is it to be understood according to
the ideas of medieval corporatism common to the
lawyers and canonists, nor according to those of a
certain number of Protestant jurists speculating on
the equality of all the members of the Church or
seeking to establish a new ecclesiastical law of civil
society.[18] The episcopal college is not formed by
the elective and regular assemblage of all its members, leading a common life in the same place, in
the manner of monastic or canonical communities

---

work which must always be consulted for an explanation of
Lumen Gentium.

[17] Thus, *Digeste*, 50, 6, 173: "*Collegarum appellatione hi
continentur qui sunt ejusdem potestatis.*"

[18] Cf. Ratzinger in Barauna, *L'Église*, 3:764–65. Yves
Congar, *L'Église de saint Augustin à l'époque moderne* (Cerf,
1970), 261, 308, 336–37.

or of some university bodies.[19] Neither is it a group of associates who would all be equal, "with the same power", who would never act except all together, like certain groups of merchants or certain priestly colleges in pagan Rome.[20] The structure and authority of this college (*collegium*; Greek: *synedrion*), often designated also in Latin sources by the two other words *corpus* and *ordo* (Greek: τάξις, τάγμα),[21] are to be determined, as has been

[19] Thus Hostiensis, *Summa Aurea*, l. 1 (Basle edition of 1573, col. 319): "*Quid collegium?—Plurimarum personarum collectio simul inhabitantium speciali nomine attributo*"; and numerous others. Details in Pierre Michaud-Quantin, Universitas, *Expressions du mouvement communautaire dans le moyen âge latin* (Vrin, 1970).

[20] Michaud-Quantin, Universitas, 70, who also cites the definition, repeated by the dictionaries: *Societas collegarum in uno honore positorum*, *honor* being the goal or the interest that is the *raison d'être* of their association;—it is in taking this last word in a rather different sense that Popes Leo and Gelasius will say that the bishops, like the Apostles, have a common dignity. Cf. Lécuyer, *Études*, 76.

[21] Tertullian mentions the *ordo episcoporum*: *Adv. Marcionem*, l. 4, c. 5 (Kroymann, CSEL, 47:430); *De praescriptione*, c. 32, 1 (Refoulé, SC, 46:130); he also mentions the *ordo ecclesiasticus*, the *ordo sacerdotalis*. Cyprian distinguishes the *clerus* from the *plebs*. Origen speaks in a similar manner in various passages of his homilies. There is an *ordo sacerdotum* or *sacerdotii*, to which one has access through an "*ordinatio*" (*ordinatio clerica* or *ecclesiastica*). . . . Cf. Vilela, *La condition*

done by theological tradition, according to the fundamental ideas of Revelation.

In the course of his earthly life, Jesus set aside a small group of disciples who were from then on clearly distinct from all the others. "He appointed Twelve of them", or "he appointed them the Twelve", Saint Mark says in a characteristic expression in which a constitutive act can be seen, "to be with him and to send them to preach."[22]

---

collégiale, 78, 105–9, 248, 259–60, 268–69. The Leonine sacramentary designates priests as *sequentis ordinis viri*, etc. Cf. Botte, *Études sur le sacrament*, 18–19, 32. In the same work, 132, P.-M. Gy praises the apostolic constitution of Pius XII, March 25, 1953, for having returned to the ancient formula *catholicorum ordo episcoporum*. Down through the ages there have clearly been rather different ways of achieving this *ordo* socially. But can we say that the very notion of *ordo* is "typically medieval and feudal" and that we should reject it as no longer being "in harmony with conciliar anthropology and ecclesiology"? (Daniel Olivier, *Les deux visages du prêtre* [Fayard, 1971], 56–57.) the words "feudal" and "medieval" seem to have held for some time a kind of repulsive fascination for several authors. We note that the word *ordinatio*, on the other hand, has returned to favor for episcopal ordination. See above, chap. 2, 205. On the two senses, historical and hierarchical, of *ordo episcoporum*: B. Botte, *"Presbyterium" et "ordo episcoporum"*, in: *Irenikon*, 29 (1956), 14–18.

[22] Mk 3:13–19; 6, 7. Cf. J.-V. Bainvel, DTC, I (1902) col. 1650–51, s.v. *Apôtres*. Batiffol, *L'Église naissante*, 59–65. J. Giblet, *Les Douze, histoire et théologie*, in: *Recherches bibliques*,

"The Twelve": this is the name which is given to them in the four Gospels as if to a very distinct group,[23] a name which is found only once in Saint Paul, in a passage where the Apostle is quoting a primitive catechism,[24] and which soon disappeared from Christian language. We know that the number twelve was symbolic of universality. Remember too that the primary concern of those who, following Judas' defection, were then only Eleven, was to complete their number by the election of a new member who took the place of the traitor "in the ministry of the apostolate".[25] We call them the Twelve Apostles, as does the ancient author of the Didache.[26] They are, the Apocalypse tells us, the twelve stones on which the new Jerusalem rests,[27] the *dodecastylum firmamentum*, Saint Irenaeus says, laid down personally

---

7, *"Aux Origines de l'Église"* (Bruges, 1965). Jean Colson, *Prêtre de Jésus-Christ* (Beauchesne, 1966), 183–93. See below, 288, note 38.

[23] Mt 19:28; Jn 6:70, etc. See above, 16, note 18.

[24] 1 Cor 15:5. The Vulgate translated δώδεκα by *undecim*.

[25] Acts 1:15–26. Cf. the prayer for the feast of Saint Matthias: "Lord, who united blessed Matthias to the college of the apostles. . . ."

[26] The complete title of the *Didache* is: "Doctrine of the Lord to the Nations through the Twelve Apostles."

[27] Rev 21:14. Leonine sacramentary, preface of Saints Peter and Paul (Mohlberg, 48).

by Christ,[28] the "twelve springs", Origen says, prefigured by those twelve springs which the Hebrews found formerly at Elim during the course of their exodus.[29] Now the episcopal college, in all that is transmittable, succeeds to this college of the Twelve,[30] to which Saint Paul, as we know, was added. Exactly how this transmission was effected will always elude us. One fact is nevertheless certain: in this obscure period at the end of the first century and the beginning of the second, the few documents which teach us something about the position of the churches—above all the letter of Clement of Rome and those of Ignatius of Antioch —show us one who exercises the episcopacy in each church conscious of the apostolic origin of his responsibility, which includes simultaneously presiding over his own church and active concern for others.[31] No one feels the need to justify

[28] *Adversus Haereses*, l. 4, c. 21, n. 3 (SC, 100:682). Irenaeus notes the symbolic parallel with the twelve tribes of Israel.

[29] *In Num.*; hom. 27, 11 (SC, 29:538).

[30] It is clear that the apostolic role of original witnesses and founders of the Church was "no more capable of being transmitted to others than that of effecting salvation was of being transmitted to them" (Bouyer, *L'Église*, 391).

[31] Clement of Rome, *Ad Cor.* 44, 2 (SC, 167:172). We know that the title *episcopos* came to be used in the West slightly later than in the East. Clement nevertheless exercised the office, surrounded like Ignatius by his presbyterium. The

himself by any pleading whatever. And nowhere, either in this early era or for a long time afterwards, is there the least discernible trace of an objection raised with reference to this.[32]

The episcopal college does not exist merely intermittently any more than did the apostolic college. It is a permanent as well as an indivisible reality. In this double sense, it is universal. Its existence and activity are not at all connected with any assemblage whatever: for it is in her very dispersal across the surface of the earth that the Church exists and is known to be the Assembly of the Lord. The college thus has nothing to do with a "government by assembly"; *a fortiori*, with a

first Christian generations knew far more than we about their origin, and we do not at all have to presume that they consistently disclosed them.

[32] Cf. Jean Colson, *La succession apostolique au niveau du premier siècle*, in *Verbum caro*, 57 (1961), 144–68; *Prêtre*, 229–41. G. Martelet, *Éléments transmissibles et intransmissibles de la succession apostolique*, in: *Verbum caro* (1961), 185–98. Ephrem Boularand, *La consécration épiscopale est-elle sacramentelle?* in: *Bulletin de litt. ecclés.* (1953), 3–36 (20–21). Heinrich Schlier, *Le temps de l'Église*, trans. Father Corin (Casterman, 1961), 11, 147, 153–55. Cerfaux, *La théologie*, 393–400. Bouyer, *L'Église*, 387–448. Bibliography by Schnackenburg in: *Istina* (1969), 31–32. On the parallel between episcopal and apostolic colleges according to the magisterium and post-Tridentine theology: M.-J. Le Guillou, in: *Istina*, 10 (1964), 103–10.

system of particular assemblies, whether national or regional—although the history of the Church is full of such assemblies, both occasional and regular, which are often very useful, as we shall see. A permanent reality, it "never ceases to function".[33] Its cohesiveness is made manifest in diverse ways, notably through the relations that bishops or groups of bishops establish between themselves in the name of their churches. In the first centuries there were frequent exchanges of letters, called *communicatoriae litterae*, or again, *litterae formatae* (in other words, "official letters"[34]). Such was that synodal letter of the bishops who, having deposed Paul of Samosata in Antioch and installed Domnus in his place (in 268), addressed the news of it "to Dionysius (of Rome), Maximus (of Alexandria) and to all those who exercise the ministry with us on the inhabited earth, as well as

[33] Philips, *L'Église et son mystère*, 296. In the letter of Celestine to the Council of Ephesus (431), *sanctum collegium* (PL, 50:505) undoubtedly refers to the assembly at Jerusalem, but with Celestine the word's meaning is not limited to a meeting (Lécuyer, *Études*, 18–19).

[34] Colson, *L'Épiscopat*, 31–38. Zmire, in: *Recherches augustiniennes*, 7 (1971), 27. S. Pieszczoch, *Notices sur la collégialité chez Eusèbe de Césarée*, in *Studia patristica*, 10 (Berlin, 1970), 302–5. It is worth noting that both the authors and the recipients of these letters are the churches as well as their pastors.

to the entire Catholic Church under heaven"; such was also the letter of the Council of Sardica to Pope Julius (in 343).[35] Saint Cyprian's correspondence contains a certain number of these letters of information, encouragement, consultation and communion in joy. Optatus of Milevis refers to this epistolary "commerce" organized in his time around Pope Siricius, owing to which, he says, the entire universe is in accord *in una communionis societate*.[36] It was by this means that the regional synods—still rare in the second century,[37] but which would multiply in proportion as an administrative hierarchy was to various degrees organized —would sometimes have universal repercussions. We can, with Monsignor Philips, regret that such an exchange of "spiritual letters, letters of encouragement and caution between the churches" has "fallen into complete disuse". But the most essential action of the college is normally carried

[35] Batiffol, *Cathedra*, 105, 111–14.

[36] *De schismate Donatistarum*, l. 2, c. 3 (C. Ziwsa, CSEL, 26:37): ". . . *Siricius . . . , cum quo nobis totus orbis commercio formatarum in una communionis societate concordat.*"

[37] When the bishops of Asia met on the subject of Easter, around 190, it was at the request of Pope Victor; the words with which Polycrates of Ephesus wrote of it to Victor do not suggest "that similar meetings are a customary thing, on the contrary" (Battifol, *L'Église naissante*, 268–70). From the third century on, it was otherwise.

on from day to day by the simple fact that each head of church teaches in his own church the same faith as the others do in theirs. This is what is commonly called in modern theology the "ordinary magisterium"; if it is declared infallible, it is indeed because there is a real unity of the episcopate. Each bishop being individually fallible, the mere sum of their teachings obtained by addition could not have an infallible character. It is all together that they possess, as Saint Irenaeus says, the *charisma veritatis certum* inherited from the Apostles.[38]

When the situation requires or recommends it, the college can act in an extraordinary way through the assembly of its members. This is the ecumenical council, the first of which was held at Nicea in 313. It is possible to describe in its procedure, just as in the organization of the pres-

---

[38] *Adversus Haereses*, l. 4, c. 26, n. 2 (SC, 100: 2:718; cf. n. 5, 728). Cf. Louis Ligier, Le *"charisma veritatis certum"* des *évêques, ses attaches liturgiques, patristiques et bibliques*, in: *L'homme devant Dieu* (Aubier, 1963), 1:247–68. "This ordinary magisterium is the normal form of the Church's infallibility" (Ratzinger, *Le nouveau peuple*, 94–95). Slightly different terminology in Philips, *L'Église et son mystère*, 301–2. The apostolic succession is succession in faith (cf. Congar, *Ministères*, 66–68, 82, 86), and it is impossible to dissociate the authority to govern from doctrinal authority in the Church. Cf. Jacques Zeiller in Fliche and Martin, *Histoire*, 1:385–86.

byterium in each church, a certain number of characteristics inspired by other assemblies, such as the pagan synods, the municipal curia or the Roman Senate.[39] This is a natural occurence. The carving out of ecclesiastical districts according to that of civil administrations for reasons of convenience, as is still frequently the practice today, is completely normal. The council nonetheless constitutes a unique type of assembly,[40] one that is concerned, moreover, only with some particularly intense moment which can only be exceptional: there was no ecumenical council before the fourth century, and the list of those that followed is not long. It is not only through decisions made in council, but more usually through the unanimous teaching of its members, dispersed in space and spread out in time, that the episcopal college watches over and orders the faith and life of the Christian community.[41]

[39] Christopher Walter, *L'iconographie des conciles dans la tradition byzantine* (Paris: Institut français d'études byzantines, 1970) particularly 124–27, 148, 163, 220, 262. Cf. Vilela, *La condition collégiale*, 103–5, 404.

[40] On the theology of the council: Ratzinger, *Le nouveau peuple*, 79–100.

[41] Pope Simplicius, *Epist.* 4, c. 2: "*Indissolubile esse non dubium est, quod vel ante decreverunt in unum convenientes tot Domini sacerdotes, vel quod singuli per suas ecclesias constituti, eadem nihilominus sentientes, diversis quidem vocibus sed una mente*

By virtue of the fact that he is incorporated into this universal college, each new bishop thus contracts an obligation, which he shares with all his colleagues, toward the whole of the Church and her mission. "Each one, in his diocese, is responsible for the whole episcopal body, to which, following the apostolic college, the duty of protecting the purity of the faith and the unity of the Church has been entrusted."[42] It is even necessary to specify—and without intending, by doing so, to settle the debated question of the priority between these two connected elements[43]—that it is

---

dixerunt." Ed. Thiel, 184. Simplicius was pope in 468. Cf. Gréa, *L'Église*, 224: "The scattered episcopacy loses nothing of what constitutes it. . . ." Dom Emmanuel Lanne, *La primauté romaine et les Églises orientales*: "It is not merely assembled or dispersed bishops who form the college, but the bishops as pastors of their own churches." Cf. 83, note 3.

[42] Paul VI, apostolic letter *Quinque Jam Annis*, December 8, 1970.

[43] Is the candidate first inserted into the college in order to receive afterwards his particular office or vice versa? Because it wished to bring out the collegial bond, it was inevitable that the Council appeared to favor the first opinion; it did not, however, enjoin it. Those from the East profess the second, to which Father Bouyer seems to acquiesce, while Jean Colson and Father Ugo Betti, like Dom Gréa, are of a contrary opinion: "One can very well conceive of 'apostolic successors' who do not preside over a presbyterium, in other words . . . who are not 'bishops' of a diocese." (Colson,

insofar as they are members of this college and in communion with it "that the bishops are legitimately put in charge of particular churches" since the latter, as we have already seen, "are inconceivable without the bond that unites them to the universal Church which is realized in them."[44] At the same time as he is given jurisdiction over his own flock, the bishop receives, therefore, his share of concern with regard to all that affects "the well-being of the entire Church".[45] "All together", Saint Cyprian said, "we must look after the body of the whole Church, whose numerous members are scattered in the various regions." "The body of bishops (*sacerdotum*)", he said again, "is numerous, linked by the bond of mutual concord and the ties of unity, so that if one or another of our college tries to initiate a heresy, to divide the flock of Christ or to ravage it, the

---

Les fonctions, 341.) The question remains open. It is not merely a subtle distinction; it is enough for us here, however, to affirm the connection between the two elements. Father Yves Congar has attempted a synthesis uniting the two positions, in the spirit of the Council: *Ministères*, 123–40: "Do episcopal consecration and apostolic succession constitute the head of a local church or member of the college?"

[44] W. Onclin, *La collégialité épiscopale à l'état direct ou latent*, in: *Concilium*, 8 (1965), 81.

[45] Cf. *Lumen Gentium*, n. 23 B. 1969 Synod, *Responsiones P. Angeli Anton*, 10.

others come to the rescue. . . . For, though we are many shepherds, we feed a single flock, and our duty is to gather together and care for all the sheep whom Christ won through his blood."[46]

Each action taken by a bishop in virtue of this diffuse responsibility, "having a universal effect and being exercised within the communion",[47] can and must be called collegial although it is not an act of the college.[48] As numerous examples demonstrate, "the bishops of the early Church had an intense awareness of their responsibilities toward the entire Church",[49] and when some of them appeared to be losing it, a voice was raised at times to restore it to them or to revive it in them.

---

[46] *Epist.* 36, c. 4, c. 3–4 (Hartel, 2:575, 746–47). Cf. *Epist.* 33, c. 1; 66, c. 8 (566 and 753).

[47] Georges Dejaifve, S.J., "*La collégialité épiscopale d'après Lumen gentium*", in: *Lumen vitae* (1965), 491: "Just as the college cannot be reduced to a mere juridical assembly without a betrayal of its nature, so, too, any of the activities of the members which have a universal consequence and which are exercised within the communion cannot be excluded from the domain of collegial action."

[48] Onclin, *La collégialité*, 80: "In an indirect way, this episcopal collegiality thus finds its expression in certain actions which are not acts of the college as such, but acts of a bishop working individually or even several bishops working jointly at the service of various particular churches."

[49] Ratzinger, *Le nouveau peuple*, 39.

Witness this reprimand by Origen, which seems indeed to be aimed farther than at one local bishop; it is not without vigor and maintains a perpetual timeliness: "How am I concerned if another acts badly? —That is what those who preside over the churches are saying when they forget that all of us, the faithful, are one body having one God who holds us and keeps us close together in his unity, Christ."[50]

This awareness of a universal duty has often become blurred. It has been pointed out, for example, that the feudal era, "by partitioning off each bishop in his fief", obscured the collegial sense.[51] Nevertheless, it has never been completely lacking in any era. It was alive in several French bishops of the last century, who said

[50] *In Jesu Nave*, hom. 7, n. 6: "*Quid hoc ad me spectat, si alius male agit? —Tale est quod (dicunt) ii qui ecclesiis praesunt, non cogitantes quia unum corpus sumus omnes qui credimus, unum Deum habentes qui nos in unitate constringit et continet, Christum, cujus corporis tu qui Ecclesiae praesides oculus es, propterea utique ut omnia circumspicias, omnia circumlustres, etiam ventura praevideas. . .*" (*Opera*, Berlin ed., v. 12, Baehrens, 862).

[51] Colson, *L'Épiscopat*, 130–31. The text of the consecratory preface for bishops is perhaps an indication of this. Until the end of the twelfth century, it said: "*Tribuas ei, Domine, cathedram episcopalem ad regendam Ecclesiam tuam et plebem universam*"; the last words were then changed to: "*et plebem sibi commissam*".

through the voice of Monsignor Dupanloup: "Now who could have so low, so unworthy an opinion of the Church and of the Catholic episcopacy as to believe that all care, all solicitude must be relegated within the narrow limits of each diocese?"[52] When Saint Irenaeus used his influence with Pope Victor to intervene in favor of the Eastern churches and of peace in the Church in the Easter conflict; or when Saint Augustine, aware of the threat to the faith, undertook the battle against Pelagius, whose doctrines hardly interfered with his little African diocese;[53] or again, when Saint Cyril of Alexandria tried, as Pope Celestine put it, "to stop the fall of his colleague (Nestorius) by offering him the right hand of his magisterium, in order thereby to come to the aid of many others",[54] the action of each of these three bishops was eminently collegial, that is, taken in virtue of

[52] Quoted by Georges Dejaifve (NRT, 1960), 2:796. Which hardly corresponds to the assertion of J. Bianchi, *Dossier* (Lyons, 1970), 216: in the nineteenth century, "the bishop does not attend to what is happening outside the boundaries of his diocese." But there are many pastoral letters to support Dupanloup.

[53] Little by reason of its importance, although its territory was relatively extensive in comparison with the African dioceses that surrounded it. See below, 332–34.

[54] "*Nisus est labentem revocare collegam, porrexit dexteram magisterii sui, in uno volens plurimus subvenire*" (PL, 50:552 A).

the principle of collegiality. We could even say, to use a more subjective expression which has enjoyed some popularity over the past few years, that they were impelled to it by an *affectus collegialis*.[55] And, to take but one example, this was also the character, though in a less precise way, of the more recent action of Cardinal Mercier, Archbishop of Malines, who, in publishing in 1908 an important pastoral letter on modernism, took care first of all and with some solemnity to warn his priests and his faithful that this letter did not concern them.[56]

[55] *Expositio et explicatio Relationis de parte doctrinali*, c. 3; 12: *"Exercitium enim affectus collegialis multo latius quam actio stricte collegialis patet."* *Responsio P. Angeli Anton*, c. 1, 7: *"(In affectu collegiali) agitur . . . de authentica collegialitate, non de collegialitate secundi ordinis . . ."*; and 10: *". . . ut affectus collegialis et sollicitudo qua singuli episcopi, ex Christi institutione et praecepto, pro universa Ecclesia tenentur, magis in dies ad effectum perducatur . . ."* (Documents of the 1969 Roman Synod).

[56] "Thank God, these errors that have invaded France and Italy particularly have hardly any followers in Belgium. You must have been preserved from them by the vigilance of your pastors and by the spirit of scientific impartiality and Christian submission which animates the representatives of higher learning in our country." Pastoral letter for Lent in the year 1908.

V

EPISCOPAL CONFERENCES

In addition to their obvious specific usefulness (indeed, to their practical necessity today, which we have not gone into here at all[1]), the various, more or less strongly institutionalized meetings of bishops which take place by regions, provinces, nations or broader areas can contribute valuably to developing in their members the sense of collegiality and the responsibilities it entails by accustoming them to look beyond their particular church and to work in common. Such meetings can also in various ways—we will have to come back to this again—play a "relay" role, which can contribute to a more organic and more rapid concord among the entire episcopacy.

These kinds of meetings, on either an occasional

[1] Let us at least recall the immense benefit which the solid and dynamic CELAM represents at the present time for the Church in all Latin America.

or a regular basis, have developed in the Church, particularly from the third century on. Their history is the very history of the local churches. The more the hierarchy of various "ecclesiastical districts"[2] became organized, the more the series of synods also varied, to different degrees. A uniform type was never established. Today the universally prevalent type in the Latin West is that of the "episcopal conference". After having been gradually introduced into different countries by the pressure of circumstances, it was sanctioned by the last council. However different they may be with respect to synods formed on a hierarchical system of archdioceses, primacies or patriarchates, episcopal conferences are called more and more to render an analogous service in the universal Church.[3] Their role is all the more important in this regard since the great number of bishops spread across the world would make it very complicated to have purely individual consultations when the need arose. Such conferences can also contribute in other ways to the activity of the

[2] There is a good summary of this history in Duchesne, *Origines*, chap. 1, 1–45: "*Les circonscriptions ecclésiastiques*". For the first five centuries, see also Marc Clément, *L'Apparition du Patriarcat dans l'Église*, photocopied thesis in canon law (Lyons, 1963).

[3] Cf. *Lumen Gentium*, n. 22, 1.

college, for example by appointing some of their members to take part in the episcopal synod which is periodically convened in Rome. They can therefore rightfully be called "one of the possible variants of collegiality", insofar as through them "collegiality is partially realized in a manner which then helps to realize the whole".[4] Nevertheless, strictly speaking, that is, in its full meaning, based on Scripture, episcopal collegiality, which succeeds that of the Twelve, is essentially universal—and, on the other hand, a collective act is not in itself a collegial act. Consequently, it is not said that the bishops carry out their responsibility "collegially" in their conference, but that they carry it out "conjointly".[5] Conversely, as we saw in the preceding section, all action worthy of being called collegial is not necessarily collective.[6] These are two different ideas.

We must also be on our guard here against the confusion perpetually kept alive by the theological ignorance of some journalists as well as by the

[4] Joseph Ratzinger, in: *Concilium*, 1 (1965), 53–54. Cf. Jérôme Hamer, O.P., *Les conférences épiscopales, exercice de la collégialité*, NRT, 95 (1963), 966–69.

[5] *Christus Dominus*, n. 38, 1: ". . . *munus suum pastorale conjunctim exercent*. . . ."

[6] Cf. Zizioulas, *"La communauté"*, 87: "Episcopal collegiality does not represent a collective unity. . . ."

secular inclinations of our age towards collective forms of government: the confusion between "college" in the vernacular and "college" in Christian language. In virtue of this confusion, in recent years, the idea of episcopal collegiality has been too closely tied, if not altogether assimilated in public opinion, to that of episcopal conferences, just as to that of all supra-diocesan organizations. The speed of technical evolution brings about, especially in our time, a need to organize social life into groupings at once broader and more specialized. To this corresponds, naturally, an analogous need in the Church with a view to better adapted pastoral action. A single bishop, within the limits of one diocese, cannot fulfill all his duties as pastor.[7] From which necessarily arise certain restrictions brought to bear upon the autonomy of dioceses, to the advantage of certain more differentiated agencies covering a more widespread area. If this evolution were more or less identified with the development of episcopal collegiality, the latter would, paradoxically, be understood as a diminution rather than a univer-

[7] It is what the Council noted in *Presbyterorum Ordinis*, n. 7: "In our present age, apostolic initiatives must, for many reasons, not only take multiple forms but also go beyond the limits of a parish or a diocese." Similarly in *Christus Dominus*, n. 37.

salization of the bishop's role. This would be an application of the general law according to which the individual recedes before the collective, whereas the true collegial sense demands, on the contrary, a greater personal activity. There would thus be a danger of gradually distorting the theological reality by absorbing it into sociology. It is too easy to give examples of this already.

Consequently, we believe that it is important, after having indicated the correspondence and the relations which exist between the doctrine of collegiality and the practice of episcopal conferences, to point also to the differences, principally those which appear from the texts of Vatican II.

The primary objective of episcopal conferences is an immediately practical one, and their efficacy is connected to its limited character. Their most usual activity, devoted to local affairs,[8] does not in itself constitute an exercise in collegiality. All the more reason that this must be said of the activity of the commissions and the various bureaus or secretariats they assign to themselves. The sometimes very elaborate organization they set up[9] is

[8] Cf. *Christus Dominus*, n. 37 and 38.

[9] Paul VI put them on guard against this too natural temptation to excess in his address of March 25, 1971, to the Council of the Episcopal Conferences of Europe: "It is advisable for you to have a very flexible structure, not adding to

not an organization of collegiality. This is what Monsignor W. Onclin, an authority on canonical matters, explains: "The bishops gathered together in particular councils or in episcopal conferences are not representatives of the college of bishops. They do not exercise there the power that they possess with regard to the universal Church when all are united as the college, but the power with which they are invested as heads of the particular churches of which they have charge. Consequently, the decrees of particular councils and the decisions of episcopal conferences are neither directly nor indirectly acts issuing from the college of bishops but are measures taken by bishops using collectively the powers they possess in the particular churches entrusted to them."[10] It must be granted that, in order to achieve greater unity of action, for example in general questions which deal with public authorities, the bishops of a given country could arrive at common decisions which,

---

the weight of heavy responsibilities that you carry." See below, 297, note 58.

[10] Onclin, *La collégialité*, 87. Cf. S. Dockx, O.P., in: *La collégialité épiscopale* (1965), 306: "All joint action, all concerted decision between bishops beyond the diocesan framework is not, for all that, the exercise of one of the forms of episcopal collegiality."

provided the requisite conditions,[11] would compel the recognition of each of them;—but this is something entirely different (to which we will return a little farther on) from the authority issuing from the episcopal college, an authority which compels recognition in itself and not in virtue of a human agreement.

The Vatican II decree *Christus Dominus* on the pastoral responsibility of bishops clearly illustrates this fundamental distinction by the simple fact of its structure and by the arrangement of its three chapters.[12] The first of these, entitled "The Bishops and the Universal Church", is devoted to collegiality, to the basic reality, as it were, in application of the doctrine set forth in *Lumen Gentium*. The bishop as head of the church forms the subject of the second chapter, which has the title "The Bishops and the Particular Churches or Dioceses". And it is only then, in the third chapter, on the "Cooperation of Bishops for the Common Good of Many Churches" that the question of episcopal conferences is treated. There it is stated that a number of heads of dioceses come together in these conferences in order to settle as best they can certain questions which they have

[11] *Christus Dominus*, n. 38, 4.

[12] See the commentary on the decree by W. Onclin, in: Unam Sanctam, 74 (Cerf, 1969), 82–83.

in common: in fact, "in our time especially, it is not unusual for bishops to be unable to accomplish their task satisfactorily and fruitfully without achieving a daily increasing concord and more coordinated action with other bishops". The Council, considering the "remarkable proofs of apostolic fruitfulness" given in various places by already-existing conferences, therefore regarded it to be "entirely advisable that such assemblies be formed in all places".[13]

The point of view adopted by the Council, as we can see, is essentially pragmatic. Some bishops would have preferred a more precise bond indicated in the texts between episcopal conferences as an institution and collegiality or the unity of the episcopate as a principle of faith. The Council disregarded this. It did so because, in reality, even if bonds of what could be called convenience do indeed exist between the institution and the principle, the *doctrinal* bond, properly speaking, does not exist—or at least it is only indirect, insofar as the members of these conferences can together extend their solicitude beyond the area in which they exercise their usual activity. A principle of

---

[13] The motu proprio *Ecclesiae Sanctae* for the implementation of the decree says: "Bishops of nations or territories where a planned episcopal conference does not yet exist should see that it is established as soon as possible. . ." (41, 1).

divine right is one thing, an institution of ecclesiastical right is quite another, suggested by the circumstances of time and place. Nevertheless, at the 1969 Synod, a bishop again asked that a dogmatic definition be formulated for the episcopal conference! There was obviously no basis for it, and it would have been a serious confusion of different orders even to attempt it for something that is certainly very useful but by nature and form contingent, and recommended, according to the statement of the Council itself, for reasons of a practical order. The constitution *Lumen Gentium* is as clear as possible in this respect. It recognizes no intermediary of a doctrinal order between the particular church and the universal Church:

> . . .The individual bishops placed at the head of each of the particular churches exercise their pastoral authority over the portion of the people of God entrusted to them and not over other churches or over the universal Church. But, as members of the episcopal college and legitimate successors of the apostles, each of them is bound, with respect to the universal Church, by the institution and precept of Christ, to have that solicitude which is eminently fruitful for the universal Church even if it is not exercised by an act of jurisdiction. All the bishops, in fact, must promote and safeguard the unity of the faith and

common discipline. . . . Besides, it is well established that, by governing their own church as a
portion of the universal Church, they are effectively contributing to the good of the whole
Mystical Body, which is also the body of the
churches.[14]

In order not to be one-sided, we are in fact
obliged to say something more. Episcopal conferences, let us again repeat, are an excellent thing.
They, like so many other more or less analogous
assemblies of previous centuries, constitute an
organization that is valuable for the Christian life
of a whole region or an entire nation. They are
particularly opportune in our time, and we can
consider, with Monsignor Philips,[15] that they are
called to a great future. If they were the main
subject of this work, it would be appropriate to
demonstrate this at greater length. Nevertheless,
if they too quickly put their ordinary activity in
the same category as the exercise of collegiality,
it is possible that, far from encouraging this exer-

[14] C. 3, n. 23, 2. That is indeed what is deduced from
ancient tradition. Cf. Joseph Ratzinger, in Barauna, *L'Église*,
765: "If one wishes to gain a clearer idea of collegiality by
considering its practical meaning, the principal concern will
be to establish the organization of particular churches within
the unity of the universal assembly."

[15] Philips, *L'Église et son mystère*, 1:315.

cise, they would restrict it and perhaps impede it. It is even less possible to brush this hypothesis aside, a priori, because history, both yesterday's and that unfolding beneath our eyes, does not fail to bring it now and then to our attention. Two kinds of possible disadvantages are then revealed which are interrelated besides.

On the one hand, we should not forget that the best systems have their limits: if these are exceeded, it is inevitable that the law of inversely proportional returns will come into play. Too elaborate an organization of these regional groups of bishops risks doing harm to the personal initiative of each of them, absorbing him in specialized tasks which take him away from his diocesan laity and priests,[16] paralyzing him sometimes in his essential ministry, perhaps even dulling his consciousness of his personal obligations as much with regard to a universal catholicity as in the government of his own church. What would tend to prevail in this case would be an impersonal, anonymous leadership developing into a bureau-

[16] A frequent separation could only add to the unrest reported on various sides for several years and recorded by the preparatory document for the episcopal synod of 1971: "*Inter Presbyteros et Episcopos intercedit, si non semper gravis quaedam simultas et contentio, saltem quaedam imminuta fiducia*" (*De sacerdotio ministeriali*, 9).

cracy; it would by that very fact be a theoretical, abstract teaching of neutral tone, without human warmth, in which the faithful would no longer recognize the voice of their pastor. Finally, just as some bishops were reproachable not long ago for fleeing their responsibilities by hiding behind a Roman congregation, it could be feared that a number might be prompted to flee them today by taking refuge behind some national commission or other, whether this commission be instituted in virtue of a conciliar decree or of Roman recommendation. The temptation might even be stronger, the pressure being more immediate. Jacques Maritain recently recalled, and no subtlety of the theological or, as they say, "pastoral" order could obscure the pertinence of his remark: "A bishop is by divine mandate the pastor of his diocese; it is for him alone,[17] on his responsibility before God, to make decisions concerning the souls entrusted to him. If he became, as it were,

[17] This word "alone" could be ambiguous if attention were not paid to the context and especially to what follows. It is quite obviously not a question here of asserting that the bishop, like any superior in charge, can turn up his nose at advisory organizations which have always, at least by right, played an important role on all levels in ecclesiastical tradition. Wisdom prescribes them, and the last council wished to consolidate them, according to the spirit of ancient tradition, into "presbyteral councils".

not *de jure* but *de facto*, the executive agent of a commission, would it not be his very mission as successor of the apostles and the evangelic prescription itself that would be injured?"[18]

Jacques Maritain's observation corresponds, even in its very words, with the observation expressed a little earlier by Dom Emmanuel Lanne concerning the ancient tradition about the relation of the bishop to the various assemblies to which he may belong: "The bishop of each church remains, in short, *solely responsible* for his community and for the application of the norms decided by the councils. . . . Each church has its own typology, so to speak, for which the bishop alone answers finally before God."[19] Dom Emmanuel Lanne, who considers this point "important", not only invokes, as others do, the testimony of Saint Cyprian,[20] but he also appeals to "numerous ex-

[18] *De l'Église du Christ, sa personne et son personnel* (DDB, 1970), 149. In his *Exhortation Apostolique* of December 1970, Paul VI reminded the bishops that the urgent duty of preaching derives from "a personal, absolutely inalienable responsibility" (*Doc. cath.* [1971], 54).

[19] *"Pluralisme"*, 178. Similarly, in his report to the Roman Synod of October 17, 1969, treating episcopal conferences, Cardinal Marty was anxious to specify: "The immediate responsibility of the bishop in his own diocese being unharmed" (*Doc. cath.*, 66 [1969], 1013).

[20] Like Zizioulas (Orthodox), *"La communauté"*, 77. Cf.

amples from subsequent history".[21] He remarks as well that for Vatican II, faithful interpreter of tradition, it is "the local community in its liturgical dimension in the full sense", in other words "the particular church", which becomes or remains "the center of reference for the life and manifestation of the Church as catholic and apostolic, because visibly one, around the bishop, and holy, through the very object of this life and this manifestation: the Word of God and the sacraments, for it is the Holy Spirit himself who gathers it together: *in Spiritu sancto congregata* (*Christus Dominus*, no. 11)".[22]

Let us also recognize, on the other hand, that if

Cyprian, *Epist.* 55, c. 21 (Hartel), 2:639: "*Manente concordiae vinculo et perseverante catholicae ecclesiae individuo sacramento, actum suum disponit et dirigit unusquisque episcopus, rationem propositi sui Domino redditurus.*"

[21] It is thus that Canon 51 of the Council of Elvira (300) "established that an excommunicated person could be reconciled only through his bishop or by the consent of the latter"; the Council of Arles (314), in its Canon 16, extends this law to the whole Church. "Each one is therefore master indeed of his community" (Clément, *L'Apparition*, 17 and 31). Canon 5 of Nicea, however, admitted an appeal by the excommunicated to the provincial council.

[22] Lanne, "*Pluralisme*", 65–66, 186. They did not, for all that, fail to appreciate the importance of institutions such as patriarchates, synods of various types or even episcopal conferences.

the various groups of churches "correspond to a need for Catholic unity grafted, so to speak, onto a natural human tendency to cooperate and unite", a tendency there is every reason to encourage, these groups can also be at times, from another point of view, "the fruit of a tendency which is also human, but perhaps too human: the tendency to find unity, not in universality, but in a division of classes, nationalities, cultures or races".[23] Does universal experience not give us sufficient warning that national organizations can be the means for both greater openness and increased provincialism by turns? In our western regions, has it always been at the time when the collegial sense of the bishops was most intense that organizations such as national councils multiplied and were juridically promoted? As for the East, who is not aware of the harm that the tendency toward "autocephaly" produced there? "The division of the Church into national organizations, the administrative centralization in each of these organizations" have been vigorously and not without reason denounced by more than one Orthodox theologian.[24] In any case, would it not be para-

---

[23] Bouyer, *L'Église*, 551–52.
[24] Cf. Schmemann, *"La notion de primauté dans l'Église orthodoxe"*, in *La primauté*, 148–50, showing well the political character of autocephalism.

doxical if, at the very time that we are being so opportunely placed on our guard today against all "immoderate nationalism" in the political order, we were to see in the ecclesiastical order episcopal conferences, through an excess that transformed their nature, give place to a religious nationalism?[25]

This is not so much a question of structure, moreover, as a question of spirit. And it is quite obviously, in its extreme form, a question only of a *possible* danger. Less serious but also closer at hand would be the danger, because of the confusion pointed out above, of seeing in the different countries so many episcopal conferences juxtaposed, without access to each other, without mutual exchanges, each contenting itself to rule the affairs of its own country, thus achieving, not union, but dispersion.[26] To avert these different

---

[25] Cf. in the Roman Synod of 1969 the intervention of Cardinal Wright: ". . . *Ita omnis 'nationalismus immoderatus', seu 'sphera influentiae', uti dicitur in mundo politico, vitatur et excluditur; ille nationalismus qui adesse potest etiam cum loco Conferentiarum nationalium episcopalium loquitur de coetibus episcoporum; nationalismus qui semper et ubique unitati, fidei et caritati Ecclesiae perniciosissimus fuit, est et erit.*"

[26] Ratzinger, *Le nouveau peuple*, 126. This is why the decree *Christus Dominus*, n. 38, 5, says that "it is necessary to encourage relations between the episcopal conferences of various nations in order to promote and insure a greater good".

kinds of dangers radically, we can never remind ourselves too frequently of the essentially universal nature of the collegial bond and the solicitude which each bishop must have personally, in virtue of this bond, for the universal Church.[27] In that case, through the "conference" of her bishops, the whole local church will have this solicitude and, beyond its local usefulness, this conference will be a very effective instrument in the service of catholicity.

[27] At the same synod, *Expositio . . . de parte doctrinali*, 12: "*Sollicitudo pro* universa *Ecclesia, qua* singulus *episcopus ut membrum collegii episcopalis tenetur.*" Cf. *Lumen Gentium*, c. 3, n. 23.

VI

THE CENTER OF UNITY

This collegial bond is a bond between each particular church and all the others, between each head of church and all the others, each of them being jointly responsible for the "tradition of Christ", as were the Twelve whose mission they continue under new conditions.[1] And within this universal network of which the unique "Church of God" is composed, there exists a center, "an obligatory point of reference":[2] the particular church of Rome, governed by the successor of Peter, "first" of the Twelve, according to Matthew's expression.[3] In fact, the Church is "fundamentally", according to the expression of Mark

[1] Cf. A. Descamps, "*Aux origines du ministère, la pensée de Jésus*", in: *Revue théologique de Louvain*, 2 (1971), 3–45. See also above, chap. 4, 242–44.

[2] Ratzinger, in: *Concilium*, 1 (1965), 43.

[3] Mt 10:2.

and Luke, "Peter and those who are with him".[4]
The bishop of Rome is "he who maintains unanimity in the body of bishops".[5] Universal pastor,[6] he
is the living bond, not only between all the pastors
who presently exist on the face of the earth, but,
what we sometimes forget too easily, "between
the Church of today and the Church of the Apostles". Successor of the first and principal witness
of Jesus,[7] he insures unity in the present Church
"by watching over her living continuity with the
Church of all time".[8]

If we wished, we could endlessly debate the
question of whether Peter's prerogative was conferred on him insofar as he was head of the apostolic college or insofar as he was head of the
faithful. We do not deny the interest that such a
distinction can offer—no more than we deny that
of the related question, left open by the Council,
on the relative duality or unity of the subject of
supreme power in the Church.[9] Without wishing

[4] Mk 1:36. Lk 9:32. Jean Colson, *Évangélisation et collégialité apostolique*, NRT, 82 (1960), 370–71.

[5] Gérard Philips.

[6] Jn 21:15–17. Cf. R. Schütz, in: *Communion*, 3 (1971), 4.

[7] I Cor 15:5. Lk 24:34. Cf. Acts 1:21–22; 2:32; 4:20; 5:32.

[8] Bouyer, *L'Église*, 443.

[9] An account of the opinions is found in Congar, *Ministères*, 177–81.

to consider in this brief study whether the texts
would not rather clearly suggest one or the other,
we hope at least that the discussions raised on this
subject will not go so far as to revive the kind of
subtlety that belongs to an abusive scholasticism.
Whatever the solution adopted, it is an essential
point which cannot be challenged. But as soon as
one tries to express it with some precision, there
is unquestionably no way to avoid entirely a
problem with language. Since the constitution of
the Church is a unique case, without true analogy
to those of human societies, it is difficult always to
find an adequate vocabulary for it—both adequate
and easily intelligible, for experience gives sufficient evidence, starting with the constitution
Pastor Aeternus of Vatican I, that the most adequate
terms can also be, in fact, those which most lend
themselves to confusion. It is this problem with
language that leads to unjustified criticisms but
also at times to the occasion of real abuses. Monsignor Philips one day explained the choice of the
adverb *seorsim* which appears in the explanatory
note appended to chapter three of the constitution
Lumen Gentium:[10] to express the character of acts
of the pope outside of the collaboration of the

[10] *Nota explicativa praevia*, n. 3: "*Distinctio non est inter
Romanum Pontificem et Episcopos collective sumptos, sed inter R.
P. seorsim et R. P. simul cum Episcopis.*"

college, *seorsim* had been chosen over the word *solus*, which might suggest that the pope is at that time cut off from the bishops and the Christian people, and also over *personaliter*, which can also specify a "collegial" act on the part of the pope and which risks, besides, allowing the belief that the pope would act as a private person; *seorsim*, however, has not escaped criticism either. Without becoming confused about the use of "personal" in cases where the context does not permit ambiguity, we will accordingly follow a suggestion of Dom Gréa, calling to mind that to the "new and less exact" terms "personal" and "separate", it is advisable to prefer those "drawn from ecclesiastical antiquity": "his own" and "singular".[11] We will therefore say that for Peter and the one who succeeds him, what is concerned, according to the Gospel, is a singular prerogative, and that the failure to recognize this singular prerogative, in whatever century or circumstances one lives, would be in principle the negation of the Church such as Jesus Christ wished her to be.

Moehler expressed a very accurate view when

[11] *L'Église*, 157, note. Monsignor Gasser, in his *Relatio* to Vatican I (July 11, 1970), had already written: "We are not speaking of the personal infallibility of the pope, although we do claim this prerogative for his person. . . ." Mansi, v. 52, col. 1213 a. See also Congar, *Ministères*, 169–70.

he wrote in his *Symbolicon*: "If the episcopate is to form a true unity in order to unite the faithful and thereby achieve the great communal life that the Catholic Church lays claim to, that episcopate itself needs a center which by its active presence gathers together and firmly unites the whole Church."[12] It is not on such an argument, however, that our faith is finally based. As Vladimir Soloviev has written, "all reasonings in favor of the central and sovereign power of the universal Church would be of very mediocre value in our eyes if they were only reasonings. But they adhere to a divine-human *fact* which is indispensable to the Christian faith despite all the artificial interpretations by which one might wish to suppress it".[13] On the other hand, it is clear that it is always the Spirit of God who "strengthens the organic structure of the Church and who maintains harmony within her".[14] "If we wanted to have absolute human guarantees, the primacy would remain extremely uncertain in the face of the perils

[12] *Symbolicon*, n. 42; quoted by Geiselmann in Chaillet, *L'Église*, 183.

[13] *La Russie et l'Église universelle*, 5th ed. (Stock, 1922), 161. Similarly, Ratzinger, *Le nouveau peuple*, 105: "In the decisive realities of the Church, what is important are not reasonings but *historical realities*."

[14] *Lumen Gentium*, chap. 3, n. 22, 2.

which come from men, and it is always necessary to take note of this eventuality. Without reliance on the Holy Spirit and his protective power, the whole building of the Church is endangered, and there is no way out."[15] But we also know that God wished men to share in his work of salvation, and we do not at all have to change or disregard, but simply receive what was instituted for this purpose and of which the New Testament texts bear witness.

In this respect, a formula adopted by Vatican II can suffice as much to express the essential truth that interests us here as to give the essential motivation: the bishops, says *Lumen Gentium*, "gather together the universal Church which the Lord has founded on the Apostles and built on blessed Peter, their head".[16] The formula expresses Jesus' thought exactly, "engraved, so to speak, in the very names 'Cephas' and the 'Twelve', taking into account the depth of their biblical resonances".[17] Thus it is with the church of Rome, where the successor of Peter holds office, "that the whole Church must necessarily conform", as

[15] Ratzinger, in Barauna, *L'Église*, 179–80.

[16] N. 9: ". . . *Ecclesiam congregant universalem, quam Dominus in apostolis condidit et supra beatum Petrum, eorum principem, aedificavit*."

[17] Coathalem, *Un horizon*, 1020.

Saint Irenaeus proclaims in a celebrated text.[18] The reference to Peter is, so to speak, the "short cut" instituted by Jesus himself in order to ensure unity.[19]

In the appendix to the Gospel of John, "Simon Peter, who already occupies in the Gospel a predominant position among the Twelve, brings the fish in his net to the Risen One in a symbolic scene. Jesus then solemnly gives him the duty of 'feeding the flock'. The Church is one. And she is the Church of Peter. It is to him (among the Twelve) that the risen Jesus has confided the harvest, the fishing and the care of the flock. . . ." These lines, from one of the best contemporary exegetes,[20] were echoed in advance by two beautiful lines of poetry by Charles Péguy:

> And we fell into Peter's net
> For it is Jesus who cast it towards us.[21]

"The manner in which the bishops of Rome

---

[18] *Adversus Haereses*, l. 3, c. 3, n. 2 (Sagnard, SC, 34:103).

[19] "*Brevis et compendiosa via*" (Pius IX). Jimenez Urresti, in: *La collégialité*, 273–74.

[20] Heinrich Schlier, *Essais sur le Nouveau Testament*, Fr. trans. (Cerf, 1968), 213–14, on Jn 21:10–17. Cf. Jn 1:42; 6:68; 13; 18; 20:1–10.

[21] "*Suite*" from *Eve* (*Poésie*, Pléiade, 885 and 886).

have spoken and acted shows that they felt responsible towards the whole Church for the deposit
they received from Peter", and similarly, outside
of Rome, "neither their capacity as successors of
Peter nor the principle of their authority, whatever its limits might be, were ever challenged in
the first centuries".[22] As early as the year 95 or 96,
while the Apostle John was undoubtedly still alive
and Ephesus was closer than Rome to Corinth,
and while the church of Corinth had herself been
founded by an Apostle, the church of Rome intervened with the church of Corinth with calm and
firm authority, through a letter from Clement, in
order to set her internal affairs in order: "If some
disobey what we say to them on behalf of God,
then they know that they are making a mistake and
exposing themselves to considerable dangers."[23]
"It should be noted", remarks the Orthodox theologian Nicolas Afanasiev, "that the Roman

[22] B. Botte, *Histoire et théologie, à propos du problème de
l'Église,* in: *Istina* (1957), 339. "They encountered resistance
(cf. the controversy about baptism in the third century); but
the Church finally came around to the solutions which they
had proposed."

[23] C. 59, n. 1. Cf. c. 63, n. 2 (A. Jaubert, SC, 167 [1971],
195 and 203). The anonymity of the letter, sent in the name
of the church of Rome, shows the profound solidarity of
the churches and of their heads during the early Christian
centuries, but it cannot mislead us about the person and
authority of Clement. No one in antiquity was misled by it.

church did not judge it necessary to justify herself in one way or another" for her intervention; "one would say that she had no doubt that her priority would be accepted without discussion";[24] and this is in fact what happened: the reprimand was received respectfully by the Corinthians; toward the year 170, Dionysius of Corinth wrote to Pope Soter that they continued to read Clement's letter in their liturgical assemblies;[25] it was the same for centuries in various regions, and the prestige of the letter was perhaps even greater in the East than in the West.[26] "One cannot escape the impression", concludes Monsignor Duchesne, "that as early as the end of the first century . . . , some fifty years after her foundation, this church (of Rome) was already conscious of being in possession of higher, exceptional authority which she would not cease to exercise later."[27] Even before

[24] In *La primauté*, 45–46.

[25] In Eusebius, *Hist. eccles.*, l. 4, c. 23, n. 11 (G. Bardy, SC, 21:204).

[26] Annie Jaubert, ed. of Clement, SC, 167:88–89. Jean Dauvillier, *Les temps apostoliques* (Sirey, 1970) 295–319. On the prestige of Clement himself in the East: Louis Duchesne, *Églises séparées*, 2d ed. (Fontemoing, 1905) 131–33.

[27] Duchesne, *Églises separées*, 126, 155: in the first three centuries "all the churches of the entire world, from Arabia, Osroene, Cappadocia to the farthest limits of the West, sensed the unceasing action of the Roman church in all things, in faith, in discipline, in government, in ritual, in the works of

the end of the apostolic age, we see the "epiphany of Roman primacy".[28]

People have often made every effort to diminish the importance of such testimony, as well as that of those who followed, of Ignatius of Antioch,[29] Irenaeus of Lyons, Dionysius of Corinth. They have said that, in these early times, there would still have been only the exercise of a primacy of fact, and that it was only later that Rome sought to make a primacy of right out of it by working out what Maurice Goguel has called a "myth of justification".[30] In order to do that, she, according to some, interpolated the Gospels, or, according to others, forced the interpretation from the texts. The interpolation thesis was supported by exegetes of some importance, such as Holtzmann, J.

---

charity". There is perhaps some exaggeration in these latter words.

[28] Batiffol, *L'Église naissante*, 146.

[29] Thus, in the address of the letter to the church of Rome (August 107), it has been suggested that προκαθημένη τῆς ἀγάπης be understood as "who is most charitable" or "who excels in works of charity", which is hardly acceptable from a grammatical point of view and does not account for the fact that elsewhere "*agapè*" seems indeed for Ignatius to be a synonym for community or "*ecclesia*" (*Trall.* 13, 1; *Phil.* 11, 2).

[30] *L'Église primitive*, 158, 187, 231.

Weiss, and, at first, Harnack;[31] it was also the thesis of Alfred Loisy, who wrote in his commentary on the *Évangiles synoptiques*: "It is not without reason that Catholic tradition has based the dogma of Roman primacy on this text (Mt 16:18). Consciousness of this primacy inspires the whole development of Matthew, who not only had the personal history of Simon in view, but also the traditional succession of Simon Peter."[32] But this theory, which was impossible to support seriously, had to be abandoned. It was not less impossible, despite the extreme ingenuity which was then displayed by some in glossing over the meaning of the texts,[33] to continue to disregard the eminent place attributed to Peter in the Synoptics, in the Gospel of John, as well as in the Acts and in Saint Paul.[34] Without doubt, it must not be forgotten that in the text of Matthew 16:18, as Karl

[31] Harnack has changed position on "You are Peter" several times; "an instructive specimen of the author's virtuosity and also of the specious arguments that can always be found to support a bad thesis" (Batiffol, *Cathedra*, 3 and 38–39). Cf. Michel d'Herbigny, *Theologia de Ecclesia*, 3d ed. (Beauchesne, 1927), 1:272–73, 283–85; 2:325.

[32] *Les Évangiles synoptiques*, 2 (Ceffonds, 1908), 13.

[33] For the Gospels, the arbitrariness is all the greater as one rightly stresses, on the other hand (but at times to excess or in a unilateral way), the theological intentions of the evangelists.

[34] On Saint Paul's testimony, see Bouyer, *L'Église*, 464–65. Soloviev, *La Russie*, 151, quotes these lines from

Barth reminds us and all Catholics profess, "it is Jesus, and not Peter, who builds, 'constructs' his community (οἰκοδομήσω μου τὴν ἐκκλησίαν), and it is that which makes it invincible; Peter is called, in consequence of his confession, only to furnish the foundation, the rock";[35] but it is in fact he who is called to do it, and no other. The only hypothesis left, therefore, would be that according to which this foundational role vested in Peter was not transmittable. This is known to be the opinion of Oscar Cullmann, who also sees in the authority recognized in the see of Rome in the course of the first two centuries only a condition of fact whose justification was sought, improperly, in the Gospel only from the third century on.[36] Nevertheless, as the Protestant theologian Jean-Jacques von Allmen observed quite recently, when Jesus

---

E. de Pressensé on the role of Peter in Acts: "During all these early times, Peter exercised a predominant influence. Proof of his primacy is seen in the role which he then played. But, to look closer, we recognize that he was only displaying his natural gifts purified and increased by the divine Spirit" (*Histoire des trois premiers siècles du christianisme*, 1:358).

[35] *Dogmatique*, v. 4, t. 2, fasc. 3 (Geneva, 1971), 23.

[36] *Saint Pierre disciple, apôtre, martyr* (Neuchâtel, 1952), 192–214. See a critical analysis of this position in Benoit, *Exégèse et théologie*, 2. Cf. Charles Journet, *Primauté de Pierre* (Alsatia, 1953), 57–102.

says again to Peter, in chapter 22 of Luke: "I have prayed that your faith may not fail, and you, you will strengthen your brothers", he entrusts this task to him "within the framework of the Eucharist", that is, "within the framework of what Jesus wishes to see endure until his return".[37]

It is furthermore natural, for want of indications to the contrary, to think that the unity of the particular churches among themselves is to reflect that which united the Apostles among themselves. This is why, concludes M. von Allmen, the primacy of the church of Rome "seems biblically strong to me". Perhaps indeed, he confides to his reader, "the fact that the kind of fear which seizes all of us Reformed theologians when we see that we have not managed to elude the problem

---

[37] In "*L'Église locale*", 532. It could be that the insertion of Jesus' word at this place was the work of Luke. In this case, we would know at least that such was already Luke's conviction on the importance of this word. See the analogous reflections of Ratzinger, *Le nouveau peuple*, 34–35, on the subject of Matthew, who wrote after Peter's death. —Cf. Jacques Guillet, *Jésus devant sa vie et sa mort* (Aubier, 1971), 135: "The Church already exists at Caesarea. Already she speaks, already all her authority comes to her from Jesus, from the confirmation which he gave to Peter. . . . Such was the Church at her source, such she remains through the centuries. . . ."

of the apostolic succession comes from the fact that, consciously or not, we sense that if there is apostolic succession, there is also undoubtedly in this apostolic succession a specifically petrine succession".[38] That the latter was at first affirmed peacefully by simple practice, and not by theoretical expositions, claims and an arsenal of proofs, is indeed what one might expect. The contrary would be suspect, as if it were a question of coercing recalcitrants to accept a novelty. In this early sobriety, moreover, there is only what we would ordinarily expect. Reflective thought is always second, and it ordinarily assumes a certain fullness only under the action of contradiction. The theological justifications then invoked do not come of necessity to transform a fact into a right (that is, into what would then be an abusive right), but, indeed, to show the right of the fact.[39] In

[38] "*L'Église locale*", 529. In which the bishops succeeded to the Twelve and the bishop of Rome to Peter: Bouyer, *L'Église*, 468–70. Cf. Clement of Rome, c. 42 (A. Jaubert, SC, 167:169–71). See above, 85.

[39] Similarly, the people prayed to the Trinity before speculating about it. The tradition of the Church is a tradition in act. The first Christians did not constitute a professorial body. Cf. Vatican II, *Dei Verbum*, chap. 2, n. 8. Neither does one find in the early Fathers the theoretical affirmation of a priesthood of the faithful, or that of an episcopal college succeeding to that of the apostles.

order to intervene legitimately with authority, Clement of Rome did not need to begin by setting forth to the Corinthians the history of Christian origins, nor to address to them or to us a course in Gospel exegesis. He acted quite simply in the consciousness that he had his responsibility, and his letter was received in the churches with a similar consciousness. Now, after the event, we note a perfect conjunction between his intervention and the New Testament texts which establish its legitimacy. Thus, from the very origin of the Church, Soloviev's request is confirmed: "Let them find for us, then", he asked, "an effect corresponding to Christ's word to Peter other than the chair of Peter, and let them discover a sufficient cause for this chair other than the promise made to Peter."[40]

It has been said that Clement's letter is the "eminent prototype" of all Roman interventions.[41] In the fifth century, Pope Celestine writes, "Placed by God in an observation post, we must prove the diligence of our vigilance, cut short what is forbidden, sanction what is to be observed; our spiritual care is not lacking even for what is happening far away, but extends to all places where the name

[40] *La Russie*, 132.

[41] Henri Holstein, *Hiérarchie et peuple de Dieu* (Beauchesne, 1970), 22.

of God is preached"[42]: in saying this, he is saying nothing but what Clement could have said before. If the popes are thus convinced of their mission, those outside of Rome are just as convinced, as had previously been the Corinthians whom Clement addressed, and justification is given for it more than once. Irenaeus does this even before any pope thought to do it, it seems, when he extols the *principalitas* in the Roman church, which is to say, the primogeniture which her origin merits her.[43] Not long after, Cyprian said in the same sense that at Rome is found "the 'principal' chair of Peter and the Church from which proceeds the unity of the body of bishops"[44] and, in the first edition of *De Ecclesiae Unitate*: "The primacy is given to Peter, and thus we can see a single Church and a single chair. . . . Can one who deserts the chair of Peter imagine himself to be in the Church?"[45] By the very fact that he adjured

[42] *Epist.* 4 (PL, 50:430 A).

[43] *Adversus Haereses*. Cf. Batiffol, *Cathedra*, 36. It was by Callixtus (217–222) followed by Stephen (254–257) that the "You are Peter" seems to have been quoted as an authority in Rome.

[44] *Epist.* 59, c. 14, 1: "*Ad Petri cathedram atque ad Ecclesiam principalem unde unitas sacerdotalis exorta est*" (Hartel, 2:683).

[45] C. 4: "*Primatus Petro datur, et una Ecclesia et cathedra una monstratur. —Qui cathedram Petri super quam fundata Ecclesia est, deserit, in Ecclesia se esse confidit?*" Such appears to have

Pope Victor not to excommunicate the Asians, Irenaeus recognized his power to take such a measure. The Council of Sardica, convened in 343, wrote to Pope Julius that it is good that the bishops of all the provinces have recourse to the head, which is to say, to the see of the Apostle Peter.[46] Saint Ambrose declared that by giving Simon the name of Peter, by delivering to him the keys of the kingdom and by strengthening his faith, Christ made him the foundation of the whole Church, etc.[47] We will subsequently have occasion to cite other testimony.

The day-to-day life of the Church is equally and even more eloquent than any such declarations. What we can reconstruct of this life during the first centuries shows us the bishop of Rome in his dual role as center and arbiter. We saw above that the various particular churches, conscious of their

---

been the primitive text. Cf. Colson, *L'Épiscopat*, 99–101. Cf. Optatus, l. 2, c. 9: *"per cathedram Petri, quae nostra est"* (CSEL, 26:45).

[46] *"Hoc enim optimum esse videbitur si ad caput, id est ad Petri apostoli sedem, de singulis quibusque provinciis Domini referant sacerdotes."* Cf. Pierre Batiffol, *Le catholicisme de saint Augustin*, 5th ed. (Gabalda, 1929) 1:199. The authenticity of this phrase has been contested, but very probably wrongly.

[47] *De fide*, l. 4, c. 5, n. 56: *"Qui propria auctoritate regnum dabat hujus fidem firmare non poterat, quam cum petram dicit, firmamentum Ecclesiae indicavit?"* (PL, 16:628 B).

profound unity, were anxious to maintain relations with each other: the letters of Ignatius of
Antioch offer us an early example of this. The
practice of occasional or regular "letters of communion" was eventually organized. An entire
communication network was thus in operation,
one which was more or less tightly knit according
to times and places but from which no region was
excluded. And Rome was the center of this network. The letters came to the bishop of Rome,
and he circulated them. In this way, Catholic
unity was manifested. One of the witnesses of this
practice was Optatus of Milevis: "Thanks to an
exchange of official letters", he tells us, "the entire
universe agrees and becomes one with the bishop
of Rome in a society of communion."[48] But
more essential is the role of arbiter held by the
"Apostolic See"[49] in all kinds of affairs, great and
small. They consult us, states Innocent I, from all

---

[48] ". . . *cum quo nobis totus orbis commercio formatarum in una
communionis societate concordat*" l. 2, c. 3 (CSEL, 26:37). Cf.
Batiffol, *Le catholicisme*, 1:101–4.

[49] On the history of this formula, which, like others, was
not at first nor always afterwards reserved for the see of
Rome: D.-H. Marot, "*La collégialité et le vocabulaire épiscopal
du 5ᵉ au 7ᵉ siècle*", in: *Irenikon*, 36 (1963), 42–48. Applied to
Rome and bringing to mind the memory of the two apostles
Peter and Paul, the formula assumed a particular importance.

the provinces, even the most distant, with whom correspondence is difficult, and each time we reply.[50] Saint Avitus, bishop of Vienne, also verifies this a little later: "You know", he writes to Senarius, "it is one of our synodal laws that if any doubt should happen to arise in matters which deal with the Church's situation, we have recourse to the great bishop of the Roman church, as members to our head."[51] All the more reason for this recourse to take place in grave circumstances in which the faith of the Church is at stake; even in the periods when various disputes were raised in the East, it was always known, without any reservations, that such was the inviolable rule, for, as John, Patriarch of Constantinople, wrote to Pope Hormisdas in 519, such is the law of salvation: "In

---

[50] Reply to the Council of Milevis which had consulted him (417). In Augustine, *Epist.* 192, n. 1–2. PL, 33:784. The three letters of Innocent (col. 779–786) should be read. See also the famous letter *ad Gallos episcopos*, which is either from Damasus or from Siricius, and which is also a reply to bishops who have consulted "the authority of the apostolic see": those who would not observe the prescriptions it contained "would be excluding themselves from the society of Catholics and from communion with the apostolic see".

[51] *Epist.* 36: "*Scitis synodalium legum esse, ut in rebus quae ad Ecclesiae statum pertinent, si quid fuerit dubitationis exortum, ad Romanae Ecclesiae maximum sacerdotem, quasi ad caput nostrum membra sequentia recurramus*" (PL, 59:253 A).

fact, it is in the apostolic see that the Catholic religion is always kept inviolable."[52]

For a long time, "this hierarchical preeminence, this general administration which had its center in Rome, was exercised without any thought of creating a special staff. It was with the priests, deacons and secretaries of his church that the bishop of Rome handled the affairs which arose".[53] But in proportion as the mustard seed developed, that is, as the tree of the Church grew, it was necessary to become more organized. Traditions were codified. Just as local hierarchies were constituted, to the point of forming the great Patriarchates in the East, so the church of Rome gradually acquired the necessary means for the accomplishment of her mission. Historical contingencies also intervened, which, on the one hand, contributed to loosening the ties with the East, and, on the other, allotted some tasks to the papacy which were at first unforeseen: administrative tasks of the ecclesiastical order and even, subsequently, of the political order. As the history of canon law clearly shows, the essential reference of all the churches to that of Peter was concretized in a group of complex institutions subject to a thousand variations.

[52] "*Prima salus est quia in Sede apostolica inviolabilis semper catholica custoditur religio*" (PL, 63:444 B).

[53] Duchesne, *Origines*, 15.

One can find many an excess, many an abuse in it. It is not a question, moreover, of wishing to canonize what was, even entirely legitimately, only of human initiative nor of wanting to maintain indefinitely what, even if it was beneficial, indeed indispensable at a given time, no longer corresponds to the needs of a new situation. Newman, who showed himself to be more clearsighted in his generosity of spirit than many critics who are less gifted with an historical sense and who are able to see only the dark side of the picture, praised the benefit to European civilization derived from the centralization of ecclesiastical power in the Middle Ages and its temporal extensions; but he also specified that this did not mean that such a benefit would still remain valid for modern Europe.[54] Nothing is less in conformity with the true traditional spirit than a frozen conservatism. Besides, it might only be nostalgia. All that matters—but it is something of vital interest—is maintaining in its authentic vigor the unique role of the successor of Peter as achieving the "form of unity" of the successors of the Apostles, that is, as ensuring the *singularis cathedra*

[54] *Lettre au duc de Norfolk* (1871), chap. 3 (trans. B.-D. Dupuy [DDB, 1971], 184). Newman refers to the Protestant historian L. von Ranke, *Die Römischen Päpste. . .* (1834–1836).

through all the churches, in space and in time.[55] What must always be sought, through necessary adaptations and doctrinal reflections as through reforms and practical inventions, is a better communion between the bishop of Rome and his brothers in the episcopacy, *"id est, unitas illa radicalis a Spiritu sancto omnia ordinante in Ecclesia ad regnum Dei promovendum"*.[56] The episcopal collegiality recalled and confirmed by Vatican II, if it is understood in its true sense, can only call forth "a closer association of the bishops with the universal government of the Church, a more immediate solidarity, beyond that offered by the processes of the pontifical curia, between the bishops and the pope and between the bishops themselves in their responsibilities as pastors".[57] Some decentrali-

[55] Optatus of Milevis, *De schismate Donatistarum*, l. 8, c. 3: *"forma unitatis"* (CSEL, 26:170); l. 2, c. 2: *"una cathedra"*, *"cathedra unica"*, *"singularis cathedra"* (36, 46, 47).

[56] Cardinal Garrone, Roman Synod of 1969: ". . . which is to say, this radical unity which comes from the Holy Spirit ordering everything in the Church to promote the reign of God." Cf. Patriarch Maximos IV defining episcopal collegiality as "active concern for the interests of the kingdom of God by all the bishops jointly, in communion with their leader, the Pope of Rome": *Irenikon*, 36 (1963), 325.

[57] Dejaifve, *"La collégialité"*, 483. Vatican II, *De Pastorali Episcoporum Munere*, c. 2, n. 12 and 13. Episcopal Synod of 1969, *Responsiones P. Angeli Anton*, 10: Numerous Fathers

zation can thus be opportune;[58] it is within the logic of the Council's provisions, and a good deal has already been largely achieved in actual fact. This ought to contribute to a renewed vitality in the churches—but on the condition that it not be understood as a loosening of the bond of unity.

Neither the initiative nor the fruitful activity of any particular church would be promoted in the least possible way by her withdrawing into herself or by her standing aloof with respect to the center. Such an attitude, on the contrary, could only contribute to her sterilization.[59] The principle of "subsidiarity" is sometimes invoked in this regard. Once again, in accord with the bishops of the Roman Synod of 1969, Paul VI recommended

---

have asked "*ut episcopi magis activam responsabilitem et magis operosam participationem una cum (papa) de facto exerceant.*" Cf. Paul VI, discourse at the end of the synod, October 27, 1969 (AAS [1969], 728).

[58] But, it has been observed (Legrand, "*Inverser Babel*", 346), "it would be of no use to decentralize the Roman bureaucracy [only to duplicate it] within each diocese", or within each episcopal conference.

[59] Also, Cardinal Garrone again said, "*a nobis (episcopis) expectatur ante omnia ut quaestio de relationibus inter episcopos et Sanctam Sedem sit vere et appareat ut inquisitio de modis aptioribus ad unitatem inveniendum in opere urgenti fidei promovendae et defendendae.*"

developing its exercise.[60] All the same, it is necessary to understand it as a whole and not in a unilateral way.[61] The vitality of the body of the Church—as of all well-ordered society—demands that the head not monopolize all the functions and all the decisions, but leave to each of its members what it is normally qualified to do by itself. It is this principle which, put into better practice during the last few years, has distributed administrative responsibilities more widely. If it is applied everywhere in the spirit that dictated it, only good can result from it.[62] It can be extended very far without striking the least blow at the unity of the

[60] Closing discourse, October 27 (*Doc. cath.* [1969], col. 1033–34).

[61] It is again the Reformed theologian Jean-Jacques von Allmen who writes, with wisdom: For the *bene esse* of the Church, "a sincere respect for the principle of subsidiarity" is necessary; "but also . . . a sincere respect for the unity of the universal Church—in order to limit local claims to autonomy" ("*L'Église locale*", 536).

[62] Father Louis Bouyer made this concrete by reminding us of a symbolic fact: "If, the primitive church at Jerusalem having disappeared, . . . the Roman church succeeded her in her function of 'Mother and head of all the churches on earth', the Roman church herself never associated this appellation with the Vatican offices but with the Lateran Cathedral where the popes, down through the centuries, have preached the Gospel to a faithful gathering, baptized, presided at common prayer and at the eucharistic banquet" (*L'Église*, 337–38).

Church. But it must not be forgotten that there are two sides to the principle of subsidiarity, and that it would be of no use to insist on the rights which proceed from it if one were not disposed to assume his share of the duties which it entails. Whether with respect to their own flock, or with respect to the entire Church, the pastors share with the pope responsibilities which they cannot shift onto him by handing over the entire exercise of this principle to him. Now, one can sometimes wonder, and we do in fact wonder, without venturing to criticize anyone in particular, if all are always genuinely aware of this. Today especially, with the grave situation in which the Church finds herself and in the face of the immense anguish of so many people to whom her renewed vitality could give hope, does it not happen that we rely too easily on the pope—without even a true desire to follow him—to take care of watching over the Catholic faith, to direct the efforts at adaptation in the sense of a true evangelical renewal and not of a surrender to the trends of the century, to promote effectively the great and necessary movements of social action, to call to mind the exigencies of the spiritual life in season and out?[63] Is not

[63] In the extreme cases where the local hierarchy failed completely in these duties, while keeping out of Rome's

such a shirking of one's responsibilities as little conformed to the principle of subsidiarity as to that of unity?

The most important initiatives from a bishop or a group of bishops, and the greatest administrative autonomy, whether hierarchical or not, which one can conceive, far from being incompatible with the permanent concern for Catholic unity, find in the reference to Peter the security they need. And it is again in her reference to Peter that each church finds the protection of her independence with regard to worldly pressures of all kinds, whatever their source may be, which can be exerted upon her. Without the support of a strong papacy, Newman again wrote, the Christian hierarchy would have long ago "degenerated into a feudal, semi-clerical, semi-secular caste, endowed with hereditary benefices and more and more a slave to civil authority; it would have become a national priesthood which would gradually have fallen to the intellectual and religious level of its nation or tribe of origin".[64] Earlier examples

---

view, the time came when the faithful had to apply the instructions of Saint Augustine: *"Videtis quam sit tacere periculosum. . . . Ad nos quidem pertinet non tacere; ad vos autem, etiam si taceamus, de Scripturis sanctis verba pastoris audire"* Sermo 46, c. 9, n. 20 (PL, 38:282).

[64] *Lettre au duc de Norfolk*, 185.

could be reported: it was the papacy above all which maintained in the first centuries of what is so often called in an appalling oversimplification the "Constantinian era" the independence of the Church and the orthodoxy of her faith against emperors who, remaining semi-pagans, supported by turns, and with what energy! semi-pagan heresies.[65] There are also more recent examples. It is sometimes said rather quickly that dangers of this kind belong only to the past; that threats of encroachment by the State, which had made a strengthening of the papacy necessary in order to protect religious freedom, are scarcely to be feared any more; that "the Church has never been so free". That is a very optimistic view. The growth of nationalism and the increase in totalitarian states are facts of the present century, and even in

[65] It often seems to be forgotten that, in the very century that followed the edict of Milan, the Catholic Church was very often in conflict with the Empire (to say nothing of Julian's interlude) and that her bishops were severely persecuted at that time: let us recall in particular Athanasius, Chrysostom or Pope Liberius, retorting to Constantius II: "I have to be alone a great deal, my faith will lose nothing by it. . . . Exile me wherever you like." Liberius had written to Hosius: "*Mihi moriendum magis pro Deo decrevi, ne viderer novissimus delator aut sententiis contra evangelium commodare consensum*" (in Hilary, *Fragmenta*, series B, 7, 6: CSEL, 65:167). He was exiled to Thrace.

the regions where the Church is free in relation to public authorities, she is vulnerable to many servitudes in relation to various social forces and to the tyrannies of "opinion". What some would like to give us as expressing "the sentiment of the Christian people" is often only a new form of secular pressure, a formidable power that asserts itself through all the combined means of "psychological action". Each day brings us examples of this, and shows us the damage caused by it. What distortions of faith, morality and Christian sentiment can be effected in consequence! What opposition can arise between the churches of hostile nations or blocs of nations![66] In some cases, what grievous inability on the part of bishops to free themselves from the bonds which prevent them from acting—if indeed they do not fall into the traps which a skillful conditioning places before them! In such dangers, which can be daily, reference to Peter is a light and a support.

It is again in this same reference that each church or each group of churches finds the safeguard for

[66] Today, some readily criticize the pope's office as "head of State" (of the Vatican!). They do not see that this recent juridical fiction assures the independence of the papacy. Would they find a better one?

its personal identity, as the young African churches are so strongly aware today. And it is, finally, this reference, this direct tie with Rome, which maintains Catholic fidelity most effectively each time an internal crisis occurs to put it to the test. Then the personal intervention of Peter is decisive.[67] Here again, history speaks to us with eloquence. Let us merely recall the protest of the deacon Hilarion, legate of Saint Leo, in 449 against the decisions of the vast episcopal assembly at Ephesus which earned the name "the robber council".[68] Situations were not so rare in which "the faithful had great need of a doctrinal orientation which was not perfectly clear in the teaching of their bishops"; one can even wonder "if it was not the bishops themselves who had need of being 'strengthened' by their head, the successor of Peter, as much to be fortified themselves and to be able then to teach with complete assurance, as for

[67] The prerogatives of the church of Rome and of her bishop "are manifested especially in instances where the faith is in danger, according to the word of Jesus to Peter (Lk 22:32)": Patriarch Maximos IV, *"La collégialité épiscopale"*, in: *Irenikon*, 36 (1963), 321.

[68] An account in Louis Duchesne, *Histoire ancienne de l'Église*, 3d ed., 3 (Fontemoing, 1910), 411–26. We know that this was the prologue to the Council of Chalcedon.

the strengthening of their doctrinal authority over the faithful".[69]

[69] Jimenez Urresti, *"L'autorité du Pontife romain sur le collège épiscopal"*, *La collégialité*, 270. This will be less surprising if we recall that, at the time, the situations are nearly always ambiguous. Those who, caught at the center of a tempest, can discern the root of the problem in time are rare. Thus, at the time of the schism launched by Henry VIII, the cause of Catholic unity and the papacy could seem to the eyes of many to be confused with that of an abusive administration collecting taxes and claiming to exercise a universal jurisdiction. Cf. the Anglican point of view set forth by D. W. Allen and A. M. Allchin in *Irenikon*, 37 (1964), 174–75. Cardinal Wright recalled, at the 1969 Synod, that at that time John Fisher was the only bishop who *"inter fratres suos nationales anglicanos sanctae Sedi et fidei antecessorum suorum et nostrorum fidelis remansit"*. Cf. Chancellor Audley, head of the tribunal that condemned Thomas More to the punishment of traitors in 1534: "Master More, you wish to be considered wiser than all the bishops, all the nobility and, universally, all royalty!" (Germain Marc'hadour, *Thomas More* [Seghers, 1971], 108).

VII

THE SERVICE OF PETER

Two orientations have taken shape in various areas of the Church during the past few years which are supported and reinforced daily by the press. If they came to prevail, they would jeopardize the Catholic equilibrium of unity in diversity, whose reference to Peter, as we have just said, is the guarantee instituted by Jesus. As brief as this present study might be, it could not pass over them in silence without remaining too abstract.

The first is a tendency to loosen in a practical way, through a series of omissions rather than through clearly declared positions, the bonds of each church with the center. This appears principally in certain churches which we have called "local", for it seeks justification—very wrongly —in the idea of collegiality. According to some, it would seem that this collegiality can assert itself in action only in the measure that it steals a part of the pope's authority; in the measure that it keeps him at a distance, neglecting to listen to him as well as to inform him, avoiding statements that might resemble his, no longer mentioning him except in prayer, and that but rarely. It is a certain affectation of not being aware of what comes, or is thought to come, from "Rome"; a pretension opposite to that so-called "curialist" pretension that has been violently denounced recently, but which is symmetrical to it: it follows the latter's example by taking its inspiration, too, be it only in small things, from that "demand of one's rights"[1] or that "ecclesiology of power" which was precisely what Vatican II was reacting against. It explains, perhaps, at least in part, certain astonishing silences.[2] It is sometimes manifested even in liturgical texts: it is thus that the invocation *pro papa nostro* in the four canons of the Mass becomes each time, in the official French translation, a dry and distant "for *the* pope"; a minimal change

[1] Cf. Cardinal Wyszinski, October 13, 1969, exhorting the members of the synod and the episcopate in general not to let the *vindicatio jurium* predominate.

[2] In his grave apostolic exhortation *Quinque Jam Annis*, addressed to all the bishops in December 1970, Paul VI wrote: "It is not the time to ask us, as some would like to insinuate, if it is really useful, opportune, necessary to speak, but much rather to take the means necessary to make us heard . . ." (Doc. [1971], 55).

which might be of no consequence in other times, but which seems very inopportune today.[3] Who cannot see that tendencies of this sort are detrimental to the "communion" which is always the ideal and which the Council wished to promote?[4]

Is it proper to see in such an attitude, as many think, a resurgence of gallicanism? This would perhaps do it too much credit. The difference is not so much in the fact that the ecclesiastical gallicanism of the past was often mixed with a political gallicanism supported by the national State, for the most ardent adversaries of nationalism and even of the State which represents the nation can still have a strange national particular-

---

[3] The reason advanced for the suppression of "our" is scarcely valid (it would prove just as true for suppressing the "our" of the "Our Father"). This pronoun has a positive value, in the case of a pope as in the case of the bishop of the place. It has been preserved by the other translations I have been able to consult. The Germans, who could not be suspected of "papolatry", correctly translate: *für unsern Papst*. I do not believe the bishops themselves wanted this suppression. Batiffol, *Leçons*, 242, quotes an ancient formula (seventh century): "*pro famulo tuo X. papa nostro sedis apostolicae episcopo*".

[4] Cf. Cardinal Garrone, at the 1969 Synod: "*Maxime nobis praecavendum est, ne quaestio de relationibus inter episcopos et Sanctam Sedem non jam sub aspectu et inspiratione communionis respiciatur. . . .*"

ism. But the old gallicanism was equipped with a doctrinal system, it included a tradition, it was devoted to venerable usages, it expressed itself in a culture that was not only ecclesiastical but human, perhaps too narrow, but solid, attested by so many remarkable works, so many illustrious names. Here, on the contrary, we are facing an adolescent reaction, a rough and rootless ideology, a withdrawal without nobility. Despite some superficial gestures, it would be proper, rather, to speak of a certain provincialism or of a certain insularism.[5]

In fact, proceeding from a completely local conception of the collegial bond, the advocated movement away from the center becomes at the same stroke—notwithstanding words that are occasionally deceptive—a tendency to dissolve the bonds of universal collegiality. It is naturally at Rome, the center of catholicity, that the vast work of research and clarification called forth by the last council in matters of liturgy, canon law, theology, and pastoral practice for the purpose of the desired renewal comes together today. It is at Rome that the experts coming from the four corners of the world to achieve this end most often meet. It is therefore from Rome that the more or less pro-

---

[5] "Nothing is more foreign to the ancient episcopate than insularism" (Botte, *Études sur le sacrement*, 122).

visional fruit of all this work flows back. It, like any other work, is not always perfect. But to ignore it or to neglect it systematically, to reject it as "Roman", is at the very least to make a mistake in the shadow of which one isolates himself. [6] If, in a given region, the bishops were to give in to those who press for this, they would be depriving their own church of a wealth that ought to be common to all the faithful. And if, allowing themselves to be imposed upon, they were to adopt a similar attitude with regard to the papacy itself, they would be undermining their own support, as has been justly pointed out. [7] According to the teaching of Saint Gregory, taken up again by Vatican I, is the object of the pope's authority not precisely that of strengthening the authority of the bishops? [8] The latter would become all the more powerless

[6] There is one international theological commission, for example, created at the request of the bishops and placed at their disposal, which includes no Roman theologian. Since it meets in Rome once a year to discuss its work, the ideologues in question would like to condemn it in France as being "Roman". There are other examples.

[7] Bouyer, *L'Église*, 478.

[8] Vatican I, session 4, c. 3: "Episcopal authority is affirmed, strengthened and protected by the supreme and universal pastor" (DB, 1828). Cf. Olivier Rousseau, in: *Irenikon*, 29:127. There are many more than one declaration of principle included there.

to put a stop in their dioceses to that "intractable particularism" that Paul VI once pointed out with reference to the spread of a certain liturgical anarchy.[9]

Nearly one hundred fifty years ago, Moehler spoke from experience when he pointed out "the intimate link between respect for the pope and community spirit". It is clearly shown, he said, in the fact that they are so interdependent that the weakening of one also involves a threat to the other, as recent history testifies.[10] Identical testimony comes to us from an earlier era, and from our very country. Saint Avitus, Bishop of Vienne, who had been in a struggle for primacy with his colleague Caesarius of Arles, had just seen, to his great displeasure, Pope Symmachus settle the dispute in favor of Caesarius (500). Several months later, he nonetheless energetically defended, in the name of the entire episcopacy of Gaul, the cause of the Roman papacy against Italian bishops who, being overly submissive to political power, claimed to sit in judgment on the pope. That did not make him fear to address himself to some lay people:

[9] Address of Wednesday, September 3, 1970.
[10] *Gem. Schrift.* 1:265; quoted by Stefan Lösch in *L'Église est une* (1929), 233.

It is by the mandate I received from all my
brothers of Gaul that I write to you. We are concerned about the cause of the Roman Church. . . .
It is not only about what is happening in Rome
that we must think. If in fact some other bishop
happens to fail, there are means for remedying it;
but if the bishop of Rome is challenged, if his
office is shaken, it is not a bishop, it is the entire
episcopacy that falters. You well know through
what tempests we navigate in the vessel of faith.
If, therefore, you see the dangers of this as we
do, you must actively endeavor to protect the
one who guides the vessel: otherwise, what would
be our fate if the sailors were deprived of their
master?[11]

In a time of calm and spiritual health, there
would be no reason to be disturbed by a tendency
whose manifestations, at least with respect to
those in authority, are still generally rather benign. It could be interpreted as a passing fever
brought on by the inopportune explosion of a
sense of rediscovered liberty. But at a time when a

[11] Avitus, *Epist.* 5 (in 501), in Ulysse Chevalier, *Oeuvres
complètes de saint Avit évêque de Vienne*, new ed. (Lyons: Vitte,
1890), 131–33 (in Migne, PL, 59:248–49, ep. 31): ". . . *Non ea
tantummodo, quae Romae geritur, causa cogitanda est. In sacerdot-
ibus ceteris potest, si quid forte nutaverit, reformari; at si papa Urbis
vocatur in dubium, episcopatus jam videbitur, non episcopus,
vacillare. . . .*"

worldwide crisis is shaking the very interior of the Church so strongly, the consequences of such a state of spirit can go much farther than some of those who spread it might suspect. It introduces a ferment of disintegration into a social body where cohesion would be more than ever necessary in view of the inevitable spiritual combat. Nothing, in any case, could better avert the danger it constitutes than a clearer, more decisive awareness of what is essential to the structure of the Church: the communion of each particular church, in the person of her bishop—and also, consequently, of each local church grouping some number of bishops—with the pastor of the church of Rome, the universal pastor and center of Catholic unity.[12]

The second orientation, or the second tendency, takes shape in a series of more explicitly formulated theses, protests and plans for reform. It also claims to promote in actuality the idea of

[12] "*Ille enim est, cui Dominus dixit: pasce agnos meos . . . et pascere est etiam quaerere communionem omnium*" (Cardinal Wojtyla, Cracow). "*Conferentiae nationales, regionales et aliae hujusmodi, valde convenientes sunt, saltem propter rationes practicas. Sed qua tales, non in communione sunt cum Roma, nec Ecclesiam catholicam proprie constituunt. Potius loquendum esset de Ecclesiis dioecesanis, vel melius de episcopis per mundum dispersis una cum gregibus suis, qui cum centro unitatis fidei, caritatis et spei christianae, vid. cum Sede Romana, in communione sunt*" (Cardinal Wright).

episcopal collegiality by reducing to a minimum the exercise of authority by the bishop of Rome. The promoters of each of these plans, whether it is a matter of an old idea resurrected or of a new invention, want to see in them (one wonders why) the panacea that is to open the path of progress and ensure the salvation of the Church.

It is, to begin with, the call for more frequent councils. Previously, in 1870, a few bishops, recalling the famous decree of the Council of Constance as well as a vow made at Trent by a group of Italian prelates, had requested that a periodicity of ecumenical councils be established. This was a desire, if not to adopt in doctrine, at least to apply in practice the conciliarist system which had seduced a number of minds at the time of the great schism of the West. But this system did not have—even apart from any heterodox element—any origin in tradition. "The theologians who would like to make the council a regular institution", writes Monsignor Gérard Philips, "are making a mistake: by its very nature, the council is an event rather than an institution",[13] and the report recently published by the joint commission on "Catholicity and Apostolicity"

[13] Philips, *L'Église et son mystère*, 1:296. See above, chap. 4, 248–249.

says in a similar manner that councils are "sporadic manifestations".[14] In a formula that has become slightly archaic, Dom Gréa said not long ago with wisdom: "The Catholic Church cannot shake the world by frequent sessions of ecumenical councils."[15]

Moreover, even Monsignor Strossmayer, the boldest of those who in 1870 desired this periodicity, perhaps under the influence of the doctrine of *sobornost* advanced, or readvanced, by the slavophiles, dared to propose only a rate of twenty years for the convocation of the council.[16] Today, a number would like the episcopal synod that Paul VI instituted even before the end of Vatican II to be transformed in practice into a kind of council by becoming, contrary to the letter and spirit of its institution,[17] the regular organ of the magisterium

[14] In: *Irenikon* (1970), 198.

[15] *L'Église*, 223.

[16] Georges Dejaifve, *Conciliarité au concile du Vatican*, NRT, 82 (1960), 798–99. There is nothing there, however, that prevents us from admiring the ideas and work of this great bishop.

[17] *Expositio et explicatio relationis de parte doctrinali* (October 1969) 6: "*Talis est episcoporum synodi natura, maxime cum in coetum extraordinarium congregatur, atque tali gaudet repraesentatione episcoporum collegii, ut tanquam organum universalis episcopatus magisterii haberi non possit.*" Paul VI, Discourse of October 27, 1969: "*Hoc autem institutum non eo spectat ut*

of the universal episcopate. They consider that as long as the synod has only a consultative role, collegiality will not be fully realized. This is to be doubly mistaken, in my opinion. The synod is an expression, one might even say that it is today the most outstanding expression, of collegiality. But, on the one hand, the decision made in October 1969 to meet again every two years[18] clearly shows that neither the pope nor the bishops present intended this to be a question of introducing the equivalent of a biennial ecumenical council into the Church, in defiance of all tradition as well as of good sense—and certainly neither the pope nor the bishops conceived of the full exercise of episcopal collegiality under the single species of conciliarity; they had not forgotten the conciliar text which they had passed and promulgated five years earlier and which too many impromptu theologians seem never even to have read. If, on the other hand, some want thereby to restrict the pope to executing the decrees of some majority, it

---

potestatum aemulationem gignat vel difficultates paret efficaci atque ordinato Ecclesiae regimini; spectat vero ut in rem deducatur mutua Romani Pontificis et Episcoporum propensio ad fovendam arctiorem communionem et sociam operam apte ordinandam" (AAS [1969], 728).

[18] Paul VI, closing discourse, October 27 (*Doc. cath.*, 66 [1969], 1011).

would be advisable for them to recall that even in the case of an ecumenical council, there has never been cause for setting up an opposition between the pope and the other bishops,[19] or, all the more, for bringing the former under the subjection of the latter.[20]

Is that not unquestionably what one is seeking to do when, through a similar concern to render collegiality more effective, one makes another proposal: that henceforward the pope be elected by a delegation from the universal episcopate. Is that not, nevertheless, what might result? Would that not, whether we like it or not, make the pope a kind of super-bishop with neither local nor temporal roots, a constitutional monarch or president

[19] "We can never overemphasize the fact that the comparison should be made, not between the pope and the other bishops, but between the pope and the episcopal college in which he himself is included" (Cf. Philips, *L'Église et son mystère*, 297 and 304).

[20] It is nonetheless desirable, of course, for the bishops to be as closely associated as possible, whether individually or through episcopal conferences or synods, with the preparation of the acts issued by the pope, as Cardinal Marty said in his report of October 17, 1969 (*Doc. cath.*, 66 [1969], 1013–14. See above, 296–97.) On the subject of majorities and minorities in the Church, Karl Barth's reflections, which are not without humor, should be read, in his *Dogmatique*, vol. 4, t. 1, f. 3 (1967), 73–74.

of a Church conceived and, as it were, remolded in imitation of some modern State? Would the one elected still plainly be the bishop of Rome and, as such, successor of Peter and heir to his mission? The question can at least arise, and it does not seem to have been examined at first with the attention it requires. "The election of the Sovereign Pontiff", considers Dom Gréa, "belongs so exclusively to the Roman Church that no authority, no assembly, no council, even an ecumenical one, could be substituted for her. . . . The one elected by the Roman Church is the sole heir of Saint Peter."[21] In point of fact, in 1963 no one we know of seriously raised the idea that the successor to John XXIII could be designated by the Council. Perhaps Dom Gréa's assertion, however, appeared to some to be too absolute, given the fact, as he himself said, that the forms of the election for the Roman Church have undergone more than one modification in the course of the ages, and that the present college of cardinals can be thought to represent the Church of Rome only rather fic-

[21] *L'Église*, 176. John XXIII and Paul VI emphasized their fundamental character as bishops of Rome by insisting on visiting parishes themselves, celebrating the Eucharist and preaching in them. —Without believing the present system to be immutable, we merely think that the one that some would like to substitute for it suffers from serious defects.

titiously. This observation is not without some truth. However, it must also be observed that it is not a question of the single diocese of Rome, narrowly defined: formerly, when a bishop died, the bishops of the neighboring dioceses customarily gathered together for the election and ordination of his successor; now the college of cardinals still comprises today the bishops of "suburbicarian" dioceses: a title which has become fictitious but could again become real. On the other hand, the extension of this college to bishops of the entire world offers the advantage of assuring in practice a choice that might be more readily approved, without making it a question of principle. Moreover, we will always be forced to admit that some anomaly is inevitably exhibited in the conditions of any institution that develops and endures. But is it necessary to cut rather than preserve what remains of an early bond, even if what remains is now in part only symbolic? To what end? In the name of what principle?

The election, we are told, should be "by a council truly representative of the Church"; this would be a council "representative of different nations, different mentalities, different ages of life".[22] Let us pass over these last words, which

[22] Hans Küng, in: *Concilium*, 64, editorial.

savor a bit of the dreamer. . . . But where then have they gotten this assumption of "representation"? Does it have the least foundation traditionally? Was Peter elected by the Eleven? Have any of his successors inherited his role through an election of this kind? Could Clement of Rome say to the Corinthians that he was speaking to them with authority because he had been elected by the various churches? If we were shown that a once truly representative method of electing the pope was no longer so today, then it would be clear that our present method should be modified so as to make it again conform to tradition; to object to this would be the act of a narrowminded conservatism. But such is in no way the case. To call for this representation of the universal Church for the election of a pope—would this not be a profound distortion of its meaning and lead, as I have said, to a conception of the one elected as a representative or as a delegate?[23] I will not say that such a

[23] In order to avoid all ambiguity, let us specify, with Joseph Ratzinger (*Le nouveau peuple*, 90) and Yves Congar (in *Le concile et les conciles*, 308–9), that there is indeed a biblical and Christian concept of representation, but that it differs fundamentally from the political and parliamentary concept. The spiritual head represents his community as the personification and the summation of the body of which he is the head. Receiving his authority from the Lord he incorporates into his

method is impossible. But would this not, in any case, take very great liberties, not only with respect to ecclesiastical tradition but with respect to the Gospel:

> According to Saint Matthew, it is not so much that Peter is raised by some distinctive power above the rest of the Twelve, but rather that he personally received the same power that will be given jointly to the Twelve (himself included, therefore)[24]. . . . Peter, in this regard, does not appear as a super-apostle but as the apostle in whom, personally, all that is shared or possessed in common by the entire apostolic college is brought together.[25]

---

person (not private, but official) the members for whom he has been appointed leader. "When the pope acts in virtue of his office, he represents at the same time the whole Church and the whole body of pastors. But no one can deduce from this that he receives his power either from the community of the Church or from the bishops: on the contrary, he receives it directly from Christ" (Philips, *L'Église et son mystère*, 1:297).

[24] Cf. Mt 18:18 (= Jn 20:23) and Mt 16:19.

[25] Bouyer, *L'Église*, 463; cf. 473. Jerome, *Contra Jovinianum*, l. 1, n. 26: ". . . *At dicis, super Petrum fundatur Ecclesia; licet id ipsum in alio loco super omnes Apostolos fiat, et cuncti claves regni caelorum accipiant, et ex aequo super eos Ecclesiae fortitudo solidetur, tamen propterea inter duodecim unus eligitur, ut capite constituto, schismatis tollatur occasio*" (PL, 23:247 A). —The question of Peter's exact situation at Rome and of the "how"

It is therefore not surprising that a proposal in which this distinctive character of Peter appears if not suppressed at least poorly preserved has given rise to many reservations. Is it not an attempt to adapt the constitution of the Church to secular customs rather than to emphasize and revitalize its own originality? Does it not go contrary to one of the most important elements renewed by Vatican II, the value of the particular church based on the bond of the Church and of the Eucharist? Does it not manifest a predominant concern for (very questionable) efficiency rather than for full fidelity?

Neither are the lively reactions it has provoked on the part of the Eastern churches surprising. In fact, except for the intellectual blindness of a few, found there as everywhere else, the principal spokesmen for Orthodoxy have not had difficulty in allowing a certain preeminence in the universal Church to the bishop of Rome. Several today understand the necessity of this preeminence all the better as they note the bitter absence of a common center in their own churches, an absence which the vain attempts based on modern theories of a supreme collective authority cannot remedy.

---

of his succession will always remain obscure. There are diverse hypotheses. Cf. Colson, *Les fonctions*, 323–26. Lanne, "*Pluralisme*", 65. Benoit, *Exégèse et théologie*, 2:305–6. On the first episcopal lists of Rome: Batiffol, *Cathedra*, 170–73.

They willingly recognize the value of ancient testimonies that are unanimous in seeing "in Rome the eldest Church and the universal center of unanimity of the churches"; it is only, one of them again says, "in the heat of polemics that these testimonies, their consensus and their significance can be denied".[26] In particular, they consider the famous 28th canon of Chalcedon, insinuating that the primacy of ancient Rome came to it not from the Apostle but from its secular greatness, was only a text reflecting political opportunism.[27] If they do not wish to express this primacy in terms of law, they nevertheless refuse to follow those of their historians who systematically minimize the importance of traditional attestations; hesitant before the idea of a "supreme authority", they are all the more so before that of a "mere president conceived in democratic or parliamentary terms".[28]

[26] Schmemann, *La primauté*, 121, 136, 141–42. Cf. Soloviev, *La Russie*, 17–21.

[27] Likewise, J. Meyendorff notes that "Photius did not know the polemical argument that artificially opposes Peter to his confession of faith any more than later Byzantine theologians did" (*La primauté*, 96–97).

[28] Schmemann, *La primauté*, 142. In the same work, N. Afanasieff prefers to say "priority" instead of "primacy", in order better to contrast the authority of testimony to a power "based on right". He notes, however, that "the testimony of the church of Rome was no less valid (in ancient times) than

But what they strongly emphasize, sometimes even perhaps exclusively, is that the primacy is bound to a well-determined local see and owes nothing to any representation whatever.[29] With how much greater reason would they refuse to accept the primacy of a super-bishop installed by a representation of the Western churches alone (or nearly so).[30] The plan presented to us as being

---

any juridical act whatever. If, in the history of the Church, there truly was an era in which the formula '*Roma locuta, causa finita*' corresponded to reality, it was indeed at the time when the Church possessed no juridical power" (54 and 60–62). We have not considered here at all the meaning of this dichotomy. Let me say only (with the hope of advancing nothing inaccurate) that in my opinion, in the essential act of his magisterium, the authority of Peter's successor is indeed one of testimony. He decides nothing at his own pleasure, rather he refers to the faith of the entire Church, that is, to the tradition coming from the Apostles, of which he is the guardian par excellence. But he refuses to give in to the pressures of those who at times would like to have him make an arbitrary decision in the name of an authority he does not acknowledge. On occasion he brings this back to the attention of bishops who appear to have forgotten it themselves.

[29] Schmemann, *La primauté*, 143. Cf. Jerome, *Epist.* 146, to Evangelus, no. 1: "Wherever there is a bishop, whether at Rome or Gubbio, at Constantinople or Reggio, at Alexandria or Tanis, he has the same value and also the same priesthood" (J. Labourt, 8:116).

[30] I put it this way for brevity's sake, knowing full well

urgently necessary for the good of the Church would undoubtedly constitute, solely by its being given serious consideration, a major obstacle to the ecumenical cause. Has sufficient care been taken in reflecting on this?

Whatever solution is given to the problems of election or synodal collaboration, it will always remain difficult to dispute the fact that the prerogative of Peter's successor consists above all in a role of personal intervention. One might therefore be tempted to devise a roundabout approach that would permit this prerogative to be neutralized without being abolished. It would be a matter of persuading the pope, in the name of the good of the Church, to bind himself by a solemn act in decreeing that in the future he would no longer ever intervene except "collegially". —The idea would be ingenious. But if it were taken in its full sense,[31] would not those attracted by it wonder

---

that today this distinction of the geographical order corresponds only rather poorly to reality. We could also say: "the Latin churches alone", which would not be entirely exact either. It is a matter of only those churches who are of Roman Catholic obedience at the time of the election of a pope.

[31] The case would be completely different if it were a decision made by the pope not to use his personal authority with respect to some problem or group of problems, even important ones, in which the essential faith and discipline of

what the moral as well as the juridical value of such an act might be. How, without betraying his mission, could the successor of Peter dismiss in advance the exercise of a prerogative which Christ wished him to have, not as an individual privilege that he could renounce, but as the foundation of a service for the universal Church, a service which circumstances might render necessary?[32] How could he in that way evade the testimony that must be his? Or indeed, what would be the significance of this previous decree if it were understood that he could deviate from it at will? Would this not create in advance for the Church an occasion for dispute rather than an instrument of union, all the more as it is precisely in cases of

---

the Church were not involved; a decision to hand over some practical solution, for example, to the choice of an episcopal synod, even though the synod by itself is only a consultative organ.

[32] Cardinal Wojtyla, October 15, 1969: "*Collegialitas videtur etiam magna confirmatio istius supremae auctoritatis in Ecclesia, quae soli B. Petri successori est propria. Si in collegialitate includitur coresponsabilitas omnium episcoporum pro Ecclesia universali, tunc magis extollitur illa unica responsabilitas, quae ipsi soli est propria et in qua a nemine nec etiam a toto collegio substitui potest. Simul ad ipsum spectat collegialem actionem episcoporum in actum deducere, quaerendo in illa semper magis maturas expressiones communionis tam episcoporum quam Christifidelium. Ille enim est, cui Dominus dixit: Pasce agnos meos. . . .*"

serious crisis within the Church that he might have to make a personal decision?

Decentralization in the Church, or the application of the principle of subsidiarity, whose advantages and conformity to a whole tradition we have already mentioned, is one thing. A collectivist-style democratization which, by more or less oblique ways, would come to render the essential prerogative of Peter vain and empty, is something else. That would not be to return to a more effective collegial tradition, but to make concessions to secular views.[33]

The forms of intervention by the apostolic see in the life of the Church, especially in doctrinal matters, have varied greatly in the course of the centuries. It would be impossible, we repeat, to take any of these forms as an absolute norm. How many contingent varieties, how many changes have taken place in the great body of *statuta Sedis*

---

[33] That does not keep the pope, we must add, from having always to use "the appropriate means of investigation"; he has "the moral obligation to pay attention to many things, a complete list of which could be drawn up only with difficulty" (Philips, *L'Église et son mystère*, 1:233–35, 304). Cardinal Seper recalled in his inaugural report to the 1969 Synod: "His primatial ministry is subject to the objective rules of fidelity which derive from the revealed Word of God, the fundamental constitution of the Church and her tradition." See 322, note 28.

apostolicae, the *decreta majorum* or the *canones ecclesiastici*![34] It is the law of any great institution that endures. Nor would it be possible, in any given era, to attribute the same importance to acts that are by nature different by overlooking the criteria of usage. To present all encyclicals indiscriminately as infallible, as several theologians have done, was not, for example, to help strengthen papal authority. That was "a veritable inflation"—the very accurate expression of Father Congar.[35]

The frequency of interventions has varied no less than their form. We can rejoice in the fact that the present-day means of communication, which contribute to disseminating opinions in all fields, also permit the head of the Church to converse, so to speak, from day to day with the assembly of the faithful and to impart to them in that way a concrete teaching adapted to the needs of the hour. It is likewise conceivable that in a world which for the first time realizes its unity—but a unity that is scarcely anything but a more immense chaos—

---

[34] Expressions of Siricius (ca. 375) and Innocent (416). Cf. Batiffol, *Cathedra*, 45 and 57.

[35] *Ministères*, 151. Similarly, a whole so-called "papalist" interpretation of the chapter of Vatican I on the Roman primacy has constituted a regrettable excess which falsified its meaning. See on this subject Ratzinger, *Le nouveau peuple*, 64–67.

an extended activity on the part of the universal Pastor becomes singularly opportune, in order to seal, as it were, the spiritual unity of the Catholic universe and to orient the faithful, by appeals such as the discourse of Paul VI to the United Nations or his encyclical *Populorum Progressio*, toward the new works that demand their attention on a world-wide scale.[36] It is normal, moreover, as is done today, for representatives of the entire Church—bishops, priests and laity—to be associated in directing these works. —On the other hand, it is also to be hoped, as we said above, that a better application of the principle of subsidiarity would

---

[36] What could be particularly helpful in this is an order like the Society of Jesus, which its founder wished to be free from all territorial ties and from all specialized functions in order to be like a militia at the disposal of the Roman pontiff for the purpose of satisfying the needs of the universal Church according to his instructions. Cf. Jean-Yves Calvez, S.J., "*L'aggiornamento de la Compagnie*", in: *Christus*, 13:51 (July 1966), 307: "For a truer discernment of the most universal and the most urgent in the continuous mission of Christ throughout history in the Church, he (the Jesuit) remits his will to the Vicar of Christ on earth. This apostolate at the service of the Sovereign Pontiff is not a secondary task chosen *ad libitum*: it is the outpouring of his life transformed by the gift of Christ." We do not see where the appeal to episcopal collegiality could change anything in that.

contribute to reducing the necessity of more serious interventions proceeding from the center. When the assembly of pastors exercises with the necessary assiduity its responsibility as the teacher of doctrine and guardian of the faith, when local initiatives are successively taken to assure necessary adaptations and to maintain Christian vitality through the endlessly varied conditions of existence, then the universal pastor is less likely to intervene. Let us add that the actual process of administrative decentralization can help to reinvigorate the interior life of the churches—provided, however, that new excessive centralizations are not established, for example, on a national level. It will nonetheless remain impossible to overturn all the conditions resulting from history and geography. No vital institution is ever unconditionally malleable, and it is illusory to think that we can retrace our steps entirely back through the stream of evolutions, just as it is erroneous to believe that by cutting the oak tree down to the ground, we will recover the energy of the acorn. If, therefore, we are concerned about Christian unity and hope that one day it can finally be achieved, it seems to me that we must anticipate, for the reunited Church of the future, rather considerable differences in organization, even more, undoubtedly, than in the centuries preceding the schism between East and West.[37]

But the essential prerogative of Peter will remain.

To want to compel the bishop of Rome, by whatever means possible, to turn towards the other bishops in order to learn from them the path of fidelity would be to go contrary to the constitution of the Church and to her traditional practice.[38] In Christian antiquity, the papacy had

---

[37] Despite all that can be said in favor of the legitimacy, even the evident timeliness, of certain developments occurring in the course of the centuries and despite the dangerous complications which would be bound to arise because of territorial confusion in particular, we believe that the following words deserve attention: "It is necessary—as one would say in German—for Rome to agree to a discussion with the other churches on the *wie* of the Primacy, and it is necessary for the non-Roman churches to agree to a discussion with Rome on the *dass* of the Primacy." Jean-Jacques von Allmen, *"Remarques sur la constitution dogmatique Lumen gentium"*, in: *Irenikon* (1966), 31.

[38] "The pope is not the spokesman of the bishops, a kind of organ whom they themselves chose and who remains at their disposal; but, directly responsible before the Lord, he has been placed in his position by him in order to incarnate the unity of the Word and the work of Christ, just as, from the beginning, Christ had charged Peter with the same mission as the community of the Twelve . . ." (Ratzinger, *Le nouveau peuple*, 99). That, we must repeat, is totally independent of

not yet experienced the developments that a long history full of unforeseeable events was to bring to her. Its authority had not yet been defined with all the precision of juridical terms;[39] in everything, in fact, guidance came less from written and codified rules than from the living tradition and example of the ancients.[40] The difficulty in communications perhaps made a certain kind of unity less visible than in our time—a unity that the young spirit of the numerous particular churches made less necessary besides. But in every important matter of discipline or doctrine, all knew very well that in the last resort it was necessary to have recourse to the "Apostolic See".

---

the more or less considerable administrative role played by the papacy in the course of the centuries.

[39] Making allowances for excess and deviations, of which history offers too many examples, there is in principle no opposition between the details of law and the authority of testimony; the former are for the sole end of protecting the latter and of allowing the effective exercise of it. They are indispensable in a populous and complex society. The decisions of the pope, like those of the council, are not the acts of an arbitrary sovereign; they are testimonies. The one who makes them knows himself to be bound by the tradition received from the apostles.

[40] Cf. the very provocative article by Monsignor Georges Jouassard, *"Pour une étude du sacerdoce au temps des Pères"*, in: *La Tradition sacerdotale*, 109–25.

Saint Augustine again offers us, at a slightly later period, a perfect example of this conviction. No one could maintain that he was an insignificant or passive bishop. The stemming of the Donatist schism was due to his long and persevering action. We are familiar with Possidius' proud declaration on that subject: "For a long time the Catholic Church in Africa lay helpless on earth, seduced or oppressed by the Donatist faction; thanks to Augustine, with the help of the Lord, she started to raise her head once again".[41] His books carried the light into all the churches; the East received them in Greek translations. He extended his vigilance and solicitude everywhere. It was after having received letters informing him of the Pelagian influence in the East that he fully entered the lists against the new heresy.[42] He instigated the councils of Carthage and Milevis; with four of his colleagues he also addressed to Pope Innocent a

[41] *Vita sancti Aurelii Augustini*, c. 7 (PL, 32:39).

[42] Ibid., c. 11; c. 18: "*Erat ille memorabilis vir . . . circa universalis Ecclesiae utilitatem sollicitus semper ac pervigil*" (col. 42 and 49). Alypius and Augustine to Paulinus of Nola: "*Sed posteaquam ad nos litterae de Oriente venerunt, eamdem causam apertissime ventilantes, nullo modo jam qualicumque episcopali auctoritate deesse Ecclesiae debueramus*" (*Epist*. 186, c. 1; PL, 33:816).

"familial letter" which is a long, compact memorandum. Thus a frequent exchange of written documents was established between the apostolic see and the African bishops.[43] Aware of his collegial duty, Augustine saw no less clearly that the intervention of Rome is alone capable of resolving the crisis: so long as Rome has not testified, the question remains undecided; it is also necessary to implore its "pastoral diligence". Innocent replied through three "rescripts" to three reports from Africa: "his judgment is manifest", Pelagius and his disciple Celestius were excommunicated. From then on "all doubt is lifted"; Augustine could say to his people: "The rescripts have arrived from the apostolic see and the matter is settled; heaven grant that the error may come to an end!"[44] But two months later, Innocent died. Celestius rushed

---

[43] *Contra duas epistolas Pelagianorum*, l. 2, c. 3, n. 5: "*Tot enim et tantis inter Apostolicam Sedem et Afros episcopos currentibus et recurrentibus scriptis ecclesiasticis . . .*" (PL, 44:574). Cf. the letter from the Council of Milevis: "*Magnis periculis infirmorum membrorum Christi pastoralem diligentiam, quaesumus, adhibere digneris*" (*Epist.* 176, n. 1; PL, 33:763).

[44] Ibid.: ". . . *litteris beatae memoriae Papae Innocentii, quibus de hac re dubitatio tota sublata est*" (PL, 44:574). *Sermo* 130, c. 10: "*Jam enim de hac causa duo concilia missa sunt ad Sedem Apostolicam, inde etiam rescripta venerunt. Causa finita est; utinam aliquando finiatur error*" (38, 734).

to Rome, fooled the people by feigning agreement with Innocent's declarations; the Roman synod itself allowed itself to be outwitted; the new pope, Zozimus, was hesitant. The Africans insisted. Finally Zozimus published a *Tractoria*, which renewed the condemnation delivered by Innocent, and the episcopate of the entire world subscribed to it.[45]

Such was the essential process, long ago just as yesterday, throughout the extreme diversity of cases, the infinite detail of difficulties, consultations, disputes or intrigues—the opposite of that which many would like to see adopted today. All initiative obviously did not come from Rome. In addition, the Roman pontiffs were often "prudent and calm" men who did not like to precipitate matters. Nevertheless, Augustine, like many others before him, saw clearly: nothing could succeed without Rome. In the final analysis, when a grave crisis arose, it was not the bishop of Rome who sought a majority with whom to take sides: it was, on the contrary, the bishops, powerful or not, numerous or not, effectively united by collegial bonds or not, who turned toward their brother of

[45] On this whole affair: Duchesne, *Histoire ancienne*, vol. 3, 3d ed., 223–41. Batiffol, *Le catholicisme*, 381–432.

Rome to call for his decision. For such is, above all, in its unalterable simplicity, the "charism", the "office", the "service of Peter".[46]

[46] Cf. Paul VI, October 27, 1969: ". . . *illud Primatus charisma ab ipso Christo in suam Ecclesiam Petro concreditum, cujus humillimi sed veri sumus successores, sive officium, potius quam jus, ejusdem Primatus fideliter exercendi*" (AAS [1969], 728). —On the role of the papacy in the ecumenical problem (cf. above, 287–88 and 330, note 37), see also in: *Communion*, 3 (1971), 2–6: *La prieur de Taizé s'exprime sur le ministère du pape*.

APPENDIX

THE PRIESTHOOD
According to Scripture and Tradition

*An Interview with Father Henri de Lubac
Conducted by Gwendoline Jarczyk*[1]

At a time when the Synod is dealing with the
fundamental question of the nature of the priesthood and of the ministry proper to it, it is important to listen to what is said on this subject
by one of our contemporary theologians whose
thinking is most explicitly rooted in Scripture and
tradition. Many of the present problems can, in
fact, recover their true meaning when, guarding
against all passion and any partial approach, we
immerse them in the great unifying current of
Christian thought.

*Father, all of your theological research is marked by
your great knowledge of the sources of the faith and*

[1] *France catholique* (October 8, 1971).

*particularly of patristic thought. Do you not believe that
it is necessary to return to this fundamental level in order
to clear up the difficulties we have today with regard to
what the priesthood is and in what way it is to be lived?*

First of all, I would like to say that I am not a
"specialist" on the question you ask. Perhaps it
would be of greater value for you to question the
competent specialists who are not lacking right
here in France. I will mention a few of them: Jean
Colson, Pierre Grelot, André Lamarié, Édouard
Cothenet, Augustin George, Jean Dauvillier, etc.

Yes, it is necessary to return to the sources. For
people speak a great deal today about Christian
origins in order to challenge the very idea of a
New Testament priesthood.

*I would like for you to give us a general summary, as
it were, of this essential point. What does the history of
Christian origins teach us about the priesthood such as
Christ instituted it in its hierarchical structure?*

It is not unusual today to hear people contest the
very idea of all hierarchical ministry in its New
Testament rootedness (and this is not, moreover,
something new). To me, this seems completely
contrary to history such as we are able to ascertain
it today, notwithstanding, of course, all the ob-
scurities that do remain.

More than in the past, perhaps, we understand from certain analogies (and notably since the Qumran discoveries) that the primitive Church had to have been completely organized or, as we would say today, "structured". I read, for example, what J. Schmitt tells us in his excellent study on *"L'Organisation de l'Église primitive et Qumrân"* (*Recherches bibliques*, IV, 1959): "Whether it is a question of Essene brotherhoods or of other baptist sects, of Judaeo-Christian churches or of Pharisee *habhwôtt*, the Jewish community circles appear to have been organized according to a common scheme."

Moreover, it suffices quite simply to read the New Testament in order to see the authority of the Church founders assert itself. It is very true that this authority is entirely derivative; the apostle, or the one whom he establishes in his place, is a servant; but it is in exercising his authority that he fulfills his service. Saint Paul does not hesitate to speak of his power (*eksousia*). We see analogous words in the other documents of the primitive Church, and we realize that the reality corresponded to these words.

But perhaps it is good to observe, above all, that this authority of the ministers is entirely ordained to the work of salvation which they were commissioned to pursue in this world. In the Acts of the Apostles, we see the apostles preside at worship, proclaim the Gospel, impose hands, pardon or punish sinners. And they do all that "in the name of Christ" and through the power of his Spirit. They do it as "envoys of Christ", as his legates, his representatives: as representatives of Christ the priest. Now that is a typically priestly role.

Let us observe another thing as well. There is a close bond, which is insufficiently stressed, between the institution of the Eucharist and the institution of the Church, or even, more precisely, as M. von Allmen put it in his very beautiful *Essai sur le repas du Seigneur* (Jean-Jacques von Allmen, Professor at the University of Neuchâtel, is of the Calvinist tradition; I do not agree with all the explanations he gives, but it seems to me that on the question of these origins of the Church and on the institution of the ministry of the Church at the Last Supper he has clearly seen a central fact): "The institution of Holy Communion is not only the moment of the institution of the Church, but also that of the institution of the ministry in and for the Church. It is in this sense that we must undoubtedly understand the fact that at the time of the last supper, Jesus is with the Twelve exclusively, is only with those who are then to teach the Church to celebrate Holy Communion." And M. von Allmen adds (let us say, in passing): "And perhaps it is even necessary to understand the primary role that Peter plays in the apostolic college on the basis of that." He gives several indications of this; but that extends completely beyond our subject.

In any case, what is appropriate to note with this author is that the Eucharist, which could not have been invented by the first disciples, was instituted by Jesus for the life of the Church up until the parousia; the ministry of the Twelve, which was in fact instituted in order to "make" the Eucharist, is therefore in that way transmittable to their successors up until the parousia.

Throughout the New Testament, and it is again M. von Allmen who says it, we discover "two poles within the unity of shared salvation: a shepherd and a flock, a father and a family, a witness of Christ and the members of his body. . . . There is the fundamental affirmation of an obligatory reciprocity in this polarity, the impossibility for one to be without the other". Now it is this very polarity in the fundamental situation of the Church that we see in the act of the Last Supper and likewise in each eucharistic celebration. The bishop, or his representative the priest, acts and speaks then in the name of Christ; he pronounces the sacramental words, as subsequent theology says, *in persona Christi*, in the place of Christ. It is a polarity within the Church for the life of the

Church; this does not mean, however (and we will see this farther on), that there is any difference whatever in the sphere of Christian dignity and eternal salvation between the ministers and the assembly of Christian people.

Is this priest of tradition, such as you have just introduced him to us, first of all the man of "mission", dedicated to proclaiming the Word, or the man of "worship"? Is it not necessary to pass beyond this dilemma which is often established today between the "two tables"?

In fact, it is more precise to say that there are three traditional functions which form the content of the priestly ministry: the Word, worship and government. What it is above all necessary to observe is that they are not independent from each other; they are not autonomous, and certainly not disparate. If you consider them as independent, you falsify them.

Father, do you not believe that many difficulties and even false problems currently arise, here and on other levels, from this separation which people have tried to establish between elements which, in fact, belong equally to the total reality?

Yes, certainly. It will be necessary for us to come back to it in a few minutes because it is a general observation of extreme importance and one which passes well beyond our present subject. But it is true that it applies here. At bottom, a clear understanding of our faith always presupposes going beyond the dichotomies in which we have a tendency to express the questions that occur to us; a truly synthetic grasp of the truth in all its paradoxical richness is necessary.

What does that mean here? It means that the whole episcopal or presbyteral ministry (with all the activities connected with this ministry) is to be priestly in the sense that it makes the service of Christ present in the effective preaching of the Gospel message, in the gathering together and direction of the Christian community, in the remission of sins and the eucharistic celebration in which the unique sacrifice of Christ becomes a reality in a wholly singular way.

There are those, I know, who say to us: "But this ministry is not priestly, since the term *hiereus*, which was the usual term for designating the priest, is absent from the New Testament." I reply: it is merely a question of words. It is quite evident that the early Christians and the apostles themselves had to avoid letting the Church of

Christ be confused with the surrounding paganism. They therefore took care not to use this word, which was a "technical" one for designating the pagan priest. The Christian priesthood is without parallel.

It is a matter of seeing not simply words as such, but the facts, the realities: seeing the Church live —and as far back as the New Testament.

It therefore seems that in distinguishing itself from the pagan priesthood, the priesthood as Christ instituted it is implying an essential reference within itself to the sphere of the sacred. This relation is not due, therefore, as we sometimes hear, to a kind of historical drift consisting in a return to the pagan religions?

I would like to make an observation about that. I have read quite a few things on that question during the past several years. The idea of a priestly ministry is often criticized and even caricatured by using certain expressions such as "the priest, man of the sacred", etc. We are told that this is a case of a post-tridentine concept. And then, since it must of course be admitted that the Council of Trent invented nothing new, they next wish to see it as a medieval concept, proper to a feudal and sacral society. But since analogous texts are nevertheless found in the Fathers—texts which are certainly not "medieval"—it is then said: all of that comes from the era of Constantine, in which the Church aligned herself with power and with the pagan priesthood in its relations with power. But then, when they discover the same thing in the ante-Nicean and ante-Constantinian Fathers, they tell us: it is the sub-apostolic period that is the cause of it; an almost immediate rupture takes place between the message of Christ and the idea that it becomes. Finally, faced with certain undeniable fundamental ideas from the New Testament itself, some come to say: the apostles have already misunderstood Christ, they have betrayed him.

And yet, some things which do indeed come from Jesus are unquestionably there from the beginning: the institution of the Twelve, the institution of the Eucharist. . . . But they get around it yet again by claiming (and I am not exaggerating anything; I have just read it): of course a priesthood was conceived at the beginning, but this was because the men of that time did not conceive of a society without a priesthood. . . . How is it that this was not said any sooner? None of this is very serious, and it all proceeds without question from a "secularist" prejudice which history contradicts as soon as it is examined. In reality, the Christian priesthood is a unique thing.

Father, I would like for us to return to the relation between "Word" and "worship" which we broached a few minutes ago. Since we must avoid placing these two elements in opposition, how should we understand their real conjunction?

Yes, I know, a whole literature hammers away at us to impose this disjunction at any price. It is truly without foundation. The priest is the man of the Word, he is also and at the same time the man of worship—I prefer to say of the Eucharist, for it is the Christian term for "worship" and encompasses much more and lends itself less to caricatures. This is what Vatican II still teaches us. Some exaggerate the contrast between Vatican II and Trent from this point of view. Of course it is always possible to quote a text from Vatican II on the ministry of the Word while saying nothing about the following paragraph which speaks of the ministry of the Eucharist. In the opposite way, it is easy to quote what the Council of Trent says of the Eucharist and not mention what it says about the Word. What is true (but we must always repeat, it is not an "opposition") is that certain emphases are different; and this is completely normal.

The Council of Trent opposed the Lutheran concept that denies the priestly character of the ministry, the specific role of the eucharistic ministry; that is why it insisted on this truth; it strongly reaffirmed it. But it does not, for all that, neglect to evoke the Word, and on several occasions. It was a different situation at Vatican II; this time we are no longer dealing with a disputed or contested truth, but rather with a synthetic tableau: this is why worship, far from being absent from it, holds a very important place there. The constitution on the liturgy, *Sacrosanctum Concilium*, tells us that in the liturgy itself, God *speaks* to his people, Christ again *proclaims* the Gospel; it tells us further that it is necessary for the *union* of ritual and the Word to be clearly apparent. The constitution *Dei Verbum*, near the end, draws a parallel between the eucharistic ministry and the reading of Holy Scripture. But above all, the constitution *Lumen Gentium*, in regard to both bishops and priests, speaks at length of the Eucharist. The opposition that some wish to create, therefore, is absolutely groundless.

We are told, however, that if Vatican II does in fact speak of the Eucharist, the primary function attributed to the priest in these texts is, nevertheless, the preaching of the Word of God. And this is true: it is through this that one begins. In order to be able to bring together a Christian people around the Eucharist, it is indeed necessary that there be Christians, it is indeed necessary for the

Word of God to have been proclaimed to them, for them to have been baptized; it is consequently normal for one to begin by preaching the Word. But immediately after, and in an even more emphatic way, the Council describes for us the sacramental functions, and particularly that of the Eucharist; it tells us that the source and the summit of all evangelization are there. Thus, very far from opposing these two functions or from neglecting one in favor of the other, it unites them perfectly. Farther on, it says that the Eucharist is the root, the center of the Christian community. And the same Council tells us again that the Lord established ministers who, by order, are to be invested with the sacred power to offer the sacrifice.

You can see that it is absolutely false to think that there is any contradiction whatever in Christian thought between what tradition has called the "two tables", that of the Word and that of the Eucharist. The whole life of the Church has borne witness to it since the beginning, since the New Testament: despite certain deficiencies in practice (nothing is ever perfect in history, many periods of decadence can be seen in it), the twofold ministry of the Word and of the Eucharist has always been bound together and entrusted to the same ministry.

Let us return to the New Testament. Here I will cite one of the best exegetes, Heinrich Schlier. Far from telling us that at the beginning there was only the Word and that worship assumed importance only after the event, he writes: "According to the writings of the New Testament, it is certain that the community is built up principally in worship. There can be no doubt that, according to the writings of the New Testament, the active center of the divine service, of the assembly of the people of God, is the meal of the Lord, which soon received the name of Eucharist." And Schlier again shows us this union of the Word and ritual in explaining how the Eucharist, in its very reality, in its very act, is a proclamation of the Word: for the apostle Paul, the celebration of the Eucharist is "a proclamation, and one of a fundamental point of view" (1 Cor 11:24–29).

He parenthetically adds a remark, not devoid of humor, which is still rather applicable to certain situations today. It relates to the community at Corinth: "The apostle must have seemed to this community to be a man who understood nothing about the kingdom of the Spirit nor about the coming of the kingdom of God of which the Spirit is the sign"; and that precisely because Paul was not opposing Spirit to authority, organization, ministry. For Paul, the celebration of the Lord's supper is the proclamation of the death of the Lord and of his Resurrection. The act of worship which is the Lord's supper is itself gospel of the death and Resurrection of Jesus.

It is therefore evident that for Paul, the Eucharist has something in common with the communication of his message. The ritual as a whole *proclaims* it. Here, we are at the center, at the very heart of the Church. The Eucharist has an essential relation with missionary duty, with the preaching of the Word. It is again M. von Allmen who says to us (and he is thinking here, above all, of the Eucharist): "Far from offering the Church a chance to resign her mission, the sacrament, on the contrary, simplifies and purifies the missionary duty by marking out the frontier between the world and herself: it shows her where she can and must step out in order to carry the Gospel to the world, and where she must retire within herself in order to give thanks and to intercede." It is indeed in this way that the "eucharistic structure" of the Church (to return once again to one of von Allmen's terms) "controls, as it were, the apostolic structure" which is hers.

We are coming back to what I said before: one of the moments at which Jesus truly founded his Church was indeed the moment of the Last

Supper. And the Church is therefore, from the beginning, what could be called an association of worship.

Father, I would like for us now to approach the question of the relation between the ministerial, "functional" priesthood and the common priesthood, the one shared by all the baptized. How are we to understand properly the mediatory role of the priest within the people of God?

As a matter of fact, there is a whole stream of thought at present that would like to diminish this "mediatory" role of the priest (the word itself, which can be misunderstood, is not essential). According to some, Vatican II brought about a significant reversal of the traditional idea according to which the minister is the minister *of God* to the people. That is surely not true. It has never been maintained in Catholic tradition that the minister, whether bishop or priest, is uniquely the minister of God to the people.

To begin with, he is not *on his own account* the minister of God: he stands in the place of Christ; his ministry of "mediation" is totally subordinate. At the same time as he is "servant of Christ", moreover, he is "servant of his members", the people of God. Thus, this is again one of those

artificial oppositions, as if we had to choose between "minister of God" and "minister of the
people of God". You have only to reread the New
Testament, in which the two expressions (or other
equivalents) are repeatedly found. And it is the
same in all of tradition. According to the point of
view chosen or the particular aspect they wish to
bring out, they will emphasize the service of the
people of God or the service of God to the people,
but both are true.

On the other hand, emphasis is presently being
placed on the priesthood understood as a "function"
within the people of God. This is right: function,
charge, service, *munus*, *officium*, ministry—all these
words are most traditional. But it is a question of
knowing in what this "function" consists: as I
said, it implies the twofold service of the Word
and the Eucharist; but it also includes the task
which consists in governing: authority, properly
speaking, an authority entirely dependent upon
the ministry of the Word and the Eucharist (Father
Louis Bouyer has explained that very well). In
order that the Christian community can live
according to the Word and the Eucharist, the
bishop, and, in a general way, the minister, has a
certain "authority": an authority which is not that
of a master, but of a servant, of the servant of God
and of the people of God.

Thus, the minister does unquestionably assume a "function". But everything depends on whether it is an exterior function, a job, or what, with all tradition, I would call a sacred function. (This word must not be a bugaboo! But if it were to bother someone, I would say: a holy function; think of the conversion of hearts! For a little more theological precision, let us add, using a word which needs explanation, a sacramental function.) It involves sacred obligations.

It does not at all follow that ministers are somehow different in their essence, in the Christian scheme of things: like all Christians, they are a part of the people of God; they have to find their personal salvation like all the others. . . . Saint Augustine expressed it very well to the faithful of Hippo: "*Vobis sum episcopus, vobiscum christianus*", "For you I am a bishop, with you I am a Christian." Here again, when we do not try to set up oppositions from the very beginning, things seem rather simple.

This function is of very particular importance. For it is not only a "representation" of men to God; it is first and foremost a service of God and of Christ. That is why it cannot be compared to any "job" whatever. The minister represents Christ in two ways, both within the central act of the eucharistic celebration to which I like to refer. Christ is the head of the Church, as Saint Paul says, and the Church is his body; he appears before the Father. Well, on earth, the minister, at the head of the Christian community, represents Christ facing the Father. On the other hand, Christ is also and at the same time the spouse of the Church, again, according to Pauline symbolism; he is the savior of the community; now, in the celebration of the Eucharist, when the minister speaks in the name of Christ and pronounces the words of consecration, he is, as it were, facing the community, he occupies the role of the spouse.

Thus, in these two senses, the minister represents, on the one hand, the community with Christ at its head, and, on the other hand, Christ himself facing the community. And this twofold ministry is so important that without it there would be no community.

Of course, the priest cannot do that by himself, but only in the power of the Holy Spirit. That is why we see from the New Testament onward that an "imposition of hands" is necessary: it is the Holy Spirit who is communicated in that way to this new apostle, to this new pastor. And this is what is meant when we affirm that this "ordination" reaches the personal being of the minister. Through this gift of the sanctifying Spirit which the imposition of hands communicates to him, he is *marked* for a sacred function: it is definitive, irreversible. The Church has always understood it in this way.

Some within the Church are set apart for a service, a mission, a sanctifying function: to help direct the whole body, thanks to this institutional and hierarchical reality, toward the fullness of the communion desired by God. This is what implies an uninterrupted succession in the ministerial order, as it appears already in the letter of Paul to Timothy; we read there: "Revive the gift of God that is in you thanks to the imposition of my hands" (2 Tim 1:6). It is indeed, therefore, a question of an interior reality, of a gift from God for a sacred ministry; and that is a reality which is transmitted, at the heart of the hierarchical Church, through the imposition of hands.

This properly ministerial priesthood in no way competes with the priesthood common to all the baptized. Here again, it is necessary to stress that this latter notion is not an "invention" of Vatican II; it is present throughout tradition. If you will permit me to cite a work written well before Vatican II, *Méditation sur l'Église*, it contains a long (very incomplete) exposition relating precisely to the priesthood of the baptized, to the common priesthood. I did not invent it, I took it from tradition, I quoted many texts bearing witness to it.

The Council stressed this idea in order better to

emphasize its importance, and this is fortunate; but that in no way compromises the value of the ministerial priesthood such as we have just spoken of it. For it is precisely so that there can be a Christian people, a priestly people, that it is necessary to have ministers charged with transmitting this life, thanks to the sanctifying and unifying Spirit, and with maintaining it through the Word, through the celebration of the Eucharist and through the government of the churches. The people of God must be gathered together: that is the *raison d'être* of all ministry.

Father, among the various things called into question at the present time, we find the connection that exists between the priesthood and celibacy to be foremost. What are your thoughts on this point?

I would say, first of all, that we should not be so surprised by this. Historically, priestly celibacy has repeatedly been called into question by greater or lesser segments. And the widespread crisis we are experiencing in the Church today must manifest itself on this point also. Finally, we must indeed admit that we are living in an era of aggravated sexuality, the repercussions of which are felt within the Church in many ways, notably in this way.

It is very true that there is no metaphysical connection, nor any connection proceeding from a clear order from Christ to his apostles, which links celibacy to the priesthood in an absolute way. But it is certain that the tradition of the Church considers this bond to be beneficial for a number of reasons. We too often see today a type of reasoning according to which all that is not absolutely necessary must be eliminated. This is sophistry. The real question is what is required for the "greater well-being" of the Church as a whole.

The reasons brought forward in the course of the centuries on this point, as on many others, are not all the most convincing; they are not even the most fortunate in their expression. But it is not in virtue of reasons given by any particular person that the Church has instituted priestly celibacy; it is in virtue of the strength of her tradition meditating on the priesthood and on the best conditions for its exercise, on the evangelical ideal. And, as has been very well said, no text, from any era whatever, will ever equal in testimonial value that which makes known to us the thinking of Jesus himself. The ministers of Christ are called to continue his work for the preaching of the kingdom, for the organization of the Christian community, for his life of charity. It is completely normal for them to be attentive to the suggestions of the Gospel and for them to take Jesus as their model.

It is also said that celibacy is a charism; as such, it does not depend on us. But then, do they really know what a "charism" is? There are several kinds. As Saint Paul says, marriage is also a charism. . . . It is true that there are gifts of the Spirit in all this: but they do not negate the fact that each one is called to make a decision to which he must be faithful. If one commits himself to priestly celibacy, of course, he must do so in complete freedom; and I am prepared to recognize that in certain cases, the freedom may not have been sufficient. But the reasoning that some construct from this negative experience is not good: they say that they accepted celibacy only because they wanted to be priests, and that the Church imposed this "intolerable" condition on them. It could be that they therefore entered into it reluctantly. But the Church herself asks that one make this a free choice in willingly accepting the conditions which she judges to be the best for the exercise of the priesthood.

For the vocation is not simply an interior, personal affair; it implies an exterior call by the Church, and it is up to the latter to define the conditions with which she furnishes this call. If I become a priest, it is not for myself, but for the service of God and men within the Church; by presuming to define for myself the conditions of this service, I am denying the Church the freedom to which she has a right by her very mission.

It is therefore important, above all, to understand the Church's true reasons in this area: imitation of Christ, total exterior and interior availability; even more, perhaps, the fact that the minister exercises, in a derivative way, a "paternal" function: if he renounces fatherhood according to the flesh, it is in order to engender numerous sons according to the Spirit. This view, based completely on doctrine, is found already in some Fathers of the Church; the United States episcopate recently called it to mind again. Very many priests understand all this very well.

Father, what do you think about the eventuality of the ordination of married men?

That follows from what I was saying: there is no absolute opposition between marriage and the exercise of the priesthood. It is unquestionably true that the tradition of the Church, Eastern as well as Western, has never accepted the marriage of a priest. But it is possible that priests can be chosen from among married men; we see this occur, with certain restrictive conditions, in the Eastern Church; but there, at least in the beginning, it was a question of civilizations very different from ours. For my part, I do not believe that in a country like France this represents a truly practical solution from any point of view. More especially as the question, which might be considered by itself, is distorted by its collusion with the demand of marriage for men who are already priests.

Father, to bring this to a close, I would like to return to the question of more general importance which you brought up earlier, and which seemed to me to underlie your whole exposition: the most urgent thing, in this area as in others, and with which the Gospel itself inspires us—is it not for us to learn to think, not by oppositions and exclusions, but by making every effort to transcend apparent contradictions?

It is necessary, alas, to state that we do in fact often have the tendency to think by oppositions. Today, it is unfortunately a very widespread method of thinking (or rather, of not thinking). We perpetually see artificial oppositions reappear in the problems that touch our faith, Christian existence, the life of the Church. You have certainly heard this many times: love of God is opposed to love of neighbor, contemplation to action, personal salvation to collective salvation, authority to freedom of spirit, zeal for the Church to openness to the world, charism to institution, faith to religion, Word to sacrament, etc. None of this reflects genuine thought.

Étienne Borne, in a conference held at the Catholic Center of French Intellectuals, spoke of this "giddiness of dissociation" which overruns and ravages a whole section of contemporary thought. It also invades and ravages a whole section of theological literature (or rather, of literature relating to theological subjects), such as we see it developing at the present time. Now, precisely this play with concepts set up in opposition is always the mark of thinking that is overly facile, ready-made, uncritical or of a way of thinking by reaction, by feeling, deliberately impassioned. In every order of things, and particularly in the things of the spiritual life, when reality is thus dissociated, one of the terms is caricatured to solve a difficulty; then one necessarily misunderstands what one wishes to retain and exalt.

All life is synthesis. The life of the Christian mystery is synthesis *par excellence*. It is always an equilibrium of fullness. We must proclaim simultaneously the complementary and paradoxical aspects of the Christian mystery. In this resides all its grandeur: the Christian mystery is a whole, a mysterious whole. Now, out of analyses which can be illuminating, out of distinctions which can be real, one too often fabricates dichotomies, one effects dissociations, one creates deadly oppositions. It sometimes seems that this is a spirit "inspired by the devil" who seeks to "transform into grounds for opposition" what should be kept "in a spirit of concord" (Y. Congar).

Pascal says it admirably: "Usually it happens that, unable to conceive the relation of two opposite truths, and believing that the admission of one entails the exclusion of the other, they (the unbelievers) adhere to the one, they exclude the other, and think that we, on the contrary. . . ." —While in reality we admit them both. And again: "The faith embraces several truths which seem to contradict each other. . . . The origin of this is the union of two natures in Jesus Christ. . . . There are thus a great number of truths of both faith and morals which seem contradictory and which all exist in a wonderful order. The source of all heresies is the exclusion of some of these truths."

What Pascal said about the truths of faith and morals is just as true about what relates to the conditions of Christian life and to the essential structures of the Church. One of the concerns of

Vatican II was precisely to bring out this synthetic character of the Church's reality and of the doctrine of faith. And this is also true of the texts which it devoted to the priesthood. To receive them in truth, it is a poor method to quote only half of them in order to oppose them to the past: it is necessary, on the contrary, to place them back in the great unifying vision of Scripture and tradition.